THE STITCH-UP

The Stitch-Up

How Medical Misogyny Harms Us All

EMMA SZEWCZAK AND
ANDRZEJ HARRIS

Chatto & Windus
LONDON

1 3 5 7 9 10 8 6 4 2

Chatto & Windus, an imprint of Vintage, is part of the
Penguin Random House group of companies

Vintage, Penguin Random House UK, One Embassy Gardens,
8 Viaduct Gardens, London SW11 7BW

penguin.co.uk/vintage
global.penguinrandomhouse.com

First published in Great Britain by Chatto & Windus in 2025

Copyright © Emma Szewczak & Andrzej Harris 2025

The moral right of the authors has been asserted

This book is a work of non-fiction based on the life, experiences and recollections
of the authors. In some cases names of people, places, dates, sequences and the detail
of events have been changed to protect the privacy of others.

Epigraph taken from *The Husband Stitch* by Carmen Maria Machado,
published by Serpent's Tail. Used with permission.
Extract from *The Bluest Eye* by Toni Morrison (Chatto & Windus, 1979)
reproduced by kind permission of Penguin Random House, One Embassy
Gardens, 8 Viaduct Gardens, Nine Elms, London SW11 7BW, UK

No part of this book may be used or reproduced in any manner for the purpose of
training artificial intelligence technologies or systems. In accordance with Article 4(3)
of the DSM Directive 2019/790, Penguin Random House expressly
reserves this work from the text and data mining exception.

Typeset in 12/14.75pt Bembo Book MT Pro by Jouve (UK), Milton Keynes
Printed and bound in Great Britain by Clays Ltd, Elcograf S.p.A.

The authorised representative in the EEA is Penguin Random House Ireland,
Morrison Chambers, 32 Nassau Street, Dublin D02 YH68

A CIP catalogue record for this book is available from the British Library

ISBN 9781784744915

Penguin Random House is committed to a sustainable future
for our business, our readers and our planet. This book is made
from Forest Stewardship Council® certified paper.

For our daughter, Orlando.

Contents

Introduction: I Fell Out of My Vagina
(And So Could You!) ... 1

1. You Didn't Do Your Kegels ... 13
2. No Pain, No Gain ... 41
3. We're Listening ... 68
4. Go Natural ... 86
5. Sacrifice Yourself ... 109
6. Choose Joy ... 121
7. Stop Complaining ... 143
8. You Had a Baby ... 159
9. Which Box Do I Tick? ... 186

Conclusion: Cause of Death: Woman ... 206

Acknowledgements ... 215
Notes ... 217
Index ... 271

They take the baby so that they may fix me where they cut. They give me something that makes me sleepy, delivered through a mask pressed gently to my mouth and nose. My husband jokes around with the doctor as he holds my hand.

– How much to get that extra stitch? he asks. You offer that, right?

– Please, I say to him. But it comes out slurred and twisted and possibly no more than a small moan. Neither man turns his head toward me.

The doctor chuckles. You aren't the first –

I slide down a long tunnel, and then surface again, but covered in something heavy and dark, like oil. I feel like I am going to vomit.

– the rumor is something like –

– like a vir–

And then I am awake, wide awake, and my husband is gone and the doctor is gone. And the baby, where is –

The nurse sticks her head in the door.

– Your husband just went to get a coffee, she says, and the baby is asleep in the bassinet.

The doctor walks in behind her, wiping his hands on a cloth.

– You're all sewn up, don't you worry, he said. Nice and tight, everyone's happy. The nurse will speak with you about recovery. You're going to need to rest for a while.

The baby wakes up. The nurse scoops him from his swaddle and places him in my arms again. He is so beautiful I have to remind myself to breathe.

From 'The Husband Stitch', by Carmen Maria Machado

Introduction
I Fell Out of My Vagina (And So Could You!)

There's a short celebrity interview the *Guardian* runs at weekends called the Q&A. It's a series of direct questions which tend to solicit profound or pithy replies. On the days when I'm confined to my bed, too frightened to walk or stand, I make Andrzej read it out to me. The questions in the Q&A vary from week to week, but they're drawn from a common pool we've come to learn by rote. So we know that no one ever gives a straight answer to 'How often do you have sex?', and that 'What is the trait you most deplore in others?' – always something heinous like war crimes or usury – is funniest when followed up with 'What is the trait you most deplore in yourself?' (always something deeply incriminating like biting one's nails or caring *too* much).

It doesn't matter who's being interviewed. That's not the point. We only read it so that we can answer the questions ourselves, trying to make each other laugh with reference to this in-joke or that.

There's a particular question – maybe the best one – that comes up only rarely. It's a shame, because I have the best answer for it. When I get lucky and it does come up, Andrzej will hover over it, dragging the whole thing out. It's a bit we do. Our way of *processing things*.

'What is the worst thing anyone's said to you?' he'll ask me, seeming interested, cultivating ignorance. But he knows the answer. He was there when she said it.

She was a midwife called Chris. She had just delivered my second child and was in the middle of sewing me back up. Mercifully, I was still numb from the waist down after the epidural. Andrzej was sitting beside me in the wipe-clean plastic armchair holding our new baby in his arms, the two of them lost in a world of their own, as another midwife, whose name I hadn't caught, toiled over a standing desk in the corner of the room, typing up my notes. So it was really just Chris and me, huddled together over a mound of paper towels covering my knees, my two limp legs propped up in metal stirrups.

I don't know if it was the adrenaline from the delivery, or the simple surprise at somehow still being alive, but while she snipped and snapped – every so often dropping the bloodied scissors into the metal bowl with a clang to get a better purchase on a stitch with her fingertips, pulling it taut like the women in films fixing corsets – I couldn't stop talking. I asked her things like, 'Why did you want to be a midwife?', 'Do you have any children?', 'What are you doing on the weekend?', and she answered it all with patient humour. She used to be a lorry driver, but one day she realised – with urgency – that she needed to be a midwife. Her own traumatic childbirth had prompted it – a common strand among the midwives I've met – and she was determined that other women should fare better than she had. While she had a busy home life with two young children, and the drive to work was a long one, she loved the job and felt completely fulfilled by it. It was her vocation. She had only just started in Cambridge after relocating from a hospital closer to home, and she was frustrated to find that the ward here wasn't as well equipped as her old one, and that the staff were far more overworked, under-resourced, and generally struggling. At the weekend she was taking her son to his cousin's birthday party. It was a nerf gun party and she was under no illusions as to where he was going to shoot her (in the face). I asked her what her children were called. 'Normal names,' she answered, eliciting laughs all round.

When I'd first told her, in the heavy moment just after our baby girl was born, what she was going to be called, Chris had pulled a face, the memory of which still to this day makes me laugh. 'We want it to confuse people,' I'd explained. 'As good a reason as any,' she'd replied, unconvinced.

I was now making her work past the end of her shift. She looked exhausted. I had to be sewn up because my daughter's head had torn my perineum in half. At some point Chris's colleague finished the notes and came over to watch, marvelling at her skill. She told him that she'd taken special courses in the technique in London. They had left her out of pocket, but she was hell-bent on learning how to do it properly. Andrzej's interest was piqued at that. Clutching the small sleeping form of our daughter to his chest, he dipped his head beneath the paper-towel canopy to take a look at Chris's handiwork.

'It looks better than the first time,' he said approvingly, referring to when I'd been sewn up last time. It hadn't been my son's skull that had split me then, but the head of the vacuum they had used to try and extract him, and the blade of the forceps, and then finally the scissors they'd used to open me up, making two doors of me. Afterwards the obstetrician, not a midwife, had been in a rush, and had left me with a thick scar that still aches when the seasons change.

Instead of a reply, I gestured for the sick bowl. I needed to throw up again. For some reason I'd started vomiting, violently and inconveniently, straight after giving birth. Chris's face now creased in concern.

'Why are you sick?' she wondered aloud, not for the first time. 'If it carries on, I'll have to go and get someone.'

'Could it have been the epidural?' asked the other midwife. 'It was a heavy dose,' Chris nodded. 'Maybe it's that.'

I started to tell her: no, I always throw up, it's just a thing my body does; it's not the epidural, *please* don't blame the epidural, everyone always blames the epidurals – I had so many thoughts on the politics of epidurals – but Chris interrupted me, her voice heavy like stone.

'Hang on a second,' she said, her eyes fixed on a point somewhere in the distance between my legs.

There was a pause. A Pinter pause. Just long enough for me to think: *Oh God, what now?*

Then she looked up at me with her dark hair tumbling out of its bun and all over her face, she looked straight through its veil and into my eyes, and she said the worst thing anyone has ever said to me.

'Your vagina's fallen out.'

It took them months to tell me that it was a prolapse. Which prolapse, exactly, is still in dispute, as is the gradation, whether or not it will heal, or whether or not it has already done so. People tell me different contradictory things, so I don't really know what to believe. And when you don't know what's wrong with you, you haven't got a hope in hell of putting it right.

Around half of all women will experience some degree of prolapse in their lifetime.[1] It is a major medical concern. In the United Kingdom alone, a fifth of all of those awaiting major gynaecological surgery suffer from prolapse.[2]

I use the term 'prolapse' as if the condition is singular, but it isn't. Prolapse is rather an umbrella term for a host of complex issues covering a number of regions: vaginal, uterine, bladder, rectal. Within each region of prolapse are several other layers of complication and gradation. Formally, prolapse is understood as a descent of certain organs, or the tissues and muscles that surround them. These many potential descents are so varied, their effects so multiform, however, that to group them under a common name is meaningless, if not actively counterproductive. Many common, and many not-so-common, vaginal health issues are impossible to prise apart from prolapse when using the limiting language of contemporary medicine. The Prolapse loiters always at the edge of diagnosis, a pervasive presence in discussions of other, proximate conditions, such as endometriosis, pelvic inflammatory disease, recurrent cystitis, recurrent thrush, bacterial vaginosis, vaginal bleeding, vaginal dryness, vaginal discharge, vaginal numbness, vaginal pain, while being generally under-diagnosed in and of itself. Prolapse can somehow be both anything and nothing. In that sense, it is the mother of all vaginal health problems. Existing in this paradoxical state, it is the primary cause of all problems pertaining to the vagina, while also being invisible, indefinable, unavoidable. And untreatable.

To illustrate this point, the UK health service found that one in twelve women in the UK report experiencing symptoms of pelvic organ prolapse.[3] However, when a random sample of women was taken across the population, it found that a far higher number – almost 50 per cent of the sample – suffered from some degree of it.[4] Sufferers themselves, therefore, are vastly under-reporting.

That is not to say that they do not *suffer* from prolapse. But, rather, they do not know what it is that they are suffering from. Perhaps they have been led to believe that they aren't suffering from anything at all.

Immediately after my vagina fell out, the midwife – Chris – asked for something to push it back in with.

'I need a vaginal pack,' she told her assisting colleague.

He shook his head and replied with a tight smile, 'We've run out.'

Thinking on her feet, Chris cut a length of surgical gauze and rolled it into an over-large tampon. Then she ducked beneath the sheets that were now covering my stirrupped legs and got to work on reassembling me. Thankfully I was still under the influence of the epidural. While it was a relief not to feel anything, it was also unnerving. All the attention in the room had converged on a space between my legs that I could neither see nor feel, a space that felt, all of a sudden, as alien to me as Mars. After a few long minutes of absolute silence, Chris straightened up – coming back into my view – and said simply, 'It's back in,' before dashing out of the room to find a surgeon. Her assistant followed quickly after – there were other babies to be born, other women waiting their turn to fall apart – and Andrzej and I were left alone, our questions clamouring for answers. Andrzej began fumbling for his phone but as he moved to fish it out of his back pocket, the baby in his arms started to fuss, threateningly, so he gave up trying. Unable to make a sound so as not to disturb her, we instead communicated with our eyes while we waited for the surgeon to come. *This can't be happening*, said his. *Of course this is happening*, said mine.

Since giving birth, which had been followed by my immediate bout of nausea, I'd barely had a chance to look at my daughter. Now I dared not look for fear of disturbing her with my heavy stare, exposing her to my confusion and disquiet. As though she was still inside of me and we were still one. 'Don't get stressed!', the books on pregnancy scream, stressfully. 'It can harm the baby!'

I wasn't in pain. I wasn't even tired. I was suddenly more awake than I had been in days, if not weeks or months. The room was glaringly bright. Outside, the sun was rising over south Cambridge, lighting up the first day of our daughter's life. Today was her birthday, the worst day of my life.

As the surgeon examined me, he spoke to Chris in muted tones that I couldn't make out. I watched their faces closely. Many frowns – frowns I've later come to know too well – accompanied by shrugs that could only mean that I was either very lucky or the very opposite.

'Your vaginal wall caved in,' the surgeon said finally, bracingly. 'But it's back in now.'

My many questions – too many questions – came tumbling out, rendering me incoherent. What does that mean? Is it normal? What will happen next? What do I do next?

'It can happen,' he said vaguely. 'It could be fine but it's impossible to say. Go home. Don't overexert yourself! See how it goes.'

It is not just those who have undergone childbirth or pregnancy who suffer from prolapse. It can often occur 'for no reason' in otherwise healthy bodies. It can happen to those who have had a vaginoplasty, and those who have had a hysterectomy – a procedure that, ironically, is sometimes prescribed to *treat* prolapse. The research into the causes of it is scant. But nature abhors a vacuum, and where there is no confirmed explanation you will instead find hypotheses, guesswork, theories – all of which are laden with attitudes. Perhaps unsurprising in the area of women's health, those attitudes tend to circle the same drain: that having a prolapse is ultimately your own fault. Sufferers might be told that they simply have a predisposition for the condition on account of weak and deficient tissues. *Or* that it was brought on by lifestyle factors such as weight, age, constipation, or even a chronic cough.

When I first started writing this book, I was inundated with stories from people who wanted to share with me their own experiences of medical misogyny and gender violence in healthcare. I soon noticed that most if not all these accounts had a unifying theme: the sufferers had been explicitly or otherwise *blamed* for their conditions, the length of time it took them to heal (if ever at all), and their very place and standing in the healthcare system. I saw my own medical journey reflected in theirs and vice versa, all through the prism of blame.

There was the intersex woman who was told that she should expect painful examinations because of her 'odd genitalia'. The trans woman who complained of vaginismus only to have a doctor snap back at her 'you *wanted* a vagina'. A cis woman who had suffered multiple miscarriages was told that her depression may have been the cause; another was told that her active sex life may have caused her stillbirth. One person told me that their elderly mother had had a hard, plastic ring pessary implanted deep inside her vagina to treat bladder incontinence. They are supposed to be removed by a doctor every five years, but hers wasn't until she noticed, when defecating, that faeces was leaking out of her vagina. The pessary had corroded through her tissue into her rectum, causing an inoperable fistula. Multiple healthcare workers admonished the woman for forgetting to book an appointment to get the pessary removed. She had dementia.

It all begins to feel a lot like a stitch-up, as though the whole game's fixed and we can never win, only lose. And lose we do. Worldwide, around 800 people die every day in childbirth of a treatable illness. Thirteen per cent of those deaths are caused by unsafe abortion.[5] You can expect to wait nearly a decade to be diagnosed with endometriosis, a common – and excruciating – condition of the lining of the uterus that is also a leading cause of infertility in women. Women are 50 per cent more likely to receive an incorrect diagnosis for life-threatening coronary heart disease than men.[6] And, even though they are less likely to have a heart attack than men, they are more likely to die of it if they do.[7]

It is incontrovertible: women get a raw deal when it comes to healthcare. But not all women experience that with equal violence. Where I can lament my own poor treatment when it comes to my prolapse, so too can I admit that if I was of an ethnic minority group it would've likely been a whole lot worse: in 2022, in the UK, Asian women were twice as likely, and Black women four times more likely, to die in childbirth than white women.

And it's not only women who experience medical violence on account of their gender either. Think of the Black men who most disproportionately suffer from untreated heart disease; men with breast cancer who 'aren't supposed to get' breast cancer; men with ovaries who 'aren't supposed to get' ovarian cancer; intersex people who are subjected to invasive procedures that aren't medically indicated, sometimes leaving them in chronic pain, infertile, with lifelong disabilities, or worse.

The different forms of medical abuse do not count each other out, and when we speak about medical misogyny, it is always of how it exists as part of a bigger picture. Medical misogyny, misogynoir, racial bias and gender violence make all too common bedfellows in healthcare settings across the world.

The next time my vagina fell out, it decided to hang around for a while. It happened on the day before my six-week check. I was walking back from a shop – probably Boots; it was always Boots back then – on my own, looking at but still not really taking in the autumn that had rolled around here without me noticing. The students were back in Cambridge after the long summer break and the tourists had all disappeared, back to their real lives, out of this pretend city as I've always thought of it, as I might've been thinking of it then, when I lifted my leg to step up onto a curb and, in that fatal shifting of weight, something fell out of me. Or rather slid, wet and bulbous, into the door of my vagina, pressing itself against the cotton of my underwear. Immediately surprising, completely predictable. Oddly painless and, like the very first time it happened in the hospital when I was numbed with the epidural drug, all the more frightening for it. I stood completely still, hovering on the edge of the curb, one foot up and one foot down, wondering whether if I followed through with the action, more of myself would come out. I contemplated plunging a hand down there and shoving the mass back in, but the thought of touching it made my innards churn. People about me were beginning to look, in that sly, hoping-not-to-be-caught-looking sort of way, and I realised that I was going to have to move or risk having someone ask if I was okay, because how could I possibly explain *this*?

I leaned forward and began to hitch my lower leg up onto the curb, dreadfully slow, like folding eggs into batter: softly, softly, add the heavy to the light. Sickeningly, the gelatinous mass moved to fill up the space that had just been cleared for it, and pressed firm and damp against the inside of my crotch. Like Silly Putty warmed in the hands and slick with sweat, it adhered only slightly to my lips while slipping them apart with its bulge. There came a nefarious tugging sensation deep in my gut, somewhere below the belly button. I forced myself to keep my breathing light and shallow, convinced that any internal movement would have a domino effect on my organs and thrust it further out. And then, and I don't know how I managed it, but I started to walk home. Every step came with the mental assessment: Has it got bigger? Is it moving downwards? What is it? What is it taking with it? I imagined comically unspooling entrails, like Punch and Judy sausages, like handkerchiefs unfurling out of a magician's sleeve – first the cervix then the uterus, then the bladder then the intestines, all tumbling out on top of one another in a gruesome chain.

When I entered the doctor's office the next morning, the thing had retreated inside of me. There was a sensation in my vagina of heaviness, and fullness, but that clearly perceptible object had gone, retreated into my depths. I think it must have done so at some point in the night when I was lying awake, or so I thought, barely daring to breathe. Like waiting up for Father Christmas, one eye fixed on the bedroom door, though he always manages to slip in and fill your stocking when you're not looking. One moment I was in bed with something warm between my legs, and the next it was gone.

Most of the doctor's appointment was spent discussing my daughter because the 'six-week check' is shared between mother and newborn, but I was itching to talk about me. I lingered guiltily on things I knew didn't really matter, as though to prove to myself and the GP that I didn't care about my own health, only that of my child. 'She has this mark on her neck,' I said, knowing it was an innocuous birthmark. 'There's some dry skin on her thigh' that was just that: dry skin.

When it finally came to talk about me, we only had a few minutes left. The GP ordered me up on the bed after I told her what had happened. She was frowning.

'You should've mentioned this first . . .'

She didn't know what it was that she could feel. I still hadn't dared touch or look at it, so her findings were new to the both of us.

'I don't know . . .' she said uncertainly. 'Maybe it's just swelling?'

'But would swelling . . . fall out of me, like that?'

'It could feel like it, I suppose.'

I wasn't convinced. I still had the memory of the pressure of an object, not a swelling, etched on my inner thigh. I felt nauseated. How could that thing, that terrible thing, be indefinable, unknown, nameless to the very person, the only person, who could name it for me?

'It's a prolapse,' she finally concluded.

I sighed with relief. 'What can we do about it?' I asked, relieved to have a diagnosis.

'Not much,' she replied, before changing her tone almost imperceptibly and simultaneously asking and telling me: 'You overexerted yourself, *didn't you?*'

I want to show how, when it comes to women's healthcare, we find ourselves in a position of *Damned if you do, damned if you don't* at practically every turn. We are blamed for everything from our lifestyles to our bodies; womanhood itself is treated like an illness, and really, there's nothing we can do to cure ourselves of it.

It's crucial that we don't realise we're being played, though, because then we'd demand what's fairly ours: truly equitable access to health systems that actually work for us.

You may have experienced something similar to the stories recounted in the following chapters. Or not. In any case, I hope through engaging with them that you will begin to see how the systems we currently put up with are not working for many – if any – of us at all.

Bringing together these threads has only been possible by co-writing this with my husband Andrzej. As a biomedical researcher, he has been able to wade into depths that would've drowned me. On my more cynical days, I might think that it is useful for practitioners and healthcare providers that most of us *don't* know the fundamental science behind the diagnostics on offer and *can't* make sense of the collected raw data. I might think that it makes us more pliant customers, and less likely to complain, and ask for more. Generally, though, I think the problem is more one of a lack of adequate translators – of people who can understand multiple languages, and then bring different ideas together (about science, say, or women's health; or policy matters, or even the personal experience of knowing what a smear test feels like). To tackle the problems at hand – and overcome the fundamental matter of a deeply entrenched medical misogyny – we will need to involve a great number of different people, all with their own languages, voices and experiences.

In the following pages, I hope you gain an insight into the lives – and languages – of just a few of those people. Some of them I have met, and some I am intimately connected with. Others, I have perhaps spoken to briefly once or twice, and others still, never at all. But this is, equally, their story – as much as it is yours.

1. You Didn't Do Your Kegels

Over women's healthcare towers a behemoth: Kegels.

Otherwise known as pelvic-floor exercises, these involve strengthening the muscles around your bladder, vagina and rectum through daily exercises of, well, squeezing.

The pelvic floor is like a hammock stretched between the pelvic bones. It's made up of muscles and ligaments that support the weight of the organs above it, in the abdomen. Two main muscles dominate the space. They don't form one continuous layer, but have openings for the urethra, anus and – in the case of the female pelvis – the vagina. Pelvic-floor exercises are meant to improve the strength, power and endurance of these muscles, which is said to be helpful in cases where they have been damaged or weakened by physical trauma, childbirth, chronic disease or age.

They were supposedly invented by American gynaecologist Alfred Kegel in the mid twentieth century, hence the name. Supposedly, because pelvic-floor exercises were already a well-known technique among women and midwives around the world, and Kegel merely sought to 'medicalise' a relatively common practice. In his first major paper introducing the technique to the academe, published in 1948, he cited the observations of his colleague Van Skolkvik who'd been working with South African tribeswomen.[1] When examining the women's perinea, Skolkvik found them to be 'unusually firm' and attributed this to the intense regimen of vaginal exercises prescribed by the women's midwives – usually their mothers or mothers-in-law – whereby the women would contract their vaginal muscles around the midwives' distended fingers starting from immediately after childbirth.

Nowadays, these exercises are almost universally recommended as a first line of treatment for prolapse[2] and stress urinary incontinence.[3] They are also widely used for a host of other pelvic problems, including vulvodynia,[4] vaginismus,[5] chronic pelvic pain,[6] pain caused by endometriosis,[7] ovarian cysts, and period pain.[8] In fact, they are advised for just about anything – and nothing. As they're considered the cornerstone of good vaginal upkeep, you don't even have to present with particular symptoms or conditions to be bracingly reminded to 'do your Kegels'. Everyone with a vagina is expected to undertake a daily regime of intimate clenching to fight the signs of wear and tear, time, and childbirth. There are many different training plans that are described in medical literature, and every women's health resource, maternity unit, mother and baby group, website or magazine dedicated to women's health and well-being is guaranteed to recommend their own regimen of pelvic exercises.

I came across Kegels long before my first pregnancy. In fact it was my granny who first told me, in the mock-serious tone she always employed to convey serious subjects, to 'Make sure you do your pelvic-floor exercises – I certainly wish I had.' It wasn't until after my prolapse that this really hit home.

After I was first diagnosed by my GP at the six-week check and told that there wasn't much that could be done for it, I was referred to a gynaecologist. I arrived at our initial meeting, a few months later, full of hope. This was the first person I had encountered since it had happened who was expressly tasked with making it better. I was also overwrought and exhausted. 'Taking it easy' simply hadn't been an option. I had a newborn baby and a two-year-old child to look after. Living with an unidentified mass that would slump out of me – the degree to which depended on how far that day I had walked, or how many times I had picked up my children – played havoc with my mental health. Merely standing came with the instinct to constantly *clench*. My entire pelvic region hovered in a state somewhere between discomfort and pain: tired, aching muscles, odd twinges, concerning pulls. Some days I couldn't get out of bed, gripped with the terror of what gravity might do to me next. Andrzej took extended periods of time off work – leave that he wasn't, legally, entitled to, and we were thrown into a perilous position. Would his boss lose patience with him? What if he was forced to go back in; worse, what happened if he was sacked? Would I, myself, ever work again?

Big problems need big solutions. I expected to hear that I would need highly specialised, complex surgery; or, failing that, I would at least be offered some kind of living aid – a pessary, perhaps – to tide me over until my pelvic floor could heal or while the next steps were being assessed.

It was disconcerting, then, to be asked by the gynaecologist – two fingers inside me, face level with my breasts – 'Have you ever heard of Kegels?'

Of course I'd heard of Kegels: I had been doing them three times a day for months. I had an alarm set on my phone for 10 a.m., 2 p.m. and 6 p.m., at which point I'd squeeze my vagina as hard as I could ten times in a row. It was difficult at first, as my muscles were still numb from childbirth and nothing seemed to be happening at all. As the feeling returned it seemed to get easier – and less like I was taking a rough stab in the dark – but the symptoms of my prolapse hadn't been alleviated and, if anything, I suspected that my bladder weakness was worse than before I started.

As I scraped the surgical gel from between my lips with a sharp paper towel, and the gynaecologist retreated behind the vinyl curtain he'd drawn to protect my privacy, even though he'd been eye-to-eye with my clitoris moments before, he asked me whether I had considered using a Kegel 'aid'.

My ears pricked up at this. Aid implied an object. Object implied a prescription. Now this is what I wanted to hear.

He didn't answer me straight away. A new tapping sound joined the ambient machine beeps and whirrs coming from deeper within the clinic; he was typing on his computer. In a brief pause between clicks, he repeated what he'd already told me, with only minor elucidation.

'A Kegel aid. That makes sure you're doing them right.'

Ah, I thought to myself. That's my problem – I haven't been doing them right. Of course, it's my fault! I only ever had myself to blame.

I walked away from that appointment not with a prescription, because such items aren't available on the NHS, but with the name of a 'Kegel aid' scribbled on the back of my hand. *Elvie.*

The Elvie Trainer is a small, smart, egg-shaped device that's inserted into your vagina. It informs you, via your phone, of your pelvic-floor strength, and if it's improving over time. On the website, it's described as follows:

> The small pebble-shaped pod is inserted like a tampon and connects to an app that visualises, guides, and corrects your technique in response to your muscle movements. Elvie Trainer enables you to get the most out of your pelvic floor exercises, providing motivation, expertly designed workouts and personalised training programmes. Use 3 times a week for just 5 minutes a day for better pelvic floor strength, control and confidence. [. . .] Elvie Trainer has won more than 12 awards and is recommended by over 800 health professionals worldwide. Loved by women and celebrities alike, Elvie Trainer was featured in the 2017 Oscar nominee goody bag.[9]

The high price-point – then £169 – was off-putting, but having access to concrete information about my pelvic-floor health was appealing, to say the least. My desperation won out, and I ordered one – pushing from my mind thoughts of Isabelle Huppert returning to Paris not with an Oscar but a luxury incontinence aid instead.

Something that neither the website nor the gynaecologist had quite conveyed to me was the fact that the Elvie programme is designed to emulate a video game. After inserting the egg into my vagina and connecting to my phone, I was guided through a series of challenges to help determine and collate my 'score' (pelvic-floor health). It had a sleek and pared-back interface, admittedly, but even so: the exercises consisted of repeatedly trying to get a ball through a hoop on the screen, or up and over an ever-rising bar, by squeezing my vagina. A jaunty tune accompanied this charade.

Now, I am no stranger to video games. I'm an only child: I practically grew up on them, and have an enduring – adult – love for my Nintendo Switch, which I get out periodically during times of overwhelming stress, or on long flights and car journeys. I am not someone who would immediately recoil from the idea of 'gamifying' healthcare for better engagement.

My problem was not one of engagement, however. I didn't *need* to play a game to try and fix my prolapse. In fact, this was the least fun I had ever had playing a game in my life. Something about (literally) jumping through hoops and collecting points so that I could pick up my baby and go for a walk again just didn't sit right with me. To make matters worse, I would have to carve out surprisingly large portions of my day to leave the room and lie on the bed because, unlike the Kegels, I couldn't do this in company, and playing a game on my phone in front of my toddler was like waving a red rag to a bull. Being technologically inept, it would take me longer than most to get set up, if I had even remembered to charge the device that seemed to drain energy like a sieve. This is when it wasn't plagued with *connectivity issues*. I'd push the pebble into my vagina and squeeze, only for my phone to declare 'Device not recognised'. Or, I would come to the end of a level, having been squeezing away like a pro for twenty seconds prior, only for the connection to drop, and my daily score to be lost. I found accurately measuring my progress impossible.

Then came the strict cleaning instructions in order to stave off infection, and having to leave it out on the drying rack in the kitchen overnight. A visitor thought it was a sex toy, something I found less embarrassing to run with than explaining what it really was. No, I would have to say, that is something that a real doctor recommended to prevent my organs from tumbling out of my vagina.

My suspicion that the exercises weren't all they were cracked up to be had morphed into a deeper humiliation and horror at what I had been asked to do. To combat the fact of *an organ* falling out of me, I'd been prescribed . . . exercise. Every day I would squeeze my vagina, three times a day, tears in my eyes, in a desperate bid to hold in my bladder and cervix. Was this *all* they could offer me? One of my friends likened it to a man presenting with a hernia and being told that ab crunches would suffice as treatment. *Laughable.* And yet, here I was.

Maybe the Elvie works for some people. Maybe Kegels do, too. There is indeed clinical evidence to show that Kegels can improve the symptoms of stress urinary incontinence (SUI). SUI is the most common type of incontinence in women.[10] It happens when the bladder comes under pressure, causing urine to leak out. The source of pressure can be coughing or laughing, or big, sudden shifts in body weight such as when jumping and running. It happens when the muscles surrounding the bladder and the urethra become weak or damaged, often as a result of pregnancy and vaginal birth, and also with age. There is likely an element of genetic predisposition too, seeing as some younger women can develop it who have not experienced damage or trauma to those muscles.[11]

Regardless of the cause, SUI is a common problem affecting around a quarter of all women. This number may be higher, given the stigma surrounding incontinence and the likelihood of under-reporting. Aside from that caused by stress, there are three other types of urinary incontinence. The second most common is urge incontinence, which is also referred to as overactive bladder syndrome.[12] In this condition, a group of muscles controlling the bladder can become overactive and spasm uncontrollably, causing a sudden urge to urinate, whether the bladder is full or not. Why these muscles spasm uncontrollably is unknown.

The two other types of incontinence are much less common. One is overflow incontinence, caused by a blockage in the bladder that prevents it from emptying fully.[13] The bladder will subsequently overflow and leak. The final form of incontinence is known as 'total incontinence'.[14] Here, the bladder cannot store urine at all due to serious neurological injury (such as spinal injury), or a fistula: when a hole forms between the bladder and the surrounding area, most often as a result of trauma such as childbirth or extreme sexual violence.

Stress urinary incontinence, the most common form, is usually treated with Kegels. The rationale behind this is that the weakened muscles can be strengthened by repeated exercise. This is well supported by literature: a review of thirty-one published, controlled trials that involved 1,817 women from fourteen different countries shows an agreement in terms of effectivity.[15]

As urine leakage caused by SUI in those who are pregnant or have recently given birth is commonplace, pelvic-floor exercises are a common recommendation for patients. There are six published controlled trials that provide evidence indicating that exercise can help to stave off leakage both in pregnancy and the postpartum period, with average rates of decreased incidence of 62 per cent and 29 per cent respectively.[16]

While using Kegels to combat the symptoms of SUI is well supported by research, when it comes to combating prolapse the evidence is not so clear. Firstly, this has not been quite so extensively studied. To date, there have only been thirteen high-quality trials on the topic, all involving small and moderate-sized groups of participants.[17] Of the thirteen studies, all boast improvement in symptoms of prolapse for participants, but on closer inspection it becomes apparent that the results are not so impressive.

Let's take one of the largest of these studies, published in the prestigious medical journal *The Lancet*.[18] It involved 447 women from the UK, Australia, and New Zealand, all newly diagnosed with prolapse. The study found that after six months of exercise, 52 per cent of women felt that their condition was better than before starting the programme, compared to 17 per cent in the control group, who did not exercise at all. For 41 per cent who exercised there was no improvement, and for 6 per cent the symptoms worsened. Even though nearly 5 in 10 women felt no better or worse with exercise, the benefit for women who exercised was a three-fold higher chance of feeling better. But data obtained at the twelve-month mark at the end of the training programme tells another, less optimistic, story. For 57 per cent of women there was an improvement in the symptoms after twelve months of exercising, not so much more than the 52 per cent reporting improvement at six months. This indicates that there was little improvement to be had from six months onwards. What's most interesting is that 45 per cent of women who did not exercise at all, for the entire year, still saw an improvement in their prolapse symptoms by the end of the study. This indicates that the symptoms alleviated themselves. This is unlikely to be a permanent cure for prolapse, which is notorious for recurring with age and further trauma, but it does show that the exercise had less of an impact on improvement than initially assumed. Also, 43 per cent of women who did exercise experienced no improvement whatsoever over the course of a year. Clearly, their prolapses were in need of something more than Kegels or merely waiting for the naturally occurring, potentially short-lived, improvement of symptoms.

A recent (2022) meta-analysis of the published clinical trials of pelvic-floor exercise effectiveness in treating pelvic organ prolapse comes to a similar conclusion.[19] There is 'no significant difference' for patients who continue to engage with the exercise, and this might indicate that any benefits are short-lived, and limited to an initial few months of pelvic-floor muscle training. Looking at this data, it's simply impossible to tell whether the improvements we do see are the result of the exercises or merely prolapse getting better over time.

A final note on this research: although the data is scant, the same trials also indicate that any benefits of exercise are limited to younger women. For those over the age of fifty-five, the exercise seems to offer no benefit at all, be it in the short term or the long term.

Even where Kegels have been shown to be effective in alleviating SUI symptoms, they are not necessarily a long-term solution or even a satisfactory 'cure'. There have been no studies on the long-term impact of the exercises, and most research trials on their efficacy do not monitor the patient for longer than twelve months. It is likely that women would need to continue doing Kegels every day for the rest of their lives to see a continued benefit. And despite the claims of many Kegel proponents, not *everyone* is able to do them. Those with vaginismus, those recovering from Caesarean section, and those suffering from sexual trauma are just some examples of people unable to consistently squeeze their vaginal muscles. What alternatives are offered to these people? Kegels are generally 'advertised' as a universally applicable treatment option, but this simply isn't the case. And neither are Kegels an end in themselves. They are something to help with the maintenance of muscle strength, rather than the cure of a condition.

My grandmother died years before I had my first child. Her advice to 'Do your Kegels' had not been with my prolapse in mind, but her own. I only found out about this afterwards. Why would she tell me? I'd never asked.

We had been exceptionally close. For vast periods of my childhood she had practically lived with us. As one who lives in such close proximity to an elderly person often tends to be, I was intimately knowledgeable on what I thought were all of her physical ailments. I would take her to the doctor every week, pushing her wheelchair all the way from home. We would make numerous stops so she could use the public toilets, always with me complaining, '*Again*, Granny?'

Of course, I knew that she had 'issues' – all older women have 'issues', and I'd merely chalked this one up, this one that somehow involved her bladder, or her vagina, or something thereabouts, as being inevitable, commonplace, uninteresting. I must've blamed her, in some subconscious way. Her body and its own deficiencies. Her *age*. And that changed things, for some reason. I don't know why.

Repentant, I asked my mum: What did they do for her prolapse? What was her treatment?

'They gave her a mesh,' my mum answered, face suddenly grave. 'There were complications. It left her entirely incontinent. She was in a lot of pain. No one could ever tell her what was causing it, though; we only found out after she died.'

Cold memories rushed in like the tide. Granny asking if we could swap seats at the birthday party because the hard chair felt like sitting on a bag of splinters. When she stood over the kitchen sink and retched in front of us all after my young cousin jumped on her lap. The time we had to leave the theatre halfway through the play because something someone said about sex made her cry. 'What thing about sex, Granny?' I asked. 'It was just the idea of having it at all!' she laughed. 'Isn't it stupid? Please let's go home.'

Kathryn Gill was an environmental scientist who prided herself in being able to 'keep up with the men'.[20] At university she played rollerblade hockey on the men's team and, later, competed against – and often beat – men in sailing competitions at state championship level. She gave up competitive sailing when she was twenty-seven so that she and her husband could enjoy more time in each other's company, yachting, fishing, and camping out in the Western Australian bush. Gill also wanted to settle down and start a family. Despite a newly decreased pace of life, she endeavoured to maintain a fit and active lifestyle throughout pregnancy and after childbirth, continuing to go on fishing trips with her husband, and regularly meeting with a mother and baby exercise group.

It was only after she gave birth to her second child that she realised something was wrong. Soon thereafter, she was diagnosed with severe pelvic organ prolapse, affecting multiple compartments of her vagina. In January 2007 she was referred to a surgeon for treatment, which was to involve the fitting of a vaginal mesh device. The operation involved the insertion of a considerably sized piece of polypropylene mesh into the pelvic tissues through incisions in the vaginal wall. The device Gill was fitted with, called Prolift Total, was supplied by a company called Ethicon. One of the largest available mesh devices at the time, Prolift Total stretched across Gill's entire pelvic region, covering the tissue with polypropylene plastic over an area equal to that of an A5-sized piece of paper. It was meant to comprehensively reinforce the existing tissues and stabilise the organs within Gill's pelvis. She was expected to quickly recover from the surgery and return to normal life, free from the symptoms of her prolapse. At the time of the operation, she was an otherwise fit and healthy 36-year-old woman.

But following the vaginal mesh surgery, Gill immediately began to experience pain. Half a year later, that pain intensified, and it was joined by a tearing sensation inside her vagina. She found it difficult to walk and move, and was not able to sit down. Every visit to the toilet was accompanied by 'waves of pain, cramps and spasms'.[21] In her later court deposition, Gill described the following experience when inserting a tampon:

> [I] could feel something sharp inside of me. It was an uncomfortable rather than painful feeling. However, if I moved suddenly, I could feel the mesh slightly tear me, and that resulted in a sharp pain. I felt very confused after I felt the sharp mesh inside of me. I knew that something must be wrong.[22]

Subsequent examination by a doctor confirmed that a piece of the mesh had eroded through the front wall of her vagina and was now sticking out into her vaginal cavity.

In September that same year, only nine months after her initial operation, Gill underwent the first of three surgical procedures to remove the pieces of mesh from her pelvic region and alleviate her pain. As these meshes were designed to be permanent, their removal is a complex and considerably high-risk surgical procedure. Firmly lodged in the tissues of the pelvic region, in many cases not all of the mesh can be extracted from the body. Leading pelvic surgeon and mesh removal specialist Dr Tom Margolis has likened mesh extraction to the removal of rebars from a pavement: it's impossible to leave the concrete intact. And in mesh removal surgery, the surrounding vaginal tissues are left in a state similar to that of a dug-up road.

After each of her three operations, Gill hoped for recovery, only to face disappointment and thwarted hope. An additional blow came when her prolapse recurred, followed by a host of other symptoms in the area, which now included problems with her colorectal functions. In 2017, ten years after the implantation of the mesh, a further piece of the polypropylene plastic was found to have eroded through her vaginal wall. This time, she was advised against any further surgery. It was simply too late to fix.

Gill's life had been irreversibly altered. Gone were the days of camping out in the bush on weekends and fishing in remote places with her husband and children. Now she was having to live with persistent pelvic pain, which oscillated between moderate and severe in intensity. Indeed, the pain could be so bad that sometimes she struggled to breathe, and it also affected her ability to concentrate, remember, and articulate her thoughts. Gill reported that her relationship with her family had been greatly affected, as she had to make constant adjustments to her daily life aimed at preventing the aggravation of pain. She had to ration the time she could spend engaging in daily activities and had not been able to return to full-time work.

In 2017, Gill and two other women brought a class-action lawsuit before the Federal Court of Australia against Johnson & Johnson, the world's leading producer of the mesh. Gill's lawsuit, filed against their medical device subsidiary, Ethicon, was far from Johnson & Johnson's first lawsuit. But it was their first major mesh case. And mesh patients all over the world were watching it closely. As well as

Gill and her two fellow plaintiffs Diane Dawson and Ann Sanders, an estimated 1,300 mesh patients would have to be paid by Ethicon if they lost. The sheer size of the case and its scope was reflected in the material collected by the court: more than 5,000 reports, affidavits and other documents amounting to over 164,000 pages of heavy reading. Numerous people were called to testify in the trial, including thirty-seven expert witnesses from across the spectrum of biomedical research. The case sought to lay bare to the world, for the very first time, the full extent of the mesh's alleged failings, by combining serious scientific study with personal testimony. More tentatively, though, the case would offer something more than proof of what had happened, and vindication and compensation for the victims. It would offer a glimpse of *how* the mesh scandal had happened, and maybe even *why*.

The second plaintiff in the case, Diane Dawson, described her mesh as having 'taken my womanhood away from me'.[23] Like Gill, Dawson had been diagnosed with pelvic organ prolapse shortly after having children. She first received treatment in 2001 in the form of non-mesh surgical repair. Within seven years of this operation, however, Dawson's symptoms recurred, and she was advised to undergo a further operation to treat her condition. The operation was to involve the use of Ethicon's other polypropylene mesh implant, Gynemesh PS. Upon initial fitting of the mesh, Dawson found the symptoms of her prolapse were alleviated. She was pleased with the results of the operation. But complications came soon thereafter. She began to experience excruciating pain that spread from her pelvic area into her buttocks and radiated down her legs. There was also a pain deep inside her vagina, which was related to an eroded piece of the mesh.

In October 2009, this piece was removed surgically from her front vaginal wall. Four years later, in September 2013, she was recommended for further surgery to remove all the remaining polypropylene mesh from her body. By the date the trial started, Dawson had undergone a total of five separate operations that were meant to address the complications of mesh implantation. And following her last surgery, Dawson was told that even the complete removal of the mesh would not necessarily cure her. Her life was now blighted by irreversible chronic pain and her self-esteem and self-confidence were gone. Although she continued to work, it was in a large part thanks to a sympathetic employer and an incidentally sedentary job, but her position was by no means guaranteed in the long term and she lived with the constant threat of unemployment.

The third and final testimony in the case came from Ann Sanders, a British-born hairdresser who formerly ran her own salon. At the age of forty-seven Sanders had begun to notice symptoms of SUI. Following a formal diagnosis in March 2001 she underwent an operation in Perth, where she was implanted with Ethicon's 'TVT' mesh. Like Dawson, Sanders was initially very happy with the results of the procedure. In her case, complications appeared some six years after the operation. In early 2007 she began to feel discomfort when urinating. A year later, the discomfort mutated into a constant pain, which she described as akin to having a blade in her vagina. This was followed by chronic pain and recurring infections in the pelvic region that soon stopped responding to antibiotics. In 2011 it was discovered that the mesh had eroded, and Sanders underwent a procedure to remove the implant from her vaginal wall. In due course, her incontinence returned, and she was left in a state of chronic pain that limited her daily activities. She suffered from regular bouts of severe depression and in her deposition said that she felt 'absolutely worthless'.[24]

What exactly *is* vaginal mesh? It is a piece of plastic designed to be fitted into the vaginal wall, reinforcing tissues that can no longer support the organs they contain. It is most often used to alleviate prolapse and/or SUI.[25]

Outside of the vagina, plastic mesh is used to strengthen other bodily tissues that are damaged or weak. Meshes are widely used in the treatment of hernia. Take the most common type of hernia, the inguinal hernia, which occurs when part of the bowel or, more rarely, a fragment of stomach fat, descends into the groin and protrudes through a weak point in the muscle, resulting in a visible and often painful bulge. In hernia repair surgery, this protruding organ is pushed back into the stomach cavity and the muscle layer reinforced with a piece of mesh, providing a barrier which the organ can no longer push through.[26] Vaginal mesh serves a theoretically similar purpose, but in practice, as this case proved, for many women it works far less well.

Mesh can be made from a variety of materials, but the most common is a plastic polymer called polypropylene. Polypropylene can be found in virtually all household and industrial products, from water pipes to Tic Tac lids. Like many other plastics, it's a product of crude oil, and is therefore a staple commodity of the petrochemical industry. It has a wide range of attractive properties: resistance to heat and chemicals, low density, and – most importantly – low price. It's also mechanically resilient and resistant to fatigue: it can be bent and stretched, and it doesn't easily break. Hugely convenient for manufacturing, it softens and melts with increasing temperature, without first bursting into flames. In its liquefied state, polypropylene can be injected into a mould and shaped, and it can also be stretched into a thin thread and spun like yarn.[27] This thread can then be woven to make a fabric. And in appearance, vaginal meshes are just that: plastic textiles that resemble miniature fishing nets.

How could such an innocuous piece of ordinary plastic, normally completely inert when in contact with human skin, cause such terrible damage to the lives and bodies of these three women?

One of the central questions the trial aimed to answer was whether Ethicon was selling a genuinely 'biocompatible' product.[28] This issue got to the very heart of the problem with implanting plastic mesh in the vagina. If the product was found not to be biocompatible, the medical complications that had already been reported by so many women would finally be named and explained.

A biocompatible material is any kind of biomaterial: a human-made product that aims to interact with any biological system.[29] In the case of the mesh, this biomaterial is intended to be permanently implanted into the patient's body and to be compatible with it. So it shouldn't degrade when inside the body, and nor should it have any adverse effects on it whatsoever. But biocompatibility is also understood as particular to a specific site. In other words, a biomaterial that is biocompatible for implantation in one part of the body might not be suitable for implantation in another.

When biocompatibility of a material is assessed, what should be taken into account is any response the body may muster as a result of its use. When a foreign object finds itself among bodily tissues, it will elicit a form of immune system response known as foreign-body reaction.[30] Foreign-body reaction is encountered in all types of medical implants, and scar tissue will inevitably form around any foreign object placed inside the body. The mesh has a porous structure – a deliberate design feature – that allows bodily tissue to grow through it. The scar tissue will surround the piece of plastic and fuse it to the neighbouring healthy tissue, just as a scar joins two pieces of cut flesh in a wound. *Any* artificial implant will elicit some degree of inflammation response. In most cases, the strength of the response will subside over time and the implant will no longer cause discomfort to the patient. The inflammation never completely disappears and will last as long as the implant remains inside the body. But when the response *doesn't* diminish in intensity with time, a persisting condition occurs: chronic inflammation. This is where we enter the territory of harm – something that no biocompatible material should cause.

Crucially, the response of the patient's body to the implant is far from predictable and will vary in intensity from one person to another. This is why not all patients who have had mesh implants suffer from complications. What further complicates the problem of ascertaining biocompatibility is that polypropylene plastic is used successfully in other surgical applications – namely, in sutures and hernia meshes. The use of polypropylene sutures dates back to Ethicon's own early product, Prolene, which was first approved for use by the United States FDA (Food and Drug Administration) in April 1969. It had been rigorously tested in clinical trials prior to registration and afterwards. In the early 1970s, Ethicon began producing a knitted flat mesh made in a similar fashion to Prolene sutures and marketed it for use in the treatment of hernias.[31] Neither product appears capable of inducing complications like those seen in vaginal mesh patients, and certainly not on any comparable scale. In the case of sutures, it is easy to rationalise the difference. On the one hand, relatively small quantities of thread are used to close wounds, and on the other, non-absorbable sutures, such as Prolene, are removed after the wound has healed. With the hernia mesh, the difference likely boils down to a matter of position. When a piece of plastic mesh is used to reinforce the weakened tissues that cause hernia, it is placed flat and upright against the abdominal wall and, consequently, relatively little tension is exerted onto it. In contrast, the pelvic-floor area is under *considerable* stress, having to support the weight of the organs above it. Additionally, with the pelvis being one of the body's main balance points, it needs to accommodate a good deal of movement. So pelvic-floor tissue is flexible and elastic: it can stretch in all directions before returning to its original shape. Vaginal meshes may be flexible, but they are far from elastic.[32] When implanted into the body, they do not behave like the tissue around them. Some mesh specialists refer to this problem as a 'mechanical mismatch'. The overstretching of vaginal mesh means that the material folds and wrinkles, irritating the surrounding tissue and exacerbating the body's immune response.

The meaning of the above is quite simple: the use of meshes originally developed for hernia repair in the pelvic area completely disregards the unique conditions of the anatomy of the female pelvic floor. In designing their implants, Ethicon and other mesh producers simply assumed, with no evidence or forethought – and with years' worth of anecdotal (but, crucially, not technical, or scientific) evidence to the contrary – that the conditions of the abdominal wall and the pelvic floor would be the same.[33]

The idea of using mesh to treat SUI was first conceived of by surgeons early in the twentieth century.[34] Initially, they began to experiment with slings made with tissue taken from the patient into whom the device would be implanted, and to lift and support the bladder in order to relieve urine leakage. However, the use of patient's own tissue for this operation was far from ideal. The person had to be put under general anaesthetic, their pelvic region cut into, assessed and prepared for the incoming implant, and then a tissue source sought.

Once the source tissue had been located and extracted, it was then inserted into the pelvis and implanted into the relevant area. Not only was this whole operation notoriously difficult, but it was often impossible for a surgeon to find a suitable piece of tissue.

Later slings were made using donor samples instead, most commonly using cadavers, thus alleviating the need to carry out one long and difficult surgery on a single patient. But these came with their own unique setbacks. There are many problems associated with transplantation, which include finding a suitable donor match and the high risk of transplant rejection and the necessity of taking immunosuppressive drugs to reduce that possibility.[35]

It was only a matter of time before non-biological materials would be co-opted for use in the sling. In 1955, a mesh made from tantalum metal was implanted into ten women. In four of these cases, the metal eroded – breaking through the tissues and becoming exposed in the vaginal cavity. This was accompanied, unsurprisingly, by excruciating pain.[36]

On the whole, however, surgeons were having far more success with non-biological hernia meshes. After an early period of experimentation with silver, stainless steel, silk, and cotton – all of which were deemed insufficient – the boom in the plastics industry during the Second World War paved the way for the first plastic hernia meshes.[37] These seemed to avoid all the complications associated with their predecessors. Unlike the metal meshes, they were flexible, thus better at mimicking natural tissue. They were also not rejected by the body in the way cotton and silk fibres were, greatly reducing the risk of infection.

Buoyed by the success of the plastic hernia mesh, gynaecologists first began to implant women with plastic vaginal mesh in the 1960s. Frustratingly for the surgeons, however, these did not mimic the success of the hernia meshes. Not only did they elicit high rates of erosion, but surgeons also found 'wound dehiscence' – where a wound spontaneously bursts open along the line of incision, exposing internal tissue and organs – to be surprisingly common.[38]

The experiments with plastic vaginal mesh were abandoned, and the field of SUI treatment subsequently languished. Biological meshes continued to be used, but only rarely, given that the procedures were so expensive and difficult. Only the most highly skilled surgeons were able to perform this cumbersome and tricky operation, a positive post-operative outcome was far from guaranteed, and the use of anaesthetic – causing lengthy and expensive hospital stays – was attractive to neither healthcare providers nor patients.

In the early 1990s, however, the plastic vaginal mesh was revisited. This time the research was funded not by independent healthcare bodies but by private companies. Forecasters at several medical-device manufacturers – including Johnson & Johnson – identified a significant niche in the market: the lack of viable treatment options for SUI. The opportunity here was a potentially very lucrative one, with the incidence of this common condition increasing dramatically with age. Around half of all women over sixty-five find that they are, to some degree, incontinent, and this number is even higher among women who have experienced pregnancy and/or childbirth.[39]

Women in SUI's key demographic were becoming increasingly keen to exercise their independence and were, broadly speaking, better equipped to pay for it than ever before. By the 1990s, women in the fifty-plus age bracket were leaving home more, divorcing their husbands more, and having more active sex lives well into later life. With the added benefit of the favourable fiscal conditions of the era, these particular women's needs became of great interest to the free market. The profit potential for SUI treatments was on the brink of skyrocketing.

The race to develop the vaginal mesh was on. Rival American companies Boston Scientific and Johnson & Johnson were already aware of one another's interest in the device, and they both wanted to get their products onto the market as quickly as possible.

In order to do this, the devices required Federal Food and Drug Administration approval. To gain this, the companies needed to seek 'Premarket Approval', which would involve their products undergoing lengthy, human, clinical trials.

But there is a loophole that can fast-track FDA approval. It requires invoking the so-called 'Section 510(k) rule': the 'demonstration of substantial equivalence to another legally US marketed device'.[40]

Both Boston Scientific and Johnson & Johnson were already producing the highly successful plastic hernia mesh at that time. Both companies were able to demonstrate to the FDA that their vaginal meshes were substantially equivalent to their hernia meshes, thus enabling them to bypass Premarket Approval and its requirement for more stringent clinical evidence.

In 1996, the first ever commercially available plastic vaginal mesh was sold by Boston Scientific and marketed under the name ProteGen.[41] This mesh was implanted in women despite the product having undergone *no* controlled, human, clinical trials for this specific purpose; despite them having *never before* been implanted into human vaginas. All they had to go on was a single ninety-day study of use in rats.

Sales of this particular mesh were anticipated to top 35,000 units in the first year of use, with an annual sales growth of 80–100 per cent per year for the following five years. One of Boston Scientific's executives, Bill Martin, enthusiastically wrote to a colleague in March 1996: 'We need to continue moving quickly and steadily on this project so we can begin realizing our market potential very soon.'[42]

Within just a few years, a 1999 study published in *The Journal of Urology* found that, of thirty-four patients who had had their ProteGen mesh slings removed across five medical centres in Los Angeles, half suffered from vaginal erosion, and over a quarter had developed urethrovaginal fistula (an abnormal connection between the urethra and the vagina).[43] The FDA decided that the mesh 'did not appear to function as intended', and ProteGen was subsequently and suddenly withdrawn from the market.[44]

Yet this did nothing to quash other manufacturers' efforts. By this point, other versions of the plastic mesh were already available – some based on the very ProteGen prototype that had just been withdrawn. With Boston Scientific's product off the market, Johnson & Johnson now found their own mesh – marketed by Ethicon – to be the key market player. By 2001, merely three years after the product was introduced, implantation of their mesh was one of the world's most commonly performed SUI treatment operations.[45] In the UK, it had all but replaced other treatment options. New mesh designs soon materialised. The significantly streamlined mini-sling, designed for easier application, appeared on the market, and mesh kits complete with all the necessary surgical tools for implantation (making it possible for less skilled surgeons to carry out the procedure) quickly followed.

The market expanded even further as new products targeting other vaginal conditions began to emerge. Ethicon later developed Gynemesh, the first mesh kit aimed at treating pelvic organ prolapse. The more specialised Avaulta Solo mesh from Bard Medical sought to treat rectocele prolapse, and the Apogee mesh, sold by American Medical Systems, targeted cervical prolapse. The mesh industry had begun to recognise the issues in diagnosing these conditions, especially prolapse, and was responding with a proliferation of differentiated and adaptable products. By 2012, a total of 126 different mesh products created by forty distinct companies had FDA approval. The vaginal mesh industry had truly come into its own.[46]

The early problems encountered by ProteGen seemed to have been completely resolved. But, as would later be proved in court, this was not really the case. What Ethicon had that ProteGen hadn't, though, was a single clinical study. And it was this clinical study that kept their mesh on the market for almost twenty years after its introduction.[47]

This study originated with one of the creators of the Ethicon mesh: Swedish gynaecologist Ulf Ulmsten. In the mid 1990s, around the same time that the companies had identified the mesh's potential, Ulmsten began experimenting with vaginal mesh. He began with implanting meshes made from different materials: Mersilene, Gore-Tex, Teflon. All of these led to high levels of rejection in the patients.[48] In 1996, he realised the potential of polypropylene – a plastic that was already being used successfully in hernia meshes. The outcomes in the women he implanted this into seemed, at first, far more positive than his dalliances with the other materials.[49] The following year, he sold the prototype for this polypropylene mesh to Johnson & Johnson.

A condition of the sale, however, was that Ulmsten carry out a follow-up trial. Upon the receipt of this second study, on the condition of positive results, Ulmsten's company, Medscand, would receive $1,000,000 from Johnson & Johnson for the full rights to his mesh.[50]

For this study, Ulmsten devised a multicentre clinical trial. This involved a number of different surgeons operating on patients in a number of different hospitals. For many reasons, chief among them the benefits of dispersed geography and patient demographics, multicentre trials are considered more scientifically rigorous than mere single-centre trials. Ulmsten had his doctors implant his plastic mesh into the bodies of 131 women. The results of these operations were published in a 1998 article in *International Urogynecology Journal*.[51] The paper reported success rates even *higher* than his initial study, with 119 patients completely cured of SUI and a further nine who had improved significantly.

Of course, what this research paper failed to disclose was Ulmsten's considerable financial conflict of interest. Upon their receipt of these positive results, Ulmsten's firm collected from Johnson & Johnson the $1,000,000; in 1999, Johnson & Johnson paid a further $24,525,000 to Medscand to purchase all assets associated with its tension-free vaginal tape (TVT) business.[52] Johnson & Johnson now owned his mesh, and they used the results from his study to support it too. They denied that the lucrative offer to Ulmsten compromised the results of the second trials.[53]

Like the ProteGen mesh that had been quickly removed from the market, the Ethicon mesh also saw a high rate of complication and failure from the very earliest operations.[54] But it took many years and multiple successful court cases for people to accept that the problem was a systematic failing of the mesh. This is, in no small part, on account of the results from Ulmsten's study. In the following decades his study was cited time and time again in support of the product. And not just by Johnson & Johnson, but in the broader scientific community also. The Ulmsten papers are cited more than 4,300 times in scientific articles. The results from this study have been referenced, assimilated, and subsequently built upon in literally thousands of other studies.

Given that the Ethicon mesh happened to be the world's leading mesh, support for it vicariously bolstered the hundreds of other meshes in existence too. Numerous other devices had been able to gain FDA approval via the 510(k) rule by citing the success of the Ethicon mesh as relevant to their own products' efficacy. In 2000, American

Medical Systems began selling their Triangle Silicone-Coated Sling and Surgical Mesh, using the Ethicon mesh to fulfil the 510(k) rule. In 2001, new devices appeared from American Medical Systems and from two other companies, Tyco Healthcare and Sofradim, all citing the Ethicon mesh to gain FDA approval. A total of eight devices used the Ethicon mesh to *directly* gain FDA approval.[55] This figure does not account for the many later products that used the newer devices to gain FDA approval subsequently. A great number of seemingly unconnected devices were approved on the strength of Ethicon's initial evidence, their FDA approvals all interconnected but returning, inevitability, to this single – questionable – study by Ulmsten.

Ulmsten's work no doubt lent a certain respectability to Ethicon's product. Without that respectability, perhaps it would have been withdrawn from the market much sooner, as ProteGen had been. As mentioned, the Australian trial against Ethicon was far from its first. Countless other cases had already been brought against it. But the majority were settled out of court, so we have no way of knowing whether or how Johnson & Johnson used Ulmsten's results as part of their many defences.

It was only in a 2014 vaginal mesh trial in America that the compromised nature of Ulmsten's study came to light. Mesh patient Linda Batiste successfully sued Johnson & Johnson over complications arising from her own mesh implant. In the trial, her lawyers forced Johnson & Johnson to admit to Ulmsten's conflict of interest.[56] Exposing Ulmsten's conflicted study, it paved the way for the many lawsuits that followed – lawsuits which pieced together a full picture of the mesh's seismic failure. But if Ulmsten's study had been revealed as deeply conflicted far sooner, the failure of the mesh would have been exposed sooner too, and who knows how many women might have been protected from life-altering complications and damage?

Ulmsten's study served to bolster the reputation of the mesh in ways that can never, truly, be quantified. How many doctors, when approached by patients with complications, rejected or dismissed their symptoms on the basis that they shouldn't – according to the clinical evidence – exist? How many women dismissed *their own* symptoms on the basis that they contradicted the very 'science' of the mesh? The negative experience of a single patient could not compete with the evidence from this compelling clinical study that was never compelling at all.

Another bombshell was dropped in the 2014 trial: the majority of the documentation from Ulmsten's study, including the core of his data, had conveniently perished in a fire. In November 2009, a secure storage facility containing the documents in Lausanne, Switzerland, burned down under unexplained circumstances.[57] Nothing, therefore, can ever be proven. The truth behind those positive results found in Ulmsten's study will never be fully known. How many other people collaborated with Ulmsten in his pursuit of that lucrative deal with Johnson & Johnson? Why were those results suddenly destroyed in 2009? It can't have been Ulmsten who did it – he died in 2004. And who knows what else those papers revealed, not just about Ulmsten's own potential misdeeds, but about the people – or companies – who made it possible for him to commit them?

The judge of the 2017 Australian trial found in favour of the plaintiffs.[58] Johnson & Johnson appealed, only to have their case dismissed by a unanimous decision of the Federal Court of Australia four years later.[59] It was proven beyond any doubt that the lives and bodies of Gill, Dawson and Sanders had been irrevocably harmed by the mesh products implanted inside them.

The court's ruling was roundly damning for Johnson & Johnson. It found that the company had failed these women on many fronts, from the pre-market evaluation of vaginal mesh devices to post-market customer care. The company's actions as well as their products were found to be seriously deficient, with catastrophic consequences for their patients.

Ulf Ulmsten died before the first significant mesh lawsuits were brought. He may have evaded justice, but at the very least his name is forever connected with the mesh scandal he in no small part shaped.

This is unfortunately not the case for the countless people who worked at Johnson & Johnson, and the other companies which marketed other mesh products, who actively helped to sell a device that directly harmed patients. Of course, it isn't so easy to apportion blame among these people. It will never be fully known who within each organisation knew exactly what about the devices they were selling, the devices on which they were building their careers. We do, however, get a sense of how widespread the collaboration and personal culpability was through the snippets of internal company correspondence revealed in the many mesh cases' court documents.

Staff handling Johnson & Johnson's Total Prolift implant – the implant that Kathryn Gill had been given – openly discussed how 'shrinkage of the mesh may lead to pain' and that it had the potential to 'turn as hard as rock'.[60] And yet they continued to sell their mesh for a full seven years. Similarly, a product director at Ethicon expressed concern in 2004 that the mesh could harden and fold, but the warnings to colleagues were ignored.[61] Executives across all organisations were contacted regularly by surgeons and doctors raising concerns. In 2005, Professor Linda Cardozo from King's College Hospital, London, told a senior manager at Johnson & Johnson that she found Prolift's safety profile 'quite worrying' and that she had 'major concerns regarding the erosion rate and possible problems with [sex becoming painful]'.[62] Her complaints, like many others, were ignored. And where these warnings were not ignored, they were made light of, especially regarding the risk to patients' sex lives. In 2003, a surgeon sought advice from Ethicon on how to treat a patient whose husband claimed having sex with her was like 'screwing a wire brush'. Ethicon's medical director simply replied: 'I've never tried the wire brush thing so I won't comment.'[63]

It was not just the company representatives who displayed such a dismissive attitude towards the patients. Often such disregard was revealed by the doctors and surgeons too. In a now notorious group email between Ethicon executives and senior French gynaecologists, discussing how to handle the effects of the mesh on patients' sex lives, one doctor wrote: 'I would not like my wife to undergo this procedure.' When conversation moved on to how practitioners should specifically respond to their patients complaining of pain during penetrative vaginal sex, a surgeon responded: 'It is no less true that sodomy could be a good alternative!'[64]

★

Any assessment of the state of women's healthcare must first address the hole. That is to say, the gaps in attention, care, research and funding. A lack of knowledge that makes us vulnerable; a lack of knowledge that leads to harm.

Dr Janine Austin Clayton of the United States National Institutes of Health (NIH) told *The New York Times* that: 'We literally know less about every aspect of female biology compared to male biology.'[65] Part of the reason is that medical research has long been plagued by systemic bias. One of the most significant issues has been the lack of inclusion of female subjects in clinical research. Not only have the doctors, scientists and researchers carrying out the work been overwhelmingly male, but so have most of the cells, animals and humans studied in medical science: most of the advances we have seen in medicine have come from the study of male biology. For the better part of contemporary research history, the medical community has operated under the assumption that research results from male participants can be generalised to women. This overlooks potential gender differences in disease symptoms, progression, or treatment responses.

Diseases mostly affecting men receive disproportionately more money compared to their impact on the population, whereas illnesses that are more common in women often receive significantly less than their impact warrants. In 2022, the US National Institutes of Health allocated a substantial $45 billion for biomedical research, but an analysis of how this money was distributed highlights a concerning bias. For instance, conditions such as uterine cancer, endometriosis, and chronic fatigue syndrome (CFS), which are more prevalent in women, went vastly underfunded. CFS – or myalgic encephalomyelitis (ME) – is considered to be a 'contested illness' because physicians disagree on its causes and no diagnostic testing is available for it. The condition is in dire need of greater research, as the lack of medical consensus only serves to hamper patients' access to treatment. If we take 1 to mean that a condition is funded exactly relative to its burden, then CFS has a very low ratio of 0.04. Funding for prostate cancer, on the other hand, has a ratio of 1.5. Indeed, gynaecological cancers fare particularly badly and receive considerably less support than those affecting other areas of the body. Among nineteen of the most common cancers, ovarian cancer ranks fifth for lethality, but twelfth in terms of its funding-to-lethality ratio. Cervical cancer follows a similar pattern.[66]

When it comes to funding and research, what we can say of the US largely sums up the state of women's healthcare on the whole. This is because the US has for a long time been the global leader in medical and biotechnological research, significantly contributing to new discoveries, drugs, medical devices, and clinical procedures. A study published in *The Journal of the American Medical Association* lists the US as a primary global source of new medical discoveries, with the share of global medical research and development (R&D) spending ranging between 57 per cent in 2004 and 44 per cent in 2012.[67] The US influences global research trends through setting research priorities, establishing collaborative frameworks, and allocating significant funding. Regulatory decisions in the US, such as FDA approvals, often set precedents that other countries will likely follow to ensure global competitiveness and the relevance of their biomedical sector. In terms of the mesh devices, most countries followed what the FDA decreed, and then largely withdrew mesh from circulation (albeit in a limited fashion).

The worldwide effects of the mesh are ongoing. The lawsuits keep coming. The largest case against Boston Scientific in the US was settled out of court for $189 million in March 2021.[68] Johnson & Johnson was ordered to pay A$300 million in damages as a result of the Australian trial.[69] Moreover, in 2017, the Australian government enacted an outright ban of pelvic mesh. 'We think there are ample reasons for a total ban,' said Danny Vadasz, chief executive of the Health Issues Centre. 'We can't imagine which surgeon would still want to use mesh in the absence of evidence and with so many injured women.'[70]

And yet today, a decade later, mesh continues to be produced and implanted in sufferers of SUI and prolapse around the world. It may have been roundly declared a product of questionable merit, and it is no longer the dominant player in the field of vaginal healthcare, but that has not stopped patients from wilfully agreeing to the

Russian roulette of will it/won't it be compatible with my body. And this time, it isn't on account of any grand corporate subterfuge or regulator-complicit malpractice. Its continued use has much more to do with the *woeful* lack of alternative treatments that it set out to fix in the first place. For some people, the potential complications of the mesh may be a risk they are willing to take, with their current symptoms deemed worse than the prospect of potential complications resulting from implantation. This is a shocking indictment of the current state of gynaecological healthcare; a state that was certainly not helped by the mesh scandal, which has caused new and experimental forms of treatment to be seen as too risky – maybe too *expensive* – for healthcare organisations to adequately pursue. Instead, women must rely on outdated treatments that aren't fit for purpose.

This is seen most clearly in the ultimate surgical treatment for prolapse on offer for its most severe forms: colpocleisis. On the UK's NHS website for prolapse, the procedure is listed in the treatment section – after pelvic-floor exercises, pessaries, 'lifestyle changes', and surgery. It is presented as just another surgical technique, placed at the very end of the list, in its own special section, but alarm bells begin to ring when we read 'occasionally', 'when other treatments have not worked', and 'not want to have sex again in the future'.[71]

Colpocleisis is the surgical closure of the vagina. It is an obliterative procedure, meaning that the vaginal opening is no longer preserved and the vaginal cavity is rendered permanently inaccessible. Where nothing can get in, nothing can get out: the prolapse is cured. The vagina is effectively 'disappeared'.

One of the first surgical techniques developed to treat prolapse, colpocleisis is second only to the pessary. It was developed by the French surgeon Léon Clément Le Fort, who published its first description in 1877 (the procedure is otherwise known as the 'Le Fort operation').[72] It remains virtually unchanged to this day, receiving only two major developments in the last century and a half: anaesthesia and, before closing up the vaginal opening, carrying out a pan-hysterocolpectomy (the complete removal of the vagina and the uterus).[73]

Colpocleisis is only offered to elderly women deemed too frail to qualify for other forms of prolapse surgery, and those deemed unlikely to continue leading an active sex life. It is much faster than other surgical procedures, as it does not require opening the abdomen. It is also cheaper, as it can be undertaken with less anaesthesia, and a quick recovery time means patients can be in and out of hospital in a jiffy.

The authors of a 2012 review of colpocleisis in the medical journal *Urology* offer their prediction about the future of the procedure, beginning with the acknowledgement that, as 'the overall population continues to age [. . .] there will be an increasing number of women with prolapse seeking treatment'. The paper concludes that: 'With the expected increase in need for prolapse treatment, the number of patients who would be candidates for colpocleisis will only increase.'[74]

This is the future of gynaecological healthcare that we can all look forward to. Regressive, outdated, based on gaps and assumptions, pernicious falsehoods, empty hope. And heaps and heaps of blame. We'll be no further on from where we are now; no further on from where we were in 1877. That colpocleisis is 'only' offered to elderly women – the women we will all, God-willing, one day become – should be no comfort to the young, but rather a chilling portent. *Oh well*, the doctors will tell us, *you didn't do your Kegels* . . .

2. No Pain, No Gain

Like millions of other Americans, New York State-born nurse Donna Monticone found herself in the grip of an opioid addiction following the legal prescription of pain medication. In the early 2000s she had been diagnosed with idiopathic foot neuropathy[1] – pain so extreme that it required the surgical removal of inflamed nerves. Monticone was given the opioid hydrocodone to manage the pain. In 2015, she completed her nurse training, and shortly after took up a post at the University of Yale Reproductive Endocrinology and Infertility clinic. As part of her job, she was responsible for ordering and inventorying controlled substances primarily used to relieve pain during outpatient surgical fertility procedures at the clinic.[2]

Alongside work, Monticone was juggling the care of three children with a messy divorce that had been playing out in the theatre of the family court system for years. Her ex-husband was, according to court documents, a volatile man who scared both Donna and her children. She had had to take out two restraining orders against him and was suffering financially as a consequence of the drawn-out court process.

It wasn't until 2020 that she became addicted to opioids. In June of that year, Monticone stole fentanyl from the REI medicine inventory for the first time. At first, she would inject the drug in a stall of the toilets at work. At the peak of her addiction, Monticone was injecting herself four times a shift, and had begun taking vials home from the clinic, before reintroducing them, incrementally, back into the office stock.

Monticone's was far from a victimless crime. It wasn't just a case of theft – of vital hospital resources going AWOL, incurring a bill that the clinic would have to foot – but of the deliberate infliction of harm. For Monticone to go undetected, she could not simply steal the vials of fentanyl, for their absence would be immediately known. Instead, she had to leave vials in a state that appeared untouched. And to do that, she would refill them with saline. A salt solution that provides no pain relief whatsoever. Sometimes she would leave a heavily diluted mix; sometimes the vials contained no fentanyl at all. It is estimated that between June and October 2020, 75 per cent of all pain relief used in the clinic had been tampered with.[3] As a consequence, for months, hundreds of women were given little to no pain relief during egg retrievals, a surgical procedure in which a long needle is pushed through the vaginal wall to the ovary to collect eggs for IVF.

Monticone was finally caught in October 2020 when an anaesthesiologist noticed that a vial had been tampered with. Monticone initially denied involvement but, after a positive drug test, confessed to months' worth of tampering. However, numerous patients think that Monticone was stealing the drug long before June 2020; some report having experienced excruciating pain during surgical procedures at the clinic as early as 2017. Speaking with *The New York Times* for a podcast on the case, a member of staff working at the clinic at the time agrees that the patients seemed to be experiencing more pain during procedures before June 2020. 'I remember distinctly times a patient would say, "Oh, my God, I feel everything."'[4]

One of the victims, a physician herself, immediately knew that she had not been given pain relief. She was about to undergo an egg extraction and had just been injected by a nurse with what should've been 25 mg of fentanyl. 'I could taste the saline in my mouth,' she relayed during Monticone's trial.[5] The nurse injected her again; again, she knew that it had not been fentanyl. And yet there was little the patient could do – if she did not go ahead with the retrieval there and then, she would lose the eggs she so crucially needed collecting, for which she had spent days injecting herself with hormones in preparation.

Despite many patients and some staff members raising concerns, senior physicians and upper management refused to investigate the reports of increased pain during and after procedures. Vague theories were bandied about: some doctors weren't being gentle enough; some patients had an increased tolerance to pain relief; perhaps the anaesthesia they were using wasn't good enough. No real commitment was shown to getting to the bottom of the problem, however, because none of these avenues was explored, and patients continued to be subjected to excruciating, pain-relief-free surgery.

It later transpired that Monticone herself had at some point in her life pursued fertility treatment. This came as a particular shock – and then, betrayal – to a number of the patients, who had initially blamed themselves for their painful experiences. 'I think I'm immune to fentanyl' was a common refrain from the women; it was what many told themselves. And it is perhaps no surprise that they should've felt that their bodies were exceptionally *deficient* or *malfunctioning*, given the role that infertility can play when it comes to shaping self-identity and self-worth. Many of those pursuing fertility treatment have likely already experienced lengthy periods of questioning and tests, all in pursuit of the answer: What are you doing wrong to your body and/or what is your body doing wrong for you? These people are primed to internalise poor care and treatment, because fundamentally they're being made to feel as though they ought to sacrifice *anything* to become pregnant, something that they and their bodies perhaps do not deserve, or aren't really capable of.

One of the patients, Katie, remembers being told by one of the nurses that her egg-retrieval must have been so painful because of how successful it was. 'I think it was so painful because we got so many eggs,' a nurse told her.[6] The pain, then, was framed as a *good thing*. IVF clinics in general have been accused of retrieving too many eggs from patients[7] – putting them through unnecessary procedures for no meaningfully increased chance of pregnancy – and while money may be one factor (more procedures, and lengthier procedures, will ultimately earn the clinic more money), the underlying sense that the more pain a woman is put through, the more likely she is to give birth to a healthy baby, is perhaps another factor.

Each morning on my way to class for my master's in Gender Studies, I would pass a plaque on the wall of the Department of Physiology, Development and Neuroscience at the University of Cambridge's Downing Site. The text on the plaque reads:

> In this building Bob Edwards succeeded in fertilizing a human egg *in vitro*. This work revolutionised treatments for infertility and laid the foundations for human stem cell research.

Robert Edwards created IVF at Cambridge University, along with Patrick Steptoe, and a woman who was historically left out of this story: Jane Purdy. Edwards was a physiologist at the university; Steptoe an obstetrician and gynaecologist at the Royal Oldham Hospital, who specialised in collecting ova laparoscopically; and Purdy was a nurse and pioneering embryologist. Purdy ran Edward's laboratory and was the first person to see an artificially fertilised embryo divide.[8] She died in 1985, at the age of thirty-nine, so when the Nobel Prize committee awarded the 2010 prize in Physiology or Medicine for the development of IVF, it was only Edwards to whom the prize could be given. Steptoe also missed out on the prize as he had also died, three years after Purdy. Unlike Purdy, however, Steptoe's name continued to be linked to the development and he received posthumous recognition for his work whereas Purdy, by and large, did not. And it wasn't just posthumous recognition she lacked, but recognition during her lifetime too. When Edwards's papers opened to the public in 2019, it was revealed that the authorities were repeatedly refusing to acknowledge her central role in the invention of IVF.[9] Despite Edwards's petition, Purdy's name was not included on the plaque unveiled in 1982 at a hospital in Oldham, where many of the original procedures were carried out. Similarly, even though Purdy was the co-founder of the Bourn Hall Clinic, the world's first IVF clinic, located in a village outside Cambridge, her name was also omitted from the commemorative plaque installed there in 2013.

Purdy, Roberts and Steptoe conducted their ground-breaking research with modest resources and minimal financial support. Because of the ethical controversy surrounding their work at the time, the UK government's medical research founder, the Medical Research Council, refused to sponsor their work.[10] Backed only by local funding from Edwards's university and Steptoe's hospital, and after ten years of intense research, the first 'test tube' baby, Louise Brown, was born in 1978. Hers was the embryo that Purdy cultivated in the laboratory and first observed dividing under the microscope.[11]

Despite the fact that the basic IVF technique they developed has not changed, much IVF would be unrecognisable to Purdy, Roberts and Steptoe today. Since their research, doctors around the world have performed over 2.5 million IVF cycles a year, resulting in more than half a million deliveries.[12] The Universal Declaration of Human Rights, adopted by the UN General Assembly in 1948, states that all people have a right to found a family.[13] In 2015, the American Society of Reproductive Medicine (ASRM) Ethics Committee reiterated that 'reproduction is a fundamental interest and human right'.[14] However, access to reproductive assistance is severely limited by the exorbitant costs of infertility treatment. While state coverage or subsidy for IVF is available in 125 of the world's 195 countries, and most European states completely fund one or more IVF cycles, patients generally require multiple cycles and state provision usually does not meet the necessary demands of patients.[15] This forces them to pay for their own or additional care. IVF prices in the United States are the highest in the world: the ASRM reports that the average cost of one IVF cycle in the US is $12,400.[16] Then, there are additional fees, such as genetic testing of embryos ($2,000–5,000) and the yearly cost of egg and embryo storage ($1,000). And that's before factoring in the costs of the multitude of add-ons offered by providers – procedures with mysterious and technical-sounding names such as endometrial scratching, intracytoplasmic sperm injection, assisted hatching – which are taken by many of the patients desperate for a successful round of treatment.

These infertility treatment 'add-ons', however, are not what they seem. They are emerging and experimental techniques offered by the clinics on top of the mainstream IVF procedures and are advertised and sold to patients as 'optional extra' solutions, supposed to improve the chances of successful pregnancy.

Add-ons give clinics who offer them a great financial edge. As insurance companies don't generally cover them (and neither does the NHS), private clinics and labs get full whack of the fees. This is especially monetarily beneficial for US clinics, as insurers often give them relatively lower reimbursement rates for the main IVF treatment. Clinics claim to rely on the profits gained through add-ons to counter profit shortfalls derived from the IVF treatments themselves.[17]

Many proponents – and marketers – do not like the word 'add-ons', preferring to use the term 'options for treatment'. 'Add-ons', they feel, has negative connotations and the implication of being unnecessary. This may also encourage stigmatising views of IVF patients as being rich, demanding, and flippant with their spending, even though most people who purchase such additional treatments do so to *save* money, after failed attempt after failed attempt of treatment. Some marketers instead use the pharmacological term 'adjuvant' to describe these products. In technical terms, an adjuvant is a substance used to increase the efficacy of certain drugs. Describing add-ons in this way may be misleading, however, for there is little proof that they do anything of the sort.[18]

In 2016 a group of researchers from the Centre for Evidence-Based Medicine at the University of Oxford carried out an investigation into fertility add-ons offered by UK fertility centres.[19] In their study, they screened the treatments available in all UK centres registered by HFEA (the Human Fertilisation and Embryology Authority), the fertility treatment regulatory agency. Having compiled a list of twenty-seven routinely offered add-ons, the researchers focused on claims made by the clinics about the effectiveness of the treatments. They concluded that twenty-six out of twenty-seven of them were not backed by rigorous research, and that there was no evidence of their effectiveness in improving pregnancy rates whatsoever.

In the UK, 74 per cent of IVF patients reported using at least one add-on. There is no US data on the use of these supplementary procedures, as there is no legal requirement for the clinics to report it. However, given heavy marketing and ubiquitous anecdotal reporting, there is a reason to believe this number is high.[20]

The regulatory response is also indicative of their widespread use. In 2020, HFEA introduced a traffic light rating system for fertility treatment add-ons. The green light is intended for procedures shown to be safe and effective by at least one quality, randomised clinical trial. As of 2022, not a single one out of thirteen add-ons has received a green light.[21]

On the face of things, the US fertility treatment market may appear to be as well regulated as it is in the UK. The US public health authority the CDC (Centers for Disease Control and Prevention) requires fertility centres to report on the details of each treatment cycle, including pregnancy outcomes, number of infertility diagnoses and embryos transferred, the use of fresh versus frozen embryos, and whether donor or non-donor eggs have been used. Similar information is gathered by HFEA in the UK too.

The impression that the US industry is tightly controlled is merely an illusion. There is no penalty if a clinic does not report its data to the CDC. In such instances, it is simply listed as 'non-reporting'. This means that, unlike in the UK, the effectiveness of treatment plans is not monitored at all.[22]

One such add-on is apparently so controversial that it 'prompted experts to stand up and scream at each other at otherwise staid medical conferences', as relayed by Deborah Anderson-Bialis of FertilityIQ, an independent organisation analysing treatment clinics.[23] This method, referred to as reproductive immunology, masks a drastic approach with a benign name. Women are administered with steroids, IV antibodies and other drugs to suppress their immune systems. This is based on the theory that, for some women, their immune systems go into overdrive and erroneously target pregnancy, causing infertility, failed IVF, or miscarriage. However, the immune system suppression has a host of side effects, from causing fever to inducing diabetes and liver failure, not to mention the fact that it simply does not increase the chances of a successful pregnancy.

Suppressing women's immune systems is a particularly risky add-on in the context of an infectious disease pandemic. It also isn't the only invasive add-on procedure offered to women. Endometrial scratching — truly as crude as it sounds — is when a plastic pipette is used to scratch the lining of the uterus. The idea behind it harks back to Israeli doctors noticing, almost twenty years ago, that women who had undergone a biopsy of the uterine lining had seemingly higher rates of pregnancy.[24] This procedure is traumatic, painful and can cause bleeding; it is also largely unsubstantiated. A large study of 1,364 patients of Australian fertility clinics published in the prestigious *New England Journal of Medicine* in 2019 found that endometrial scratching did not increase the rate of live births: the singular desired outcome of all IVF treatment.[25] Despite this, the procedure is recommended by most clinicians in Australia, New Zealand and the UK.[26] Patients, then, are actively being encouraged to undergo painful procedures for absolutely no benefit to their fertility – and they have to pay for them, too.

A physiotherapist told me that my prolapse was probably caused by the epidural I'd had. She said that because I hadn't known when to push, exactly – despite the electronic monitor hooked up to my body that informed me of my contractions, and the midwife who would tell me when to push once I could no longer open my eyes – I had likely pushed too hard, or for too long, or either not hard or for long enough. Her sense was that the epidural had numbed me to the unique 'rhythm' of my labour, leaving me out of sync with myself and, ultimately, causing injury.

In an epidural, an anaesthetic drug is administered via a catheter inserted into the space which surrounds the spinal cord, outside of its protective shielding. The anaesthetic blocks the transmission of nerve signals to the spinal cord, effectively abolishing all pain and sensation below the site of administration.[27]

I had an epidural both times I gave birth; the first time, it was so delayed that the effects only kicked in about five minutes before the neonatal team had to rush in with ventouse and forceps to rescue my struggling son. The second time, also greatly delayed, the catheter was imperfectly positioned and only the left side of my body received the benefit of the drug. It was quite an experience, to be convulsed by breast-to-knee contractions *exclusively* on the one side. In any case, the short-lived and half-arsed (literally, in my case) numbness they brought on was much welcome. I had no side effects afterwards; indeed, I was able to move my legs and bear weight less than half an hour later.

Like many other people I've spoken to, something which greatly dissuaded me from actively planning for an epidural was the prospect of the injection to the spine. I thought it would be unbearably painful. But when push came to shove, and I was labour, I quite literally begged for it: and I have no memory – in comparison to the contractions – of it being painful at all now.

Both times, my epidural had been begrudgingly given. I was questioned repeatedly whether I could really manage without it. I was reminded a number of times that I would not be able to get in the birth pool once I'd had it: there was no going back from there. But I didn't care at all. The scales had fallen from my eyes the moment the contractions had started and all my previous hopes of a peaceful water birth were long gone. I simply couldn't manage the pain.

Should I feel bad about that? Should I feel like any less of a woman – or any less of a mother? Was my birth not a *real* birth? I don't think so. When there is a perfectly safe medical alternative *right there*, why should I choose to feel unnecessary and avoidable pain if I don't want to?

Epidural is the only medication capable of providing *total* pain relief while maintaining consciousness for labour. It is a true marvel of modern medicine, and, unusually in the field of medical innovation developed for women, it is very safe and effective. With contemporary epidural techniques it is even usually possible to walk while anaesthetised, and patients will almost always regain full feeling soon after the catheter is removed. Despite all of this, public health messaging around epidurals is mired in misinformation seemingly aimed at dissuading patients from accessing it.

Much of the erroneous advice is centred on the effectiveness of epidurals. Epidural is administered by an anaesthetist, and, with proper technique, it has unbeatable pain relief properties. Epidural is sometimes unsuccessful on first attempt (in around 12 per cent of cases), but with manipulation and catheter replacement the success rate reaches 98.9 per cent.[28] Many sources, including the NHS website, report the first number, warning women that one in ten epidurals is unsuccessful, which is not true with repeated attempts. It also does not state what it means by 'unsuccessful' (merely, that it does not bring about pain relief). Horror stories concerning the insertion of poorly positioned catheters into the spine leading to permanent paralysis are regularly touted and so many may understand 'unsuccessful' to have more significant consequences than what is actually meant here. Paralysis caused by epidural is *incredibly* rare: the overall rate of persistent neurologic injury is 1 in 257,000 patients.[29] Persistent neurologic injury does not necessarily mean paralysis, which falls on the most extreme end of this categorisation, but more commonly involves tingling sensation, numbness, or chronic nerve pain.

The very rare instances when an epidural is understood to fail (by not providing pain relief) occur when the catheter cannot be positioned correctly at all, or the patient's labour progresses more quickly than expected and the epidural effect does not set in in time. For the latter problem at least, the solution is simple: allow women to have the procedure at the earliest possible stage of labour.

Many online patient resources (including, again, the NHS materials) report that epidurals increase the risk of a need for instrumental delivery.[30] This is a significant deterrent factor for women who might be considering having an epidural. However, this claim no longer stands and has been proven to be based on outdated information; in fact, it is over fifteen years out of date. A 2018 meta-review of epidural analgesia carried out by Cochrane, a British charity that carries out research in evidence-based medicine, found that the risk of needing instrumental delivery disappears altogether in clinical trials published after 2005.[31] This disappearance is explained by improvements in epidural technique in recent years, mostly in using lower doses of anaesthetic. In fact, there is growing evidence that epidural use has a protective function in childbirth. In 2024, University of Glasgow researchers analysed data from over half a million births in the UK and found that epidurals led to an astonishing 35 per cent reduction in severe post-labour complications, with the effect increasing for patients having pre-term babies or those already considered high-risk.[32]

Public messaging around epidurals isn't always clear, and it's difficult to say if attitudes and bias against pain relief in childbirth in general are at play here. Certainly historically, this was the case. Even though the epidural technique was invented in 1921 and its first application in childbirth occurred in 1942, it only became widely available in the West in the 1980s.[33] The method's popularity rose as a response to the natural birth movements of the mid twentieth century.

In the US in 2018, 71 per cent of women received epidurals, which is on the higher end of the spectrum worldwide.[34] In Poland, the total percentage is not reported, but given the fact that only 20 per cent of hospitals offer it at all means that rates will be very low.[35] In the UK this rate is around 30 per cent, which is one of the lowest in Western Europe.[36] The starkest contrast is with France, where, in 2021, 82.4 per cent of women choose epidural analgesia – the highest rate in the world.[37] This popularity is because doctors in French hospitals are engaged in active promotion of the method and commonly recommend it to patients.

Rates of epidural analgesia exploded in France in the 1980s and 1990s, as a direct counter-response to the *décennie contestataire* (decade of dissent): the 1970s. The 1970s in France were characterised by the rise of ecological movements and a general rebellion against technological and industrialised society. Notions of medicalised childbirth came under fire too. Advocacy for epidurals came in turn, and the pendulum eventually swung in their favour. The defenders of pharmacological pain relief won, because the alternatives were replete with uncertainties and practical limitations, and they stirred political tensions. All of these factors prevented the proponents of natural childbirth from forming a unified front and disseminating their ideology widely.[38]

In the UK, many blame low rates of epidural on poor provision: overstretched NHS resources and shortage of anaesthetists. Indeed, austerity measures of the last decade have doubtlessly impacted pain relief options available and likely have something to do with cheaper methods, such as hypnobirthing being widely encouraged, whereas more expensive methods such as epidurals are tacitly deterred. In other contexts where resources are perhaps less squeezed than on the NHS, and/or where other preconceptions about pharmacological versus non-pharmacological methods are held, it is likely that the tables are turned: what is preferred and pushed here is rejected and deterred there.

Ultimately, biased attitudes towards pain relief methods greatly impact women's care. An investigation by the Department of Health and Social Care conducted in early 2020 revealed that women are commonly not receiving the pain relief they are entitled to and are often not informed about the choices, as a result of the 'cult of natural childbirth' in some parts of the NHS.[39] But all attitudes are societal, and exist outside the hospital too. When UK journalist Joanna Moorhead wrote about her experience of childbirth in a 2009 article in the *Independent* titled 'Epidurals are for wimps', she could not make this clearer:

> Of course there are moments in a labour when pain relief seems enticing: but labour isn't called labour for nothing, and in the midst of the hardest job you ever do, you need to keep your wits about you. But our society has ceased to believe drug-free childbirth is possible, and forgotten that it's how every woman used to do it.[40]

Aside from asking the obvious question of *why* should someone feel pain when they don't have to, need we remind Joanna Moorhead that there are lots of other things we women used to do more often in childbirth too, such as die? Before the advent of modern medicine, until the late eighteenth century, 25 women per 1,000 would die in childbirth (a loose and likely conservative estimate).[41] Moorhead makes it clear that to suffer makes one superior; specifically, that for a woman to suffer in childbirth is a superior act than *not* to suffer in childbirth. Where does that pain, and suffering, end? Who is the most valorised woman in this supposed competition? Who wins?

My epidural didn't cause my prolapse, just like feeling excessive pain during IVF procedures does not improve your chances of falling pregnant. And it isn't just in areas of reproductive health where women are subject to unnecessary and avoidable pain. In 2019, the patient-led campaign 'Hysteroscopy Action' was launched in the UK.[42] It aimed to raise awareness of painful hysteroscopy procedures for women, and the lack of preparation – and pain relief – offered to those going through it.

Hysteroscopy is a form of endoscopy (similar to gastroscopy or colonoscopy), but what is being visualised is the interior of the uterus. It is used to investigate and diagnose problems with the womb.

Hysteroscopies allow a physician to directly see what's going on inside the uterus and identify any potential problems. Often these can be a source of unexplained bleeding or pain, and so commonly include causes such as fibroids, polyps, and cancers; anatomical abnormalities causing difficulties with conception, such as a septate or bicornuate uterus (a range of conditions when the inside of the uterus is divided, instead of forming a single continuous space); even dislodged IUDs.

During the procedure, a speculum is used to dilate the vagina, followed by insertion of the hysteroscope. The hysteroscope is equipped with a camera and a light, located on the tip of a thin, long tube, and is pushed through the opening in the cervix into the uterus. This is, of course, painful.

However, if you were to simply push the hysteroscope tube into the uterus, you wouldn't see that much. Contrary to popular drawings of the womb, which depict it in cross-section as a big empty cavity sitting on top of the vagina, the uterus more closely resembles a collapsed plastic bag. There isn't much space in there, although the uterus can of course expand dramatically during pregnancy to contain even multiple fully developed foetuses (and their attendant baggage). Outside of pregnancy, the volume of the empty space inside the uterus is around 15–50 millilitres – somewhere between a tablespoon and a quarter of a teacup's worth of liquid.[43] This means there isn't much room to operate a camera. During the hysteroscopy, then, the uterus must be distended, or inflated like a balloon. This is achieved by pumping into it 1–2 litres of liquid.[44] So more like a water balloon, then. A very big, very painful, water balloon.

The first recorded attempt to view the inside of the uterus dates back to 1869, and was undertaken by Diomede Pantaleóni, an Italian physician and later statesman.[45] Pantaleóni's patient was a 60-year-old woman who presented with post-menopausal bleeding. He examined her cervix and vagina, and, having found nothing wrong, decided to experiment by looking inside the uterus through a long metal tube – a technique he had used previously with success in other patients to explore the bladder. Twenty-four hours prior to this planned procedure, he had prepared the patient by inserting into her cervix a device called 'laminaria tent', an early form of a cervical dilator. These tents, commonly employed at the time, were made from dried stalks of seaweed. Placed inside the cervix, the stalks would absorb moisture and expand, leading to the dilation of the cervix. They were also notoriously difficult to sterilise.

Once the patient was suitably dilated, Pantaleóni removed the tent. With the patient lying on her left side, he had her move as close to the edge of the bed as possible. This had nothing to do with patient comfort; rather, her position was dictated by his fear of setting fire to the furniture, as his technique required using a paraffin lamp with an open flame. Pantaleóni reported inserting the 20-cm tube 'with greatest ease', which allowed him to see the interior of her uterus. There, he found 'polypous vegetation', which he promptly proceeded to cauterise by pouring corrosive solutions of chromic acid and silver nitrate down the tube and into the uterus. In his paper he then reported 'the most perfect success, with no return of illness'.[46] The patient's experience of pain was not recorded.

The hysteroscopy may be described as a simple procedure, but it may not be painless. The NHS website acknowledges that there are considerable differences in pain experienced during the procedure: 'Some women feel no or only mild pain during a hysteroscopy, but for others the pain can be severe.'[47] A study by researchers from Bologna showed that 34.8 per cent of patients who undergo anaesthesia-free diagnostic hysteroscopy report severe pain.[48] Another study, conducted at a teaching hospital in São Paulo, reported moderate to severe pain in 68.4 per cent of patients: that is pain of above 5 on the scale of 10.[49]

Pain is the key reason why hysteroscopies are terminated prematurely. Studies estimate that 84 per cent of failed hysteroscopies are due to excessive discomfort or pain. While pain relief for hysteroscopy is available, either as local or general anaesthesia, it is not generally proactively offered in the UK. The patient advocacy group Campaign

Against Painful Hysteroscopy surveyed hundreds of patients, finding that 80 per cent of respondents have not been informed about the pain relief options available to them.

Part of the reason why NHS hospitals are reluctant to offer women pain relief for their hysteroscopies is due to cost. NHS hospitals are indeed incentivised to perform outpatient hysteroscopies on women, and in 2013 the NHS nearly doubled the rates that hospitals would be paid to perform hysteroscopies as an outpatient procedure, where general anaesthesia cannot be given.[50] British MP Lyn Brown has spoken in Parliament of the pain patients have been put through during hysteroscopy procedures in the name of cost-cutting measures that limited access to pain relief.[51]

Despite the British government agreeing to roll out better access to pain relief for hysteroscopies, this is largely yet to be seen, with Covid-19 measures often used as a justification for why this hasn't been the case. While money is evidently one cause of a lack of access to adequate pain relief, it is not convincing to say this is the whole story behind it. Failed hysteroscopies cost the NHS money, as do procedures required to treat cancers, and conditions in those who have refused hysteroscopy over the fear of or a previous experience of severe pain. It is not always straightforwardly cost-effective to deny women access to pain relief. Someone, somewhere, decides which procedures do and do not warrant pain relief. These decisions are based on attitudinal beliefs about who experiences pain, and whose is worse: who deserves to feel pain, and who does not.

One could argue that hysteroscopies are not so commonly done, so perhaps this problem does not largely affect that many women. The question whether this is a viable argument at all aside, there is another procedure, which *is* commonly done to women. In fact, all people with a cervix are expected to undergo it, on a regular basis. This is cervical cancer screening, commonly known as the smear test (or Pap smear in North America). Smear tests are carried out all over the world and count among the most commonly conducted screening procedures, alongside blood pressure measurements, cholesterol level testing, mammograms, clinical breast exams, and eye examinations.

But smear tests can also be very painful, and there has been remarkably little improvement in the way they are done.

Virtually all cervical cancer is caused by HPV – human papillomavirus.[52] HPV is highly infectious; almost everyone gets it at some point in their life. The vast majority of those infections are asymptomatic and over 90 per cent will have completely disappeared within two years. HPV strains fall into two different groups, depending on cells targeted by the virus: skin (causing warts, etc.) and then the cells lining the mouth, throat, anus, and genitals. These HPV strains are sexually transmitted, with HPV being the most common sexually transmitted infection in the world.[53]

Genital HPV can be transmitted through any intimate skin-to-skin contact (not just penetrative sex), and this includes vaginal–penile sex, penile–anal sex, penile–oral sex, vaginal–oral sex, and use of sex toys or other objects. A small group of genital HPV strains (fourteen in total) are classed as high-risk and, in a very small number of cases, the virus-infected cells can develop into cancer. When HPV infects a cell, it causes it to divide uncontrollably – creating more and more copies of itself. With high-risk HPVs, this uncontrolled cell division can result in a patch of infected cells that escape the control of the immune system and make what is called a 'pre-cancerous' lesion. This lesion, given time, may develop into cervical, anal, vaginal, vulvar, penile, or throat cancer.[54]

A smear test involves a sample of cells being taken from the opening of the cervix. A long brush, inserted through a speculum, is lodged in the vagina. Cervical cells collected on the brush are then placed on a glass slide, which is inspected by a cytologist under a microscope. The cytologist will stain the cells with special dyes and look for abnormal or pre-cancerous cells, which are a sign of the ongoing HPV infection and indicate an increased risk of cervical cancer in the future.[55]

The process by which HPV develops into cervical cancer, however, can take a long time, often between ten and twenty years. This is why smear tests are only offered in the UK every five years for people aged between twenty-five and sixty-four.[56] For older women, this generates an exclusion group, and is based on erroneous presuppositions.

If testing is offered every five years, that must mean that there is a window within five years, between being infected and the cancer beginning to develop, where it can still be caught and treated. So what, then, for a person who catches the virus at age sixty-five? The life expectancy for women in the UK is eighty-three. That leaves the average woman almost twenty years to catch HPV and for it to develop into cancer beyond the screening cut-off age.

The NHS based its decision not to screen women over the age of sixty-five on statistical modelling (that is likely skewed towards cost-cutting measures) rather than actual, empirical data.[57] For a start, research finds that around 40 per cent of women aged 65–80 are sexually active.[58] Also – and incontrovertibly – the rates of people developing cervical cancer over the age of sixty-five are markedly high. In the UK, half of all cervical cancer deaths are among women aged sixty-five years or over.[59]

Smear tests are particularly painful for older women. Numerous physiological changes that take place in the vagina post-menopause likely contribute to cervical screening being painful.[60] Vaginal atrophy, narrowing and increased dryness are likely to make the insertion of a speculum particularly painful. And it isn't just older women who report pain – both physical and psychological – during smear tests. It can also be more painful for those of all ages suffering from vaginismus, endometriosis, vaginal ectropion, retroverted uterus, vaginal dryness, FGM, pre-existing scarring, pre-existing trauma, bodily dysphoria, and other vaginal and psychological conditions.

This experience of pain, or the anticipation of it, can translate into people of all demographics choosing not to attend testing. Globally, where testing is commonly available, testing for all demographics is low. In the UK, around 25 per cent of eligible women fail to attend their smear test appointments.[61] In a study of the women who decline invitations, 16 per cent of respondents gave 'negative past experiences' as the main reason for their refusal. The survey failed to probe these 'negative past experiences' further, and did not give an option for respondents to cite 'pain'.[62]

Recent public initiatives aimed at increasing attendance tend to focus on 'misunderstanding' of the process or otherwise 'embarrassment' experienced by the patient. Part of this may be down to the findings of a 2016 study, one that was actually widely misreported. UK charity Jo's Cervical Cancer Trust surveyed 3,002 women aged 25–29 about their experiences and perception of smear tests. In a summary of the survey's key findings, it gave the following figure: '72% of the 25–29 year olds surveyed do not feel comfortable getting undressed in front of doctors or nurses however in stark contrast just under one in ten (8.4%) would consider surgery to alter the way their genitals look'.[63]

Putting the bizarrely irrelevant point about genital surgery aside for one moment, this summary of the precise finding is misleading. For a start, nowhere in the summary does it indicate whether or not those interviewed had not attended their smear tests – although given the title of the survey ('Barriers to Cervical Screening in 25–29 Year Olds') it seems that *72 per cent of people who did not attend their smear test* did not attend *because* of this discomfort. Further down in the actual findings – where most journalists and some researchers clearly did not foray – we learn that only 17 per cent of those interviewed had never attended a smear, and 33 per cent had delayed it, compared with 44 per cent who had never delayed a smear. So: 77 per cent of those interviewed had attended a smear test and only 17 per cent had not (the rest answered 'not applicable' to this question). Most of those who gave embarrassment as a barrier to smear tests had attended, nonetheless.

Furthermore, the question that elicited this response is murkier still. The respondents were asked the following:

Which of the following statements do you agree with? (Tick all that apply)
- I'm happy with how my body looks (33.8%)
- I'm happy with how my genitals look (31.1%)
- None of the above (29.4%)
- I feel comfortable getting undressed and changed in front of a doctor/nurse (27.7%)
- I have been for a bikini wax or would consider going for a bikini wax (27.1%)
- I feel comfortable getting undressed and changed in front of friends (25%)

- I feel comfortable getting undressed in front of other women e.g. at the swimming pool or gym (21.8%)
- I would consider getting labiaplasty (cosmetic surgery on female genitals) (8.4%).[64]

It is simply not plausible to infer from this finding that 72 per cent of women do not attend cervical screening due to embarrassment at being undressed in front of their doctor or nurse – but this is exactly what the British press did in the weeks, months and even years after the publication of this survey. 'Embarrassment makes women avoid smear tests, charity says' was the headline of one BBC article two years later.[65] 'Young women putting off smear tests due to embarrassment, study finds',[66] screamed another in the *Independent* – three years after. The 'finding' even made its way into the NHS mainframe and is still cited on many trusts' smear test websites and in their literature today.

While the press wastes column inches explaining to those who already go to smear tests not to be embarrassed by them, many others who do not attend due to pain and trauma are left feeling invisible and dismissed. It's worth noting that while Jo's Trust was able to highlight highly suspect questions about bikini waxing and genital surgery in its press release and key findings section (what does that information have to do with smear tests, pray tell?), it failed to point out how 36 per cent of patients reported experiencing pain during their last smear test.

Failing to recognise pain as a meaningful barrier to testing implies that perhaps it doesn't really exist. In the survey's press release, it is relayed how 25 per cent of women who put off a smear did so due to 'worrying it would be painful'. More women *experienced* pain than worried about it, but guess which finding the survey decided to foreground?

When public health messaging does acknowledge the prospect of pain, it does so dismissively. NHS and charity messaging repeatedly asserts that 'for *most* women, smear tests are painless' – something that is factually dishonest. Given the prevalence of the above listed conditions that can render testing especially painful (take endometriosis, for example, which is thought to affect 10 per cent of all women[67]), and those 36 per cent in the Jo's Trust survey, there are indeed a great many women who *will* experience pain. Merely stating that 'most women do not feel pain' only serves to make the great many women who *do* feel pain consider their experiences to be atypical or imagined. In material terms, enough women experience pain and discomfort to dissuade them from attending appointments, and this alone should move healthcare providers to at least alter their messaging, and at best rethink testing methods entirely.

How could testing be done differently to decrease the pain? For a start, home testing has been found to be a game-changer when it comes to opening access to screening. From the comfort and privacy of your own home, you insert a swab into your vagina (around only 2 inches deep as opposed to over 4 inches deep in a smear test) and simply twist it around before posting it off for lab analysis. Home testing can be less painful for patients for a number of reasons: the use of a far smaller swab, the self-administration, and the ability to move around and change position at leisure.

Clinically, these tests work differently from the classic smear test, but they yield similar results. As the swab does not go in as far as the cervix, it does not pick up cervical cells, but instead detects the presence of certain high-risk strains of HPV. In 2019, the World Health Organisation conducted a systematic review of thirty-three studies with 369,000 total participants across the world, confirming that self-administered HPV tests delivered clinical results no different to the classic smear tests, but had significantly improved uptake.[68]

Another group of patients for whom home testing can improve screening rates are trans men and non-binary people with a cervix. A 2021 British research group found that while these patients are equally likely to develop cervical cancer as cis women, they are less likely to access screening.[69] In the UK, those who are not registered as 'female' with a GP – despite having a cervix – can miss out on vital, automated, reminders for testing: a seemingly glaring oversight. But merely getting these patients into the surgery is not always enough, when the process itself can cause and trigger intense gender dysphoria, pain, and trauma. And that's not to mention the fact that healthcare providers have been found to actively abuse and discriminate against trans and non-binary patients, with non-binary patients tending to take the biggest brunt of that abuse. Another 2021 survey, this time by the organisation TransActual, found that 75 per cent of non-binary patients experience transphobia in medical settings in comparison with 71 per cent of trans men and 63 per cent of trans women. That discrimination can also take the form of inadequate care: 55 per cent of non-binary people surveyed felt that GPs in the UK simply do not understand, and are thus unable to meet, their healthcare needs.[70]

Over half of trans men and non-binary patients polled in the former 2021 survey responded that they would prefer home testing. Some of those who did *not* prefer home testing cited the misconception that it is less reliable than smear tests. Somewhat ironically, home testing could actually provide *more* accurate samples for trans and non-binary patients. A 2014 US paper found that: 'Pap smears on transgender men have a ten-fold higher incidence of an unsatisfactory result compared to non-transgender women.'[71] This is likely due to the difficulties that practitioners face in obtaining an adequate sample, when their patients are particularly distressed and/or in pain. There is also some evidence to suggest that longer testosterone use can cause a thinning of the vaginal walls, potentially leading to increased pain during testing. Seeing as the home test circumnavigates the need for speculum insertion, which can cause particular pain and gender dysphoria, home testing is likely to achieve better results for trans and non-binary patients.

In February 2021, the NHS launched one such flagship scheme called 'YouScreen'. Thirty-one thousand women, trans men and non-binary people across London, in certain areas where cervical screening is historically the lowest, were offered self-testing kits. The head of the study, Dr Anita Lim at King's College London, said:

> Self-sampling is a game-changer for cervical screening. [. . .] Women who don't come for regular screening are at the highest risk of developing cervical cancer, so it is crucial that we find ways like this to make screening easier and protect women from what is a largely preventable cancer.[72]

Dr Lim also found that home testing makes a big difference for older patients. In a randomised controlled trial, offering a smaller swab test without the use of a speculum raised uptake from 4.9 per cent to 20.4 per cent for patients over the age of fifty.[73]

It is frustrating that despite the positive results of home testing, health providers globally have been slow to embrace them. Self-administered HPV testing is certainly nothing new, with one of the first studies to prove its benefits having been conducted over twenty years ago in Mexico.[74] Dr Lim's 2021 London scheme was arguably only so big due to the Covid-19 pandemic. Due to social distancing restrictions, cervical screening appointments had been off-limits for many in the early 2020s. It is telling that despite low smear-test turnout for many years, the appropriation of a new method was led not by patients' needs but rather extraordinary and cost-cutting measures ushered in by a global pandemic. We shall see what comes of Dr Lim's study – and others around the world – if the merits of home testing are appreciated and the method embraced, or if we continue with coercive guilt-tripping campaigns, all with the consequence of low testing numbers and unacceptably high rates of cervical cancer.

Dilator therapy is a treatment, rather than diagnostic tool, that's prescribed for many gynaecological conditions and comes with high rates of reported pain. Its overall success is highly dubious, too.

Vaginal dilators are often described as tube-like (or tampon-shaped) semi-hard objects which are inserted into the vagina.[75] They come in a variety of materials and sizes, which are gradually increased during the therapy in order to 'open up' and 'train' the vagina into a certain shape or, in the case of vaginismus, function. Dilators are currently the most widely recommended treatment for vaginismus. Vaginismus is a condition in which the muscles around the vagina tighten in anticipation of penetration, often making it painful or impossible. Vaginismus is related to dyspareunia (pain during sex), and difficulties in distinguishing between the two have led some to argue that the two conditions ought to be considered as one.

The use of dilators in treating vaginismus is based on a few low-quality studies, on only small samples of participants, and some in particularly questionable settings.[76] Dilator use was advocated and much popularised by 'sex therapy' pioneers Masters and Johnson. William H. Masters and Virginia E. Johnson were a research team focusing on sexual disorders from the mid-to-late twentieth century. Much of their work has been incorporated into the canon of sexual medical healthcare and continues to be drawn on to this day, despite the fact that they have been extensively criticised for bringing restrictive cultural ideas about sex and gender (and heterosexual sex at that) into their work. Sufferers of vaginismus were never treated on their own, but as part of a married couple. Masters and Johnson explicitly excluded non-heterosexual couples from their studies into dilator use, and elsewhere engaged in homosexual-to-heterosexual conversion therapy. As Canadian sexologist Peggy J. Kleinplatz puts it of the Masters and Johnson approach to sexology, 'the ultimate outcome goal in the treatment of the sexual dysfunctions in women (and men) was the ability to achieve intercourse in the missionary position'.[77] She also lambasts their approach to evaluating the treatment of vaginismus in terms of 'successful penetration', something that by and large continues to this day, without considering other factors such as pain, pleasure and emotional well-being. Masters and Johnson would have their patients, suffering from vaginismus, use the dilators incrementally until they were able to accommodate the insertion of their husband's penis. Penetration was the only goal – whether the patients felt pain or even pleasure was not included in the study. They reported an almost 100 per cent success rate of dilator use in treating vaginismus.[78] Later studies based on this method have, unlike Masters and Johnson, found that where patients have been able to successfully penetrate dilators by the end of their treatment, up to 50 per cent still experience pain.[79]

In the case of MRKH (Mayer-Rokitansky-Küster-Hauser syndrome), dilator therapy is used as a non-surgical method to create a 'neovagina'.[80] MRKH is a congenital disorder characterised by an absence of or the underdevelopment of the uterus and vagina. This can make sex difficult, and in most cases causes infertility.

As a first-line treatment, the dilator therapy usually involves a hospital stay of between three days and a week. A specialist nurse will administer the dilators in several sessions each day until the patient is judged ready to carry on using them at home. Many studies show this treatment to be successful, if by 'success' you solely consider vaginal length achieved. An Australian study of sixty-eight patients between 2000 and 2014 found that the median increase in vaginal length after dilator therapy was 4 cm, and that 97 per cent of women involved felt 'satisfied' with sexual intercourse at the end of the treatment. The paper goes on to conclude that intensive dilator therapy sessions to treat MRKH should thus be considered before surgical options are explored.[81]

How much pain (and potential trauma) are these patients subjected to throughout those sessions? We have little idea, because few research studies use pain as a parameter. 'Sexual satisfaction' will be judged instead. In the aforementioned study, 97 per cent of patients reported satisfaction with sexual intercourse after dilator therapy treatment. But what does 'satisfaction' mean in this context? Many patients prior to the treatment were unable to have vaginal penetrative sex at all; others would have experienced excruciating pain. Any improvement on either starting point could be understood as 'satisfactory'; that doesn't mean that pleasurable or even pain-free sex is being had.

Studies into dilator therapy for MRKH that meaningfully engage with patient experience paint a more complex picture. A 2017 study found that: 'Despite reported success rates for vaginal dilation in neovagina creation, patients might be ambivalent about using vaginal dilators.'[82]

Many of the patients who had or were using dilators expressed negative feelings about the therapy. One patient described it as 'a constant reminder that I am different'.[83] Others disliked the amount of time it took. Patients dilating at home are recommended to do so for 20–30 minutes at a time, in three separate cycles. This involves up to 1 hour 30 minutes of dilation every day for the course of the treatment. Successful treatment can take up to six months of self-dilation.

It's understandable that patients would feel frustrated with this. They are expected to make a significant time-investment for a treatment that may not work and which for some serves as a 'constant reminder' of their condition. And all of this for a treatment that is no permanent cure. According to an NHS patient leaflet, once the six months are up and a vagina has been successfully created, 'it will remain a normal size if you are having sex regularly [. . .] If you are not sexually active for a short time you may have to use the dilators briefly again.'[84]

The use of the term 'briefly' here is misleading, for there is no evidence that, without regular dilation (either through sexual intercourse or dilator therapy), the new vagina will remain adequately stretched enough for later penetration. It also includes sexual intercourse as legitimate therapeutic advice. Patients are encouraged to rely on sexual relationships to maintain their physical health.

In a paper on successful vaginal creation for MRKH patients through dilation, it's recommended that vaginoplasty surgery ought to be offered to 'patients who are unwilling or unable to obtain an adequate neovagina with dilatation'.[85] Despite this recommendation, numerous NHS trusts in the UK *only* offer patients surgery once they have completed dilator therapy and proved that it does not work for them, and many patients all over the world will find themselves being dissuaded from surgery by their practitioners in place of dilator therapy. In a letter in the medical journal *Obstetrics and Gynecology* from November 1972, two doctors recommended sexual intercourse for creating a vagina in patients with MRKH.[86] So convinced are they by the success of intercourse in creating a neovagina, that they conclude the letter with their hope that surgical treatments for MRKH will be confined to medical history in place of this superior treatment method.

We may think we have come a long way from the days of doctors recommending a patient without a vagina to be effectively fucked into having one; but how far have we really come when contemporary NHS guidelines say that *after* a vagina has been created, patients need to be fucked if they want to keep it?

In so much of women's healthcare, we see an expectation that patients should expect and put up with pain; in fact, that pain – as in the case of childbirth and IVF – can sometimes lead to *better* health outcomes. Failing that, the pain will at least bring women closer to some mystical, ancient experience of true womanhood. All of this is rooted in a deep-seated, cultural misogyny that medical science ought to see past but, all too often, incorporates instead.

When writing this book, I met with a leading gynaecological surgeon to question him – specifically – on the issue of inordinately painful procedures. The conversation, over dinner, seemed to be going well. The surgeon – a white, British cis man in his mid-to-late sixties – showed a sensitivity to how it must feel for women, especially those who have experienced sexual assault, to be treated by a male gynaecologist, and the efforts he personally makes to try and put them at ease. While the appearance of trans men in his practice was 'quite new' for him, in recent decades, he fervently believed these men had every right to be treated with gender-affirming, specialist care. He also told me that it has always been, and likely always will be, a fight within the hospital to get his patients suffering from gynaecological conditions to be seen first, as women's healthcare – where it is not oncology – is still implicitly treated like an 'optional extra'.

I thought I was on safe terrain. Things only soured between us when I moved onto the topic of hysteroscopies, and how the very simple administration of pain relief can solve the problem. So why isn't it standardly administered? The surgeon looked at me incredulously when I posed this.

'But we can't just *hand out* pain relief willy-nilly!' he said, half-laughing and half-sighing, as though he was talking to a dimwit. 'If we did that, then when the women come in to have babies down the line and they want to get pethidine I'd have to tell them, no, sorry, it's all gone on the hysteroscopies!'

But pethidine *wouldn't* be used for hysteroscopies, I pointed out. In America they use topical local anaesthetics like lidocaine gel—

He waved this away.

'It doesn't matter. The budget will have been exceeded. There's only so much money.'

I was stumped. For someone who seemed, initially, so sensitive to the needs of patients in women's healthcare, this struck me as obfuscating. Why was he so unwilling to see the bigger picture?

I took a different tack.

'So it's an issue of women's healthcare merely being underfunded?' I asked him. 'If there was simply more money, you could administer as much pain relief as you like?'

'Steady on!' he said sharply, as though I had asserted something shocking if not outright dangerous. Then, to placate me: 'Not *everyone* feels pain during hysteroscopy. There'd be no point.'

'But what's the point in making those who do feel pain suffer for it? Needlessly?'

It was here that he shut down the conversation. Not with a hard word or a rude look, the clattering of a fork on a plate or the ostentatious throwing back of a full glass of wine, but by somehow, silently reminding me that he is *not* someone used to being spoken back to like this. For all of his earlier talk of making the women who come into his office feel empowered enough to speak to him as an equal, or an inferior, even, I was far from being in charge now. And so I navigated us back into safer territory, as was expected of me, and judged an easy target.

'So the abortion ban in the US . . . awful, isn't it?'

I'm not sure if I had been the first person to put to him that his patients don't *have* to experience pain at all, sometimes. Perhaps he went away and mulled over this seemingly earth-shattering realisation of the most complex kind. I would have no way of knowing what he subsequently concluded, though, because when the time came for us to part he told me in a joking way: 'Now, I *don't* look forward to seeing you ever again!'

An old parting joke for a doctor, I'm sure, but I couldn't help but read into it a harder truth. That he didn't want to be burdened by the question of whether or not he is complicit in the unnecessary administration of pain ever again.

3. We're Listening

Before I gave birth to my first child, my mother-in-law Jola came to visit us from Poland. Her suitcase was laden with parcels of hand-sewn baby clothes that she and her sisters had made, thirty years earlier, for Andrzej. They didn't show a speck of wear, so well had they been looked after; the only tell was their eighties style: terry cloth and lace aplenty.

These gifts for the new baby came as a surprise to me. In our previous meetings, I had assumed Jola wasn't all that interested: she rarely asked me questions about the pregnancy, and never shared anything about her own. In fact, she had never even shared her birth experience with Andrzej. Whenever he had asked politely about it in the past, she had always – equally politely – changed the subject. He quickly got the hint, and stopped asking questions.

What we had taken for a lack of interest was, we soon learned, something else entirely: it was birth trauma.

I don't know what made her start talking about it that night. Maybe it was an unconscious answer to my desperate need to hear it now, on the eve of my own labour. Perhaps it was her way of trying to warn me about what was to come.

Poland was still behind the Iron Curtain when Jola fell pregnant. Martial law might have been lifted and an internal passport no longer required to move between cities, but travel was still difficult. She hadn't seen her family for many months and was unlikely to do so in the near future. She was living with her husband Zbigniew in a small, shared apartment, in accommodation provided by the university they both worked for. The communal facilities did not quite stretch to a washing machine, and as soon as she became pregnant she knew that having one would be the key to maintaining her sanity.

But this was Poland in 1987: one did not simply walk into a shop and purchase a washing machine. With skyrocketing inflation it took them five months to save up enough and then they had the queueing system to contend with. This involved standing outside the shop in two-hour shifts, every other day, at any given time day or night – for an unspecified length of time. It could go on for three weeks, or three months. And *no one* jumped the queue or sent a stand-in, even if one's wife went into premature labour. Which is exactly what happened to Jola.

'Don't give birth' was all she could think of as Zbigniew dropped her off at the nearby hospital after her waters broke unexpectedly. Only patients were allowed inside, and so they parted tearfully in the draughty entranceway.

In reception, someone – unintroduced and unannounced – put their hand up Jola's dress to confirm that she was in established labour. She was swept away to a windowless room with bare concrete walls, containing eight beds and seven women. Each woman was sitting upright, blocked partially from view by a curtain, but these curtains only reached neck height, so she could see every exhausted face, and would make disturbingly intimate eye contact with them as they moaned and screamed. They excoriated God, their husbands, each other. 'He'll never put it in me again!' shouted one of them, repeatedly. There was a lock on the outside of the door.

Staff shaved her pubic hair and administered an enema before buckling her legs into stirrups. The nurses came periodically to check on her progress – manually, before taking their hands out of her to write on their clipboards – and then left her to scream along in chorus with the rest.

No pain relief was administered, not even paracetamol, and none was expected. At some point in the running, doctors were summoned and one – without warning, without telling her this is what they did for almost all the women – slipped cold metal scissors between her vagina and anus and cut, in between her contractions: the most excruciating time to do it.

All she knew was a pain that yearned for death. In Jola's memory the scene skips a beat from here to the point where a baby is born. Her son – her *syn*, and sin – was held out at arm's length for her to look at, for a moment: deathly blue and silent.

He was whisked away by an entourage of medics; as the door

closed behind them, she heard the scratch of the lock. 'Where are they taking him?' she asked the few who remained. 'Is he alive? Will he live?' She received no reply – instead, she felt hands slowly closing around her limbs, restraining her, and realised, in dawning horror, that she was about to be sewn back up. Consciousness left her, and she promptly passed out.

When she came round, she was in another room: the post-delivery ward. Surrounding her were the women who had birthed alongside her, no longer half hidden by chin-height curtains. The room was very quiet, save for stifled weeping and bedsheet-muffled sobs, and one of the women was missing. Jola never found out why.

Panic began to close in. She tried to calm herself with the fact that all the other babies had been taken away immediately after delivery too. Although none of the other babies, like hers, had been premature, or looked half-dead, and hadn't made a single sound or cry.

An hour or so later, the first feeding time came. Each woman was given their baby to nurse, every three hours. Some babies would be sleeping, others screaming. It didn't make any difference: *this* was the time that they would be fed. On the institution's clock.

The women were given their babies – all of them, that is, except for Jola. No one could tell her why.

She waited for the next feed. Again, every baby came except for hers. Unable to stave the panic off any longer, she burst into shameful, noisy tears. Certain that her baby had died, she latched onto a fresh, terrible thought: what if they had already taken him to the incinerator? She hadn't even touched him.

Disgruntled by the scene she was causing, a nurse agreed to go and ask someone what was going on if only Jola *promised* to stop disturbing the communal feed. Jola forced herself to stop crying. Despite her new composure, the first thing the paediatrician did was to admonish her, 'Stop being hysterical.' And then, like an afterthought, he added: 'Your son is alive.'

Jola learned that he was being kept in an incubator. She had seen incubators on the television, in programmes from the West, but did not know the name for it, and the paediatrician did not elaborate, so she imagined her small baby locked tight in an iron lung, or a straitjacket.

By this time, her milk had come. With nowhere to go, it made angry red rocks of her breasts, which burned acutely. A young trainee midwife who heard about her agony approached her in the night – against the rules – and quietly showed her how to self-express into a bottle. Once Jola had filled it to the brim with milk she carried on, emptying herself out into her hospital gown so that it soaked through to her skin, easing her painful engorgement.

It wasn't until the end of the next day that Jola was allowed to see her baby.

You can't touch him, they told her, only look at him through the scratched glass of the incubator, once a day for two minutes.

There he lay entombed and naked but for a clean cloth nappy, all gangly limbs, fingers and toes so small, so translucent, they appeared almost webbed.

Zbigniew, meanwhile, was going out of his mind. He had walked to the hospital every few hours since leaving Jola after her waters had broken, but his fretful manner irritated the staff, and a note had been left on the desk not to tell him *anything* about the fate of his wife and child.

And he had still had to queue for that '*pieprzoną* washing machine' (not that Zbigniew was one to swear often), trudging between the university where he worked, the shop and the hospital. The days were shortening and it had started to snow.

Eventually, after two weeks of agonising refusal, the reception staff gave in, and he was silently led to a metal grate that looked into the maternity unit. Jola's face peeked through the bars; this is how Zbigniew learned that she was alive. Behind her he could see a line of other women waiting to speak to their respective husbands: those who were careful not to irritate the staff. Zbigniew only had a few minutes to talk to Jola, in the full hearing of the waiting women, and she was quickly able to tell him: I had a boy. He's alive.

Weeks passed like this, with Jola trapped in the twilight zone of the hospital, a few moments to speak to Zbigniew through the bars, a few moments to look at her son through the glass, and the rest of the day devoted to the frustratingly tedious task of self-expressing. She kept this up under the instruction of the nurses who failed to tell her that she would have to slowly phase it out if she wanted her milk production to stop. This wasn't an option, and neither was breastfeeding her child. She was trapped in an endless, pointless cycle – and they would dispose of her milk at the end of the day anyway. She had no idea when she would be released; she only knew that it was twinned with the fate of her baby, whose progress or otherwise deterioration she was not informed of. Leaving the ward, even for a moment, was strictly not permitted.

Jola regulated her expressions to coincide with the feedings on the ward, to distract herself from the arrival of the other babies. This may have spared her some heartbreak, but it did not spare her the humiliation of the daily examinations. The women were instructed in unison to sit, knees hitched up to their chests, their bare vulvas revealed to the room. A doctor would glide among them unhurriedly, peering in here, offering up a comment there, while a nurse followed him round with a clipboard.

Every day, Jola thought it would be a relief to be told that today they were leaving, but when it finally did come, she didn't feel a thing. Her doctor had discharged her and she could go, now. It was the middle of the day and a call was put in to Zbigniew's work but, of course, he was not there: he was in the queue for the washing machine. Jola could've waited for him to come and collect her, but she couldn't stay in the room another minute longer. She was handed Andrzej wrapped up in blankets like a big *pierogi* dumpling. Suddenly he was in her arms, and she was touching him for the first time, but also she was having to negotiate all the complex arrangements for leaving in a rush: gathering her things (so few of them), booking a taxi (but she had no money!), being outside again (and it was so cold!), the baby squirming in her arms in the car (if he cried, would the driver cast them out?) and she didn't even know how to hold a baby (was she doing it right?).

Arriving at home with her baby – something she had long dreamed of – she had to hurry up three flights of stairs to get money from the flat, then back down, the driver's suspicious face making her anxious. And then she was climbing the stairs again, putting the baby down, picking him back up because he was crying, taking her breast out to feed him for the first time, wondering when Zbigniew would be back, wondering if he had got the washing machine yet . . . And all she wanted to do was to enjoy her newfound freedom from the hospital. To marvel, in peace, at the baby she barely knew.

Their number came up for a washing machine a few days later. Zbigniew hauled it into the basement of their building, only to find that the space that had been allocated for it was already taken; someone had bribed their way into it, and now they would have to wait until another space came up. Months passed: the snow melted, the baby grew, communism fell. Dust built up on the unconnected washing machine, still in its wrapper in the basement. The whole world had changed.

Jola insists that it wasn't *all* bad in communist Poland. Rights for women were arguably world-leading at the time. State socialism in Eastern Europe generally reduced women's economic dependence on men by offering them equitable access to education and the labour market, and equal access to state services and benefits. Generous maternity leave, free childcare, liberal divorce laws and robust sex education all contributed, according to Kristen R. Ghodsee, to improved sex lives. In her book *Why Women Have Better Sex Under Socialism*, she shows how economic liberation from men made for more liberated (albeit heterosexual, heteronormative) sex.[1]

While I'm not quite ready to have *that* conversation with my mother-in-law, she agrees that state provision for women was impressive. Six months' paid maternity leave, three years' unpaid (and only unpaid because they were earning over a certain threshold). However, all of these provisions, as Ghodsee points out, could only be taken by the mother. Alternatively, they had generous access to childcare, but spaces in nurseries were hard to come by because many of those women didn't want to stay at home for three years and wanted to go back to work and develop their careers instead – a desire perhaps exacerbated by the societal focus on the importance of work, and the ever-present threat of countrywide financial hardship that even the state could not protect its citizens from.

Jola might have felt liberated from men in some ways, but she didn't feel liberated from what was expected of her as a woman. And that was to have and raise a baby, *and* go to work. When she finally did go back to work, she experienced the 'double burden' of labour outside the home and labour within the home. I wonder how good her sex life could have been without that washing machine – hand-washing the baby's cloth nappies, hand-washing her own menstrual products (sanitary pads and tampons were not then available in Poland), hand-washing her and her husband's clothes – along with all the other chores of running a household with minimal technological help, in a time of rationing, and all of that in addition to a full-time job.

Almost four decades have elapsed since Jola gave birth, and the country's economic context has greatly changed. The shops are now full of affordable products for baby care, and even the right-wing government that was recently voted out provided generous state benefits for parents compared with many other Western countries.[2] Surely, then, the rates of birth trauma in the country are far lower today than they were in 1987?

Given the lack of reliable data on birth trauma during that period, it is impossible to draw an accurate comparison, but maternity care over time does not seem to have altered as drastically as the country's politics. A study from 2019 found that a shocking 81 per cent of maternity patients in Poland experienced violence or abuse from hospital staff.[3] These abuses ranged from obstetric violence, tying legs down during labour, to verbal and emotional abuse, shouting, mocking and insulting treatment, and neglect. The study also found that an overwhelming amount of this abuse stemmed from a failure to secure consent from the patients. In many cases this involved the forceful shaving of pubic hair, administration of enemas, vaginal examinations, cannulation and episiotomy – *all* of which Jola had experienced so many years previously.

Contemporary Poland is far from exceptional in its high rates of obstetric violence. It may take different forms, depending on the context – under capitalism or under communism, in a religious hospital or an entirely secular one – but it is increasingly being recognised as a major public health issue worldwide.[4]

Birth trauma is a broad term referring to physical and psychological injuries sustained during childbirth.[5] These injuries can range from minor tears to severe complications affecting the patient's long-term health and well-being. Babies also suffer from birth trauma. This can involve anything from bruising to broken bones; lacerations and scarring from birth instruments; nerve, organ, and tissue damage; haemorrhage, and paralysis. It is not uncommon: in the period 2005–14 the incidence of neonatal birth trauma in the US was around 30 in 1,000 hospital births.[6]

The most common type of physical birth trauma for the patient is perineal tearing, from minor (first-degree) to severe (fourth-degree) tears that extend into the rectum. Severe perineal tears that affect the anal sphincter (the muscle responsible for closing the rectum) lead to anal incontinence and a host of other complications.[7] Estimates suggest that 3 in 4 women suffer some degree of tearing during childbirth, making it an almost inevitable consequence of labour.[8] In terms of prevalence, tearing is followed by haemorrhoids, which are found in over 40 per cent of women postpartum.[9]

Childbirth can also cause injuries to the pelvic floor – damaging the muscles, ligaments, and nerves that support the pelvic organs – and can result in conditions such as incontinence and pelvic organ prolapse, which are often lifelong. Around the world, approximately 300,000 people each year are referred to surgery following pelvic-floor injury.[10] This represents roughly 10 per cent of all those who give birth vaginally.

There are further, rarer, but nonetheless serious types of physical trauma that are brought about by the process of pushing out a baby through the vaginal canal. Labour can cause lacerations not only in the perineum, but also to the vagina and cervix, and require surgery.[11] Episiotomies can become complicated with infection, pain and excessive bleeding.[12] The bladder and urethra can be injured, especially following instrumental delivery.[13] Sometimes, placenta delivery (afterbirth) can cause the entire uterus to turn inside-out. It can cause severe bleeding and shock, requiring immediate medical intervention.[14]

The pressure of the baby's body on the pelvic region is so strong that it can cause damage to the symphysis pubis (the ligament at the bottom of the pelvis), which means that the pelvis is no longer aligned properly, affecting one's ability to walk.[15] Sometimes, labour can break your coccyx (tailbone), leading to prolonged pain and discomfort.[16]

Complications following childbirth are not only disabling; they can also be life-threatening. Postpartum haemorrhage refers to sudden blood loss following labour. While all labour leads to some blood loss, excessive bleeding is not that uncommon and affects between 1 and 5 per cent of women. It usually happens within a day of giving birth, but it can occur unexpectedly and up to twelve weeks after having a baby. It is a medical emergency, and if not treated immediately, it can lead to hypovolaemic shock – not enough blood to sustain the function of the body organs – and death. The WHO estimates that each year about 14 million women experience postpartum haemorrhage, which results in about 70,000 maternal deaths globally.[17]

Bleeding is the leading cause of postpartum mortality worldwide, accounting for approximately 27 per cent of all maternal deaths.[18] This is followed by hypertensive disorders, such as eclampsia (14 per cent) and sepsis caused by bacterial infection (10 per cent). In 2020, almost 95 per cent of all maternal deaths occurred in so-called low and lower middle-income countries. The WHO reports that most of these could be prevented.[19] Indeed in that year, every day nearly 800 women died from preventable causes related to pregnancy and labour. This means that, worldwide, one preventable maternal death occurs every two minutes. While this is still unacceptably high, improved access to appropriate medical care in the last twenty years has led to a 34 per cent improvement in maternal mortality rates, most of which has been achieved in the rapidly developing Eastern European and Southern Asian countries.

Pregnancy and labour are not only the cause of physical injury; they can have a long-lasting and debilitating impact on an individual's mental health too. Experiencing psychological trauma after giving birth is very common.[20] Most women will experience a degree of postpartum depression symptoms and anxiety, but in some cases the experience of childbirth can trigger post-traumatic stress disorder (PTSD). As physical and psychological trauma are interrelated, PTSD is commonly brought about by difficult, long and complicated labour, and unplanned emergency procedures (such as C-sections).

PTSD can cause a host of psychological and physiological symptoms, including vivid flashbacks, nightmares, constant alertness, avoidance, feelings of distrust, pain, nausea, panic attacks, insomnia, and many others. Postnatal PTSD has only recently been recognised as a serious consequence of childbirth, but estimates place its prevalence between 3 and 43 per cent of births.[21] Additionally, witnessing trauma is known to cause PTSD, and birth partners have occasionally been diagnosed with PTSD or have experienced PTSD-like symptoms.[22]

Trans men suffer particularly high rates of PTSD when it comes to pregnancy and giving birth.[23] If the healthcare experiences of trans men are poor in general – what with issues of dead-naming and misgendering, a lack of accessible gynaecology, obscene waiting times for gender-affirming care, conversion therapy masquerading as counselling – when it comes to reproductive and perinatal healthcare (the period before, during and after childbirth), rates of trauma can be high.[24] This is compounded by uncertainty around provision and the general lack of coherence – for example, in the UK, there are no clear guidelines around maternity care for trans men, leaving individual NHS trusts with the task of interpreting the scant legislation.[25]

Moreover, there are a number of trans men who, due to misinformation around the use of testosterone therapy, fall pregnant accidentally – and such lack of control over one's reproductive functions can be traumatic enough in itself. There is a common misconception, held by too many healthcare practitioners, that testosterone therapy automatically prevents pregnancy.[26] This is not necessarily the case when it comes to penile–vaginal intercourse. Granted, testosterone replacement therapy can cause amenorrhoea (the cessation of menstrual periods). It typically leads to amenorrhoea within one to twelve months from the first administration; however, this doesn't make anovulation (cessation of ovulation) a given and can depend heavily on dosage. In fact, it seems that testosterone does not even appreciably affect fertility. Some studies suggest that men who undergo gender-affirming hormone therapies (GAHT) that include testosterone may retain similar ovarian reserve and oocyte (egg) quantity and quality to cisgender women.[27]

A 2018 study of LGBT healthcare clinics in the US shows that 5.5 per cent of patients were actively recommended testosterone as a form of hormonal contraception.[28] This is despite the fact that guidance from Planned Parenthood (the largest provider of reproductive healthcare in the US) explicitly states that gender-affirming hormone therapy, including testosterone, is not a form of birth control and that men can still become pregnant while on testosterone therapy if they have a uterus and ovaries, and are ovulating.[29] Consequently, unplanned pregnancy is quite common for trans men. In a 2015 study, 61 per cent of trans men reported testosterone use prior to pregnancy. Among these, 24 per cent had an unplanned pregnancy.[30] In one case a 21-year-old man who had been on gender-affirming hormone therapy for over two years suddenly discovered that he was pregnant during a follow-up appointment at seventeen weeks. He was on a weekly regimen of intramuscular injections of 100 mg of Depo-Testosterone.[31] In another case, a 25-year-old man who had been receiving testosterone therapy for three years experienced an unplanned pregnancy during a brief discontinuation of treatment. Unaware of his pregnancy, he resumed testosterone therapy until the pregnancy was confirmed. Postpartum, he struggled with insomnia and depression, and found that giving birth had also complicated his legal efforts to change his family register – his US governmental record – to male.[32]

Becoming pregnant is not the beginning and end of a trans man's potentially negative experience of pregnancy and childbirth. Trans and/or non-binary individuals reported significantly worse satisfaction with perinatal care compared to cisgender women, with 30 per cent not accessing *any* perinatal care during pregnancy, in stark contrast with only 2.1 per cent of ciswomen.[33] Those who do access perinatal care overwhelmingly describe it as unprepared for their needs. The threat of dysphoria is always one step away, and who's surprised when the entire field is stubbornly still described as '*maternity* health'?

Though healthcare professionals themselves routinely express the need for education to improve care for transgender and non-binary individuals in cisnormative perinatal services, transphobia, institutional erasure, and strongly gendered norms around pregnancy contribute to the trauma experienced by too many patients. Stigma around men accessing 'maternity' services can lead to transgender men avoiding seeking care or disclosing medically relevant information, which in turn affects their health and well-being.[34] It may also dissuade them from getting pregnant in the first place. Medical services are often not prepared to serve pregnant trans and non-binary people, regardless of whether their pregnancies are planned or not. For the men who choose to become pregnant, some will pause gender-affirming therapies, and vulnerability to feelings of gender dysphoria and isolation will be high enough as it is. Studies have shown that the balance between transitioning and reproduction is delicate, and this is one area where participants expressed a great variety of values and priorities regarding these aspects of their lives.[35] Medical practitioners may not have the necessary sensitivity and training to handle this well. Primed to respond to the cis woman who is supposed to want to always, in every instance, have a baby (and to sacrifice everything for that baby), the appearance of someone who is not tied to this rigid social stereotype can cause panic or even hostility. This, naturally, can be a source of trauma.

Childbirth may be a life-changing medical event, but experiencing trauma because of it *isn't* a given. Its impact can be lessened and instances of it reduced through good hospital practice and a strong, patient-led approach to care. In 2024 the Birth Trauma Inquiry, initiated by the UK Parliament, reported that responsibility for high rates of birth trauma fell squarely in the hands of hospitals and healthcare professionals.[36] Professor of Maternal and Child Health Susan Ayers and her team of international experts showed how actually listening to patients – not just letting them speak, but *acting* on their words – can vastly reduce negative experiences during pregnancy and childbirth.

For years, the hospital I was born in – the Royal Shrewsbury Hospital, later to become part of the now infamous Shrewsbury and Telford Hospital Trust – was held in high regard on account of its comparatively low C-section rates. Its annual number of C-sections was consistently lower than the national average – in 2006 reaching a record low of 11.8 per cent with the national average coming in at

24.2 per cent.[37] I used to leaf through our free copy of the *Shropshire Star*, searching for hilariously underwhelming local news stories of bin fires and country fair escapades – all the drama you'd expect from a quiet rural county in the arse end of nowhere. I may have even come across the following story from 2011, but I probably wouldn't have thought much of it at the time. 'Shropshire caesarean rate is the lowest in England' the article announces. 'Health chiefs at the Shrewsbury and Telford Hospital NHS Trust put the success down to having an environment which encourages natural childbirth and using a wide range of strategies to keep caesarean deliveries low.'[38]

Fast-forward to 2017, the same year that my own midwife in Cambridge told me I could not have an elective C-section, and the bubble in Shrewsbury had well and truly burst. Senior midwife Donna Ockenden was being tasked by the then health secretary Jeremy Hunt with investigating a series of suspicious deaths and serious injuries at the Shrewsbury and Telford NHS Hospital Trust's maternity unit.[39] A number of bereaved parents had come forward with concerns about negligent and grossly inadequate care, prompting the review.

Ockenden found that a litany of failings had led to the avoidable deaths of twelve women and over two hundred babies, and the serious and lifelong injury of many other women and babies. As summarised by an article in the *British Medical Journal*, the Ockenden report describes:

> poor antenatal care for vulnerable women, repeated failures to correctly assess foetal growth, reluctance to refer women to tertiary centres to address foetal abnormalities, poor management of multiple pregnancies, poor management of gestational hypertension, failure to recognise sick or deteriorating women, failure to act on abnormal foetal heart patterns and failure to escalate concerns.[40]

An aspect of the scandal was the unit's profound lack of resources and severe levels of understaffing. Staff themselves voiced concerns about patient safety, as a consequence, and suffered from extremely low morale. Postnatal midwives were regularly pulled away from their wards and onto the labour ward instead, leaving their patients without adequate support, and with a pressure to discharge them as soon as possible, to get them out of the way. One member of staff reported how it 'really increased our stress levels because obviously, it's upsetting when you can't give the care that you want to give'.[41]

Understaffing went hand in hand with a lack of support, for which there were few guidelines implemented for staff to follow. This was particularly poignant when it came to bereavement care, with women not being provided with separate spaces in which to grieve (some having to be cared for in wards surrounded by crying babies) and others being subjected to insensitive comments from staff members and other patients. One woman was told to wait for the corridors to empty before she could carry her recently deceased premature baby over to the birth suite in her arms.

When it came to failings in care in childbirth, a common thread wove its way through many of Ockenden's case studies: a disconcerting fixation on 'normal' (vaginal) delivery. Ockenden attributes this to a prevailing objective to keep C-section rates low, something that was perceived by staff to be a sign of good maternity care. This misconception about C-sections was by no means limited to the Shrewsbury and Telford Hospital Trust, but rather was part of a more all-pervasive, societal-wide belief that C-sections were a luxurious, unnecessary, and ultimately more dangerous form of childbirth. This position was highlighted by the now infamous 1999 article in the *Daily Mail* about Victoria Beckham's C-section birth, headlined 'Too Posh to Push?'[42] Where vaginal birth was framed as the superior, healthier, and fundamentally more natural form of childbirth, C-sections were instead painted as a mere 'lifestyle choice'. Indeed, in that *Shropshire Star* article from 2011, the head of midwifery at the trust, Cathy Smith, is quoted as saying: 'We try and have a department-wide ethic of natural childbirth.'[43]

Evidently, this ethic overrode fundamental principles of safety when it came to patient care. Ockenden found that some women were denied C-sections that could have prevented them serious injury or even death. Women felt that they could not request C-sections, even when they felt they were 'medically' necessary, because the culture in the hospital forbade it. Others were subjected to excruciating or unsuccessful vaginal births because doctors and midwives were convinced that these were the superior form of childbirth. In one case study from 2015, a woman was 'persuaded' to have a vaginal delivery even though she did not want one – and with tragic consequences:

> A woman had a failed ventouse delivery and emergency caesarean section in a previous pregnancy. In the next pregnancy the baby was found to be macrosomic (large) on scan at 36 weeks. The woman was admitted in labour and despite requests for a caesarean section she was persuaded to attempt a vaginal birth. This was complicated by a pathological CTG in labour with inappropriate use of oxytocin and shoulder dystocia. The baby died a few days later from hypoxic brain injury and complications of the shoulder dystocia.[44]

In another birth story from 2000, a woman giving birth to a baby in the posterior position was forced to suffer a particularly difficult natural birth because, in her own words, 'the Trust were trying to keep the Caesarean section rate low'.[45] In 2012, another woman had her C-section request *explicitly* refused:

> A woman who was known to have a big baby was refused her request for a caesarean section and encouraged to labour. She had a forceps delivery and the baby had shoulder dystocia with a resulting fractured humerus. In her letter to the Trust afterwards the mother wrote that she felt her request for a Caesarean section was refused because the Trust wanted to keep their Caesarean section rates low. There was no incident form or investigation.[46]

Time and time again, requests made by patients about their own care – informed and balanced requests; requests that could have saved lives – were flatly refused. In her final report, Ockenden stresses the importance of centring patient voices. 'For far too long,' she writes, 'women and families who accessed maternity care at the trust were denied the opportunity to voice their concerns.' The listening that Ockenden refers to, however, is not merely lip service. She prescribes real and meaningful engagement with patient voices in order to bring about the necessary changes to maternity care: 'In order to ensure families' voices are heard, listened to and acted upon within maternity services, the NHS will need to continue progress on the role of the independent senior advocate role within maternity services that was an IEA [Immediate and Essential Action] in our first report.'[47]

My current local hospital, Addenbrooke's in Cambridge, runs a service called 'Birth Afterthoughts'. Maternity hospitals around the world have similar such birth debriefing services. The idea behind this is to give those who have given birth a space to share their thoughts on the process with the hospital, and to better understand what happened to them and why. Relevant staff may liaise with one another in a confidential manner to help interpret your notes and answer your questions, ideally leaving you with a coherent picture of why things turned out like they did. As the Birth Afterthoughts website explains:

> Labour and birth may have been different to expectations and plans made during pregnancy. There may have been a need for medical intervention, or even a medical emergency. Such events can be difficult to understand without information to 'fill in the gaps', have questions answered, or understand the medical assessment and decision-making process in labour.[48]

If the Shrewsbury and Telford Hospital Trust had offered a birth debriefing service, could outcomes have been any different?

There is no scientific evidence that debriefing actually helps women deal with the trauma of childbirth. A systematic review of eleven trial studies found that a single one-on-one debriefing session did not reduce women's psychological distress following a traumatic childbirth and nor did it prevent the onset of PTSD in the twelve months following the event.[49] But what if the benefits of debriefing come in the long term rather than the short term? A study of over 500 Australian women who received the debrief found no evidence of such an effect, even four and six years after childbirth: 'Short debriefing interventions have not proven effective in improving mental health outcomes for women following childbirth.'[50] A cynical interpretation of birth debrief services may be that they are merely a response to high rates of litigation in gynaecology. Maybe it is hoped that by giving women the illusion that they are being listened to by the hospital, and by giving them a chance to air their grievances, they will be dissuaded from pursuing costly lawsuits as a consequence of inadequate and injurious care.

Perhaps birth debriefing services can't meaningfully, and retrospectively, help those who have already experienced birth trauma. However, there is reason to believe they can prevent future patients from suffering similar patterns of poor care. In 2018, British writer and new mother of twins Jessica Cornwell sat down with a senior midwife to go through a stack of notes from her own experience of traumatic labour.[51] In the meeting, she was told for the first time that she had had placenta accreta, a rare and serious condition where the placenta grows through the lining of the uterus into the uterine wall, meaning that the placenta couldn't be removed completely during childbirth. This explained perfectly the heavy bleeding that nearly cost Cornwell her life hours after childbirth and the continued string of infections that she was still experiencing months after labour. This revelation invoked her anger. How was it possible that none of the doctors who attended to her knew about this? How did *she* not know anything about it? In her memoir *Birth Notes*, Cornwell recounts the story of how her pregnancy notes were not only lost repeatedly by various medical professionals, but also contained wildly inaccurate information which meant that appropriate attention was not given to her in time.[52] It was discovered that her diagnosis of placenta accreta had never been transferred from her paper file to the computer system. The midwife apologised to Cornwell and promised an internal review of the case. Receiving a name for her condition might have provided her with only a small sense of closure, but the internal review could potentially spare countless future patients suffering on account of a mere technicality.

To listen does not just mean to *let a patient speak*. It means to engage with the particular wishes of a patient and to try to deliver their desired health outcome, where possible. It absolutely requires informed consent.

It is easier for a health service to achieve this when it is comfortably well funded. It doesn't matter how many well-intentioned promises an institution makes if their medical practitioners simply do not have the time or resources to listen to their patients. How can overworked midwives working in understaffed NHS wards in the UK today meet the complex needs of patients, particularly when they themselves are suffering from work-related stress and burnout? The Ockenden Report into the Shrewsbury and Telford Hospital Trust scandal diagnosed that maternity staff themselves were not being listened to by upper management at the trust; furthermore, they were being *actively discouraged* from giving voice to their concerns, even anonymously.[53] This belies a toxic working culture of silence which mirrors the experience of the maternity patients too. All of which has been further compounded by brutal cost-cutting measures.[54]

In the previous chapter, I relayed how a gynaecological surgeon felt that his patients came 'at the bottom' of the hospital's roster and that gynaecology was sometimes seen as an almost optional area of healthcare – unlike oncology, or, say, paediatrics. With a healthcare system on its knees, with terminal cancer patients 'routinely' facing deadly waiting times, the promise to listen to maternity patients comes across as woefully inadequate.[55] *Especially* when this promise does not seem to be making a big difference in even the richest healthcare systems in the world either.

Take the US, for instance, which spends the most money per person on healthcare of any country in the world.[56] Despite this, one in five women in the US reports experiencing mistreatment in maternity care.[57] Once again, much of this mistreatment comes down to issues of communication and of not being listened to. The US Centers for Disease Control and Prevention runs a campaign called 'Hear Her', urging patients to speak up with their concerns, and for health practitioners to listen to them.[58] Clearly, it is not merely enough to have a relatively well-funded healthcare system to ensure that the needs of maternity patients are heard. Granted, lower income patients experience higher levels of birth trauma in the US (28 per cent of uninsured patients experienced mistreatment), but a higher income by no means protects you from it (16 per cent of patients with private insurance experienced mistreatment).[59] While money may play a part in the silencing of patients' voices in maternity care, it is certainly *far* from being the only cause.

4. Go Natural

In April 1958, 27-year-old Matilda Behan was admitted to the National Maternity Hospital in Dublin ten days before her due date for a C-section. She was reassured by this, after having suffered two previous pregnancy losses. She was even feeling excited.

Four days after her admission, Behan was taken to the operating theatre for the procedure. She wasn't quite sure why it was happening *now*, exactly, given that she hadn't gone into labour yet, but she assumed that the doctors must have their reasons.

The room was packed full of people waiting for her arrival. This unsettled her. As soon as the door was closed, two nurses and two doctors approached the bed. The nurses held down her arms and the doctors held down her legs. 'In the name of God,' Behan recalls screaming, 'what are you doing?'[1]

'New procedure,' she was told simply. And then her eyes fell on the chainsaw.

A surgeon proceeded to saw up through her pelvis. She had only been given a local anaesthetic, and so she was fully conscious, and able to see what was happening. The anaesthetic was either not strong enough or hadn't yet kicked in, because Behan also recalls feeling everything too.

'I'll never forget the pain I went through,' she later recounted. 'It was excruciating pain . . .'

The torture didn't end there. With a broken pelvis and dislocated hips, Behan still had to birth her child. But Behan wasn't actually *in* labour yet. She had to wait over a week for her baby to come, bedridden in the hospital, in excruciating pain. Laid up like a chicken ready for gutting.[2]

Behan gave birth to Bernadette, the child she had waited so long for. Her life was now irrevocably altered in more ways than one. She was in her late twenties and incontinent, living in constant chronic pain, unable to have sex with her partner, unable to play with her child, unable to work, unable to dance, unable to enjoy life as she previously had done. 'I have lived on painkillers and sanitary towels,' she later told the *Irish Times*. 'All the things I took joy in were gone.'

It took decades for Behan to realise what had happened to her. She was reading an article in the same paper on the Catholic Church's influence on healthcare in Ireland, when it all clicked into place. The article mentioned how people were now coming forward with stories of having been subjected to a brutal procedure in childbirth called symphysiotomy. Behan immediately knew that she was one of them.

Symphysiotomy is the surgical separation of the pelvis. It is usually only carried out when the baby is stuck in the birth canal and a C-section is unavailable as an alternative. The pelvic bone is cut along the symphysis pubis, a strip of cartilage and ligaments that joins the two halves of the pelvic bone, and is, after cutting, hinged open to increase the diameter of the birth canal.[3] What had been done to Behan was an even riskier form of symphysiotomy: pubiotomy. This is only carried out when the symphysis pubis cannot be located or cut. In pubiotomy, the pelvic bone itself is cut through directly and so the pelvis, rather than hinging open, is instead manually broken apart.[4] Symphysiotomy is carried out in only the most life-threatening circumstances, and pubiotomy only when symphysiotomy has been, unsuccessfully, attempted first. Neither was the case for Behan. She had been summoned to the hospital under the false pretext of a planned C-section that was never going to happen. A symphysiotomy, brutal enough in itself, had not been attempted. Her pubiotomy had been fully premeditated.

The lasting damage inflicted by symphysiotomy and pubiotomy is, as you would expect, extensive. Fistula, prolapse, incontinence, infection, injury to the urethra, ruptured bladder, osteoarthritis in the joints, reduced mobility and chronic pain are all possible if not likely outcomes. The entire gait is altered, something that can – with time – cause internal tearing. Lifelong physiotherapy will likely be necessary. Everything that can be said for symphysiotomy can also be said for pubiotomy, only worse. It also poses additional risks to the baby.

The first reported symphysiotomy took place in Paris in the late eighteenth century. The surgeon, Jean René Sigault, first proposed the procedure to the Royal Academy of Surgery of France in 1768 after testing it out on cadavers.[5] The academy ridiculed Sigault's suggestion of brutally cutting open the pelvis, but he remained committed to the procedure and – almost a decade later – carried it out on a patient only ever recorded as 'Madame Souchot'. Despite Souchot experiencing severe complications afterwards, including vaginal fistula, infection, and a complete inability to walk, the fact that both she and the child had survived the birth made a hero out of Sigault.

Until then, the only possible methods for managing obstructed birth were either C-section or craniotomy (where a perforation was made in the foetal head and its contents emptied out, enabling the collapsed skull to be removed). C-section was a perilous procedure for the patient, and craniotomy unsurprisingly resulted in the death of the infant. Symphysiotomy seemed like a preferable, if imperfect, alternative. It was risky for both the patient and the child but, with skill, it could save the life of the patient (if condemning them to a lifetime of pain) and it didn't mean certain death for the child either. Also, the Catholic Church looked much more favourably upon symphysiotomy than on C-section (and increasingly so as the maternal mortality rate lifted) and *especially* craniotomy, which priests vocally opposed and framed as the unambiguous murder of the innocent.

However, symphysiotomy still had its detractors in the medical field. The French *accoucheur* Jean-Louis Baudelocque, known for 'Baudelocque's diameter' (a method of pelvic measurement), was one of its most vocal opponents. He argued that C-section was *always* better in cases of obstructed birth. Colleagues accused him of being an assassin for this view – and maybe, to a degree, that was true. Baudelocque argued that: 'with respect to the child, it is the gentlest and most certain of all the methods we can employ for terminating labour'.[6]

With respect to the child. At this point in history, C-section was certainly a safer bet for the infant rather than the patient. As midwife Leah Hazard writes in *Womb*:

> While the name of the procedure is commonly thought to reflect a belief that Julius Caesar was delivered abdominally, it is more likely to be a reference to the emperor's decree that all babies should be

extracted in that way if the mother's death in childbirth seemed inevitable.[7]

While C-section is one of the oldest medical procedures – dating back as far as ancient China (around 1,000 BCE) – the first recorded instance of both patient and child surviving it only occurs around AD 1500: *two and half thousand years* later. And this account, of a Swiss woman's desperate husband carrying out the C-section on their farm, is disputed anyway.[8] It's impossible to say exactly when the first patient and child both survived a C-section, but we do know that for the most part of history it was carried out on those who were already dead or dying and so for an automatically better chance of survival for the infant.

Before the arrival of anaesthesia to the operating theatre, developing the best C-section technique was nearly impossible. The surgery was almost always rushed, and the competing medical needs of both patient and child made for a doubly fraught situation. C-section was only ever carried out once other attempts had been made to encourage vaginal birth, and so it nearly always took place late into labour when the baby was advanced as far as possible down the birth canal and the stakes – and skill needed – had gone through the roof.

Even with the development of anaesthesia, and the huge strides that were now being made in almost every field of surgery because of it, the number of successful C-sections being carried out remained frustratingly low. The city of Paris reported a 100 per cent maternal mortality rate for the procedure between 1787 and 1876.[9] This was mainly because surgeons were reluctant to stitch-up the uterus, knowing that to do so threatened later pregnancies; instead they preferred to allow it to contract and heal on its own. This was a mitigated disaster, and – in the vain hope of preserving future fertility – meant that women were suffering blood loss, contracting infections, and dying needlessly.

Despite this, symphysiotomy hadn't taken off in any meaningful way. Its detractors were too vocal and it was considered a fringe practice that most surgeons were unwilling to perform. Outside of Europe and the US, it was practically unknown.

Thank God then for German obstetrician Max Saumlnger, whose highly influential monograph on uterine sutures in 1882 persuaded surgeons to take up the silver-wire stitches popularised by US gynaecologist John Marion Sims.[10] This more favourable look on sewing up the uterus and the employment of antiseptic were the two great breakthroughs for the procedure. A knock-on consequence of C-section becoming safer was also doctors' new willingness not to delay it. The sooner it is carried out in childbirth, the safer it is. Instead of waiting until the very last moment in obstructed birth, it would be undertaken at the earliest opportunity instead. The discovery of penicillin by Alexander Fleming was the final piece of the puzzle, and since the mid twentieth century C-section has been considered the safest alternative to vaginal birth in middle to higher income countries.[11]

Even though C-section was completely safe, accessible and recommended at the time, at least 1,500 people were subject to unnecessary and non-consensual pubiotomy and symphysiotomy in Irish hospitals between 1944 and 1984.[12] The majority of these Irish hospitals were, perhaps unsurprisingly, Roman Catholic hospitals. Through the tireless campaigning of advocacy group 'Survivors of Symphysiotomy' (of which Matilda Behan was a co-founder), and the help of committed researchers like Marie O'Connor and Jacqueline Morrissey, the issue came under the spotlight, numerous cases have since (successfully) been brought to court, and the UN Human Rights Committee has called for the Irish government to open an investigation.[13] However, the government has continually dodged full accountability. It hasn't specifically named or prosecuted any of the medical staff involved and refuses to speak transparently on the scandal's religious nature. All of this is unsurprising, and part of a bigger picture relating to the country reconciling itself and coming to terms with other human rights violations that were perpetrated in and through religious means: slave labour and forced imprisonment in the Magdalene laundries; widespread sexual abuse committed by the clergy; the mass children's graves of Galway, to name some of the better-known examples. These scandals have all revolved around issues of reproductive rights, gender violence and clerical authority, and symphysiotomy is no exception.

Contraception was only legalised in Ireland in 1980, and then with numerous restrictions (such as condoms requiring a prescription). This was in line with Roman Catholic teaching which prohibited the 'deliberate frustration' of generating new life.[14] Abortion was illegal up until 2018, again in keeping with the Roman Catholic position which opposes abortion in almost all circumstances.[15] Symphysiotomy versus C-section was, effectively, proxy for a bigger war on reproductive choice. C-section was perceived as an unnatural means of childbirth that not only circumnavigated the soul's 'natural' route into the world (the vagina), but which also 'deliberately frustrated' the generation of new life by threatening subsequent births by scarring the uterus. It has long been recommended that a person has no more than three C-sections[16] and that vaginal birth is avoided after C-section (although this advice is changing and now depends more on specific circumstances, such as the status of the current pregnancy; what type of incision was used in previous C-sections; if the uterus has been subject to any other procedures; among others).[17] This perception of C-section potentially limiting future pregnancies has had a heavy bearing on how it is viewed, especially by those with an acute interest in a person having multiple pregnancies. It was thought that C-section would covertly promote the illegal use of contraception and abortion, if those aware of its risks were to try and avoid future pregnancies, and so would encourage sinful behaviour.

Historian Jacqueline Morrissey identifies two doctors key to the promotion of symphysiotomy in Ireland: Alex Spain, Master of Dublin's National Maternity Hospital, and Arthur Barry, who succeeded Spain in the role in 1948.[18] This institution was, like most embroiled in the scandal, a private hospital under the control of the Catholic archdiocese. Spain and Barry were both devout and conservative Catholics, which no doubt contributed to their selection as 'Masters' of Ireland's leading maternity hospital. Spain would describe C-section as a form of sterilisation that caused marital disharmony and social ruin. Barry was equally vocal in his opposition to it, and when advising colleagues said of symphysiotomy: 'It is easy to know when to do the operation: do it when a section would otherwise have been employed, but be even more generous in your indication. Interfere early; it is only a minor operation and never has to be repeated.'[19]

This was another perceived benefit of the symphysiotomy: its effect of widening the pelvis was a permanent one, which meant for a permanently optimal child-bearing state – as though the patient was expected to be labour-ready for the rest of their lives. Elsewhere, Barry talks of C-section having 'disastrous effects on the child-bearing career of the recipient'.[20] Child-bearing is a job which the woman's body ought to be optimised for. There is no question about whether they will be having more children; but then of course, why would there be? These patients were thought of as fertile, married women who – if they were sin-avoiding, law-abiding citizens – did not have access to contraception or abortion. Of course, they would be having babies until the very day God and God alone decided to retire them from their reproductive duties. For Barry, he and his doctors were best facilitating the essential work of their patients. They were making it as easy as possible for them to go on getting pregnant and giving birth, in the most godly way possible.

In 1956, Pope Pius XII published a document which first sanctioned the use of anaesthesia in labour. In response to the infamous biblical passage condemning women to suffering in punishment of Eve's fall – 'I will greatly multiply thy sorrow and thy conception; in sorrow thou shalt bring forth children' (Genesis 3:16) – Pius XII responded that 'man' has the right to 'prevent and even suppress physical pain'.[21]

This position marked a shift in thinking about pain relief for labour, but also indicates how enduring the biblical justification for opposing pain relief in labour has been throughout history.

The discovery of morphine in the early nineteenth century was a significant advancement in the general field of pain relief. A derivative of opium, morphine was first experimented with by the Byzantines,[22] but it went largely forgotten until 1804, when it was extracted from a poppy plant by a German pharmacist and subsequently sold as pain relief.[23] However, it was generally not considered appropriate for use in labour. There was much concern around the risk of administering opiates, and indeed still today it is advised that they are not given too close to delivery, as they can cause temporary breathing and heart-rate problems for the patient and the baby.

Anaesthesia appeared in the West a short while after morphine. In 1846, the American dentist William Morton demonstrated the use of ether during a procedure.[24] For centuries, patients had been given alcohol and other mind-altering substances during surgery in an effort to reduce consciousness and feeling, but these offered rather unpredictable and often ineffective outcomes. The use of ether proved to be a turning point. It soon led to the introduction of effective and reproducible anaesthesia in surgery. Physicians quickly attempted to use the new drug in labour.

Four months after Morton's dental procedure, Scottish obstetrician James Simpson successfully relieved the pain of a birthing woman in Edinburgh, and began a public campaign to promote the methods.[25] He published pamphlets that would dismiss the religiously motivated arguments against the use of pain relief in labour, and found receptive ears among British high society. Simpson would travel across the country, offering his services to rich patrons. He began to experiment with the concept, and was subsequently responsible for the introduction of chloroform for use in anaesthesia. Chloroform was more potent than ether, but also more difficult to use, with the initial trials ending in deaths. Developing the safe administration of chloroform became the work of one of Simpson's students, John Snow. Snow devised a reproducible method of delivery and estimated the correct dosage of chloroform for patients in labour. Like Simpson, he was in the employ of the rich and famous, and focused his efforts on the promotion of the drug. In 1853, he was called upon to treat his most illustrious client: Queen Victoria. Snow successfully anaesthetised her during the birth of her eighth child, Prince Leopold.[26]

Royal patronage proved supremely helpful in addressing moral and religious opposition to pain relief in labour. But despite such illustrative celebrity endorsement and the work of pioneering doctors, anaesthesia was only slowly entering delivery rooms. The age-old biases persisted in the medical profession. A notable Russian surgeon and pioneer of thyroid surgery, Nikolay Pirogov, wrote in 1847: 'Haven't midwives and parturients [labouring women] and indeed all others always viewed the agonies of delivery as an indicator of safety and a well-nigh-holy accompaniment of childbirth?' Charles Meigs, one of the most prominent American doctors, noted around the same time that the 'pain of labour had never been great enough to prevent women from having more children'.[27]

The quest for painless delivery became closely aligned with European and American first-wave feminist movements. In large part this drive was focused on addressing the social injustice of pain relief, which was at the time accessible only to those who could afford it. Societies such as the National Twilight Sleep Association in the US and the National Birthday Trust Fund in the UK sprung up in the first decades of the twentieth century and worked tirelessly to improve the conditions of labouring women and improve better access to effective analgesia.[28] As pain relief in labour was still in its relative infancy, this meant that the well-meaning efforts of campaigners were sometimes sabotaged by the ineffectual methods they were promoting. 'Twilight sleep' was one such method of pain relief that was heavily promoted by the eponymous organisation, but eventually brought about their demise. The activity of the National Twilight Sleep Association ceased when one of its most outspoken proponents, Mrs Francis X. Carmody, died during childbirth while being subjected to the procedure.[29] The popularity of twilight sleep took a hit, but concerns around the method were not enough to affect its widespread application. It remained particularly popular in the US, where some hospitals were still administering it up until the 1960s.[30]

The method involved administering two drugs: morphine and scopolamine. Morphine causes pain relief and scopolamine produces memory loss. Mixed together they were meant to produce a state of diminished consciousness and insensitivity to pain: 'the twilight sleep'. It was promoted as a safer alternative to anaesthesia with chloroform and ether, for both the patient and baby.[31]

The concept was fundamentally flawed. The amount of morphine given to women was not enough to dull the pain of contractions and labour. Scopolamine, on the other hand, was very effective in inducing amnesia. Rather than prevent the pain of labour, twilight sleep merely made the women *forget* it.

There were other serious problems with this method. Practitioners of twilight sleep recommended that in order to induce it effectively, labouring women had to be kept in sensory isolation. This involved placing birthing women in darkened rooms and isolated from external sound. Physicians would also often blindfold them and put cotton and oil in their ears. Moreover, the combination of the drugs had the side effect of producing hallucinogenic effects and uncontrollable body movements. Compounded with ineffective pain relief, this meant that women would thrash, scream and attack both the medical staff and themselves. Doctors would often respond by restraining the women, sometimes even preventatively, relying on the fact that the patient would have no memory of the event.[32]

The persistence of twilight sleep in the cultural psyche of twentieth-century America is evidenced by a memorable portrayal of the procedure in the TV series *Mad Men*. In the episode 'The Fog', set in 1963, Betty Draper goes into labour with her third child. In hospital, she is tied to a bed and given the drugs to induce twilight sleep.[33] Betty experiences vivid hallucinations involving images of her past and present life, coming to the dawning realisation that her suburban dream of a marriage is an illusion. At the end of the scene, Betty is shown conscious and holding her newborn baby, with no memory of what had happened to her. Throughout the rest of the series, and indeed the rest of the show, it is uncertain if Betty's realisation ever resurfaces, speaking to the cultural anxiety around the method of twilight sleep, and its unknown, unpredictable consequences.

In the years following the Second World War, bringing with them a baby boom, increased access to healthcare, and a flourishing of healthcare technologies, labour moved into the domain of institutionalised medicine. Doctors began to freely administer strong medication to women during labour, with the dominant attitude of the era being characterised as 'knock 'em out, drag 'em out'.[34]

Predictably, the increased use of pain relief during delivery caused a new wave of opposition, this time invoking *natural* rather than heavenly laws. The charge was led by a British obstetrician going by the spectacular name of Grantly Dick-Read. Dick-Read vehemently opposed the use of anaesthesia during childbirth, claiming that 'healthy childbirth was never intended by the natural law to be painful'.[35] He was of the opinion that mothers should be fully conscious, and that they could even *enjoy* childbirth – if only they let themselves. Dick-Read argued that pain during childbirth was a result of fear, which activates a fight-or-flight response, releasing chemicals in the body that prevent the normal function of the uterine muscles. Needless to say, Dick-Read's theory had little scientific grounding. Despite numerous challenges from researchers who could not prove the fear origin of birth pain, Dick-Read and his work proved immensely popular. His magnum opus *Childbirth Without Fear*, first published in 1942, remains in print today and he is feted as the father of the modern natural birth movement.[36]

Other obstetricians, such as Robert Bradley in the US and Fernand Lamaze in France, followed in Dick-Read's footsteps and developed their own approaches to drug-free, natural childbirth. The techniques of Bradley and Lamaze focused on controlled breathing, relaxation, creating a comfortable environment, allowing women to adjust their body position, and partner inclusion in childbirth.[37] This latter aspect was particularly revolutionary, as fathers were universally and traditionally excluded from delivery wards. In no small part, this was because doctors did not want them to witness their wives being drugged up, tied down, barely conscious from heavy medication while sometimes being brutally administered to.

Directly responsible for the demise of twilight sleep, the natural childbirth movement was alluring to different people in different ways. For some, it offered greater autonomy in healthcare. As opposed to being nearly unconscious, women would be active participants in their own bodily experience – and get a (limited) say in it too. No longer at the total mercy of their doctors, women could instead direct their care to a degree, and take responsibility for it too. They would be awake for the arrival of their children. The method promised positivity, and who doesn't want the birth of their child to be a positive experience?

The fear of pain of vaginal delivery is present worldwide. In its most extreme form, it constitutes a medically recognised condition called tokophobia. Primary tokophobia is experienced by those who have never experienced pregnancy whereas secondary tokophobia is experienced by those who have. The Cleveland Clinic gives a list of negative pregnancy outcomes related to tokophobia: one of them is elective C-section.[38]

A small 2018 study found that 75 per cent of pregnant women experienced low to moderate tokophobia, and 25 per cent experienced high levels.[39] Extreme fear of childbirth may be more widespread than generally thought. Most attributed their fear to the prospect of episiotomy (where a surgical incision is made between the vagina and anus to prevent tearing).

The UK NICE (National Institute for Health and Care Excellence) guidelines state that a patient can request an elective C-section for any reason: *including* tokophobia.[40] If the hospital is sure that you are making a fully informed request, and if they are practically able to facilitate it, then they should. As the British charity Birthrights states on its website:

> If your request is due to anxiety about childbirth, the hospital should refer you to a healthcare professional who is an expert in perinatal mental health. You do not have to accept this offer of support. The guidance says that if you still want a caesarean birth after you and the hospital have talked about it, and you have been offered support, the hospital should offer you a caesarean.[41]

According to Article 8 of the European Convention on Human Rights (ECHR), everyone has the right to decide the circumstances of their child's birth. That includes the right to access C-section in contexts where it can be safely facilitated. It is important to note that the ECHR is an international treaty between the States of the Council of Europe, which is separate from the European Union. Post-Brexit it is still relevant to British law.[42]

However, in practice, patients are not currently granted full access to elective C-sections in the UK. In 2018, Birthrights reported that one in six NHS trusts did not follow NICE guidelines by offering elective C-sections.[43] And in those hospitals that do claim to follow the NICE guidelines, what is considered 'possible facilitation' of C-section is interpreted broadly.

★

The conditions of my prolapse were likely set during my first, traumatic, birth – a concern I had raised immediately after it, but had been so repeatedly, systematically dismissed that I'd even come to dismiss it myself. The ventouse and forceps used the first time round had weakened my vaginal muscles; the second pregnancy and childbirth had completely destroyed them. This could've *all* been prevented with a C-section.

I'd never wanted a vaginal birth. I *certainly* didn't want one in the weeks leading up to my due date for my first pregnancy. For over a month, my son had been lying in my womb in the posterior position: head down but facing out, when he should've been facing inwards. I'd done my reading. I knew that the forceps were a likely outcome if he didn't turn around. My midwives were all adamant that he would do, though. I wasn't so sure. Perhaps it was doom-mongering; perhaps it was the fact that I knew my baby's movements well. He *really* didn't seem inclined to turn.

As soon as my labour began it was accompanied by immediately intense, telling, lower back-pain, caused by my son's skull butting ineffectively into my pelvis. This – combined with my notes – should've been a warning to my midwives. But in an echo of Jessica Cornwell's experience, his posterior position hadn't been recorded in my notes. So convinced were they that I was making something out of nothing, that my persistent worrying went unrecorded. It never occurred to my partner or me that the midwives on shift that night wouldn't know this information, and so we didn't share it, trusting that they would advise a C-section if it was necessary.

Only when my son's heart rate sped up to a dangerous rate, and I was already fully dilated, did someone in the room connect the dots and summon a team of doctors. It was too late for an emergency C-section, and so they had to drag him out of me by brute force instead. I tore to the first degree; was cut to the second. Postnatally, I wasn't examined again by a doctor, not in the days afterwards on the ward when I could barely stand, not even at my six-week check when I reported feeling near total numbness. It took about a year to regain the feeling in my vagina and lower pelvis. I got the impression this was normal (it isn't).

When I fell pregnant the second time round, no one mentioned a C-section. Vaginal birth was an absolute given. I've since spoken to private specialists, all of whom agree they would've suggested a C-section. Perhaps they just want to fleece their customers. But I probably wouldn't have had a prolapse – at least, not yet in my life – if I'd had one.

I only once, hesitantly, broached the subject of having a C-section with my midwife. It was around the midway point in my second pregnancy, and we were talking about forceps. I said that I didn't want them to use them on me again. I didn't want them to use them under *any* circumstances. I let that hang. We both knew what I was angling for. When she didn't take the bait, asked her more directly: could she promise me that I wouldn't have them again? She said that she could not; not unless . . .

'I have an elective C-section?'

Her face fell. I don't think she thought that I'd actually say it.

'Why would you want *that*?'

How I would've liked to have answered this question is: Why *wouldn't* I want that? After what I'd been put through the first time, it couldn't possibly be any worse. Perhaps I'd be able to orgasm during sex sooner than a year postpartum if they cut the baby out of my stomach instead.

I couldn't say that. Nothing in this exchange told me that I was allowed to say this.

Instead, I answered: 'I really don't want to have to have forceps again.'

'We don't do elective C-sections on the NHS, not here,' she said quickly. 'You'd have to go somewhere else, maybe Luton. I don't know what to tell you. I can ask someone, but—'

I couldn't bear the social discomfort of the conversation any longer and so gave in, giving her what *she* wanted instead.

'No, it's fine,' I said, smiling away my defeat. 'I'm sure I won't need forceps anyway . . .'

The US leads the world when it comes to the number of C-sections performed.[44] It could be tempting to see this as evidence of patients having their needs well met, but the reality is not so straightforward.

For a start, the country's maternal mortality rate makes for some grim reading. Despite having the highest per capita medical expenditure in the world, the US has double the maternal mortality rate of Belgium or Canada, and more than triple the rate in Finland as well as several other Western European countries (all of which have much lower C-section rates).[45] Many factors contribute to this high maternal mortality rate, including inadequate access to preventive check-ups during pregnancy, a lack of prenatal care, and increased rates of chronic conditions such as obesity, diabetes, and heart disease. There are also considerable disparities between Black and white, rural and urban, and rich and poor women. The maternal mortality rate is three times higher among African American mothers compared to white mothers.[46]

Rather than being an indication of women receiving better or more personalised care, a high C-section rate likely has more to do with what *practitioners* want, and the financial structures they are operating within. In the US context, researchers believe that the high rate can be better connected to payment incentives offered to physicians and hospitals for carrying out more complicated procedures.[47] In other countries with similar healthcare systems, this is likely to be the case too.

Iran previously held the top spot in the highest overall rate of C-sections worldwide. Far exceeding the WHO recommendation of 10–15 per cent, Iran had a rate of 55 per cent in public hospitals (with some private hospitals reaching as high as 87 per cent).[48] The government had implemented projects to try to reduce this number, including preparation classes for pregnant women, mother-friendly hospitals and redevelopment of standard birth protocols, all to no avail. In 2014, it embarked on a fresh bid for reform. In public hospitals across the country, both doctors and patients were offered financial incentives for vaginal deliveries and caps were put in place on the number of C-sections doctors could perform in total.[49]

The project was a dramatic success; in first-time mothers, the rate of C-sections was brought down from 48 per cent to 35 per cent in under six months, and after fifteen months C-sections were down by 10 per cent across the board.

Researchers found that the financial incentives offered to doctors, more so than the patients, played a pivotal role. The doctors with the highest C-section rates responded quickest and most effectively. They had been able to charge more for C-section procedures than for vaginal deliveries, and were likely recommending them to their patients. Now that the tables were turned, doctors encouraged their patients accordingly. It was assumed that this explained why the other measures implemented by the government had not been so successful. They targeted the attitudes towards C-section of the mothers, rather than the doctors carrying them out.

Causing surprise among researchers and public health officials, Iran's C-section rate did not continue to drop much further. It was reported to have risen again in 2018 to 48 per cent in public hospitals, and in private hospitals it has returned to approximately the same rate as what it was before the measures were implemented in 2014. Perhaps the patients began asking for them despite the doctors' encouragement towards the more lucrative option?

A research study in 2018 found that the reasons behind women's preference for C-sections in Iran were multifarious, but converged around a few central themes: a deep-rooted fear of the pain of vaginal birth, a belief that the baby's safety was better guaranteed by a C-section delivery, and the risk of irreversible damage to a woman's bodily and sexual function.[50] None of these root issues are considered or addressed, however, when healthcare providers instead endeavour to coerce patients through financial means.

Another area in which financial pressure is exerted on patients to achieve an intended goal is infant feeding. In 2022, the WHO released a report describing the advertising of formula milk as 'exploitative', 'manipulative' and ultimately deleterious to infant well-being.[51] In their work more broadly, the organisation unambiguously states that breast milk is superior when it comes to infant well-being and health.[52] The WHO has been nothing but consistent in this message, introducing guidelines in 1981 to prevent the promotional sale of formula milk. The UK adopted these guidelines, but, over forty years later, still has one of the lowest rates of breastfeeding in the world.[53]

While the debate over the benefits of breastfeeding versus the supposed harms of formula feeding rages on, women – especially poorer women – find themselves economically penalised by the state for formula-feeding their babies. Like tobacco and other such products considered harmful to public health, formula milk is excluded by law from supermarket offers, sales, and point-saving schemes, which many people on low incomes rely on. At the time of writing, the cost-of-living crisis means more people than ever before are resorting to the use of foodbanks, which do not accept the donation of formula milk. In 2023, the UK government's Competition and Markets Authority reported that the cost of formula had risen by 25 per cent in the past two years alone.[54]

Ultimately, economic punishment hasn't succeeded in raising levels of breastfeeding in the UK. The country may want to take a long, hard look at itself. A crisis in maternity staffing means that many women and new parents do not have access to adequate breastfeeding support postnatally. In a pointed statement made by the Royal College of Midwives in 2021, the link between austerity and the inability of maternity units to provide infant-feeding support was noted:

> It is vital [. . .] that maternity services are always adequately staffed so that midwives and maternity support workers can provide high quality support to every mother on infant feeding. The current and worsening midwife shortage in England and growing staffing issues in other UK countries are certainly making this difficult to achieve. Not everyone can or chooses to breastfeed and other influences, including socioeconomic and education factors also play a part. It is a complex picture, but undoubtedly, mothers' access to breastfeeding support is crucial.[55]

Debate around the benefits of breast milk tends to be ideologically driven, with all major medical bodies extolling the many virtues of breastfeeding but providing little data by way of evidence. A meta-analysis of over 9,000 research papers on breastfeeding benefits conducted by the US Agency for Healthcare Research and Quality concludes that much of that work is scientifically weak. Some of the studies are too small to be informative, or fail to control for the many possible confounding variables. The findings are often inconclusive and, in most cases, examples to the contrary can be found for any research purporting positive effects.[56]

Breastfeeding is also a class issue. In 2011, the UK tabloid the *Daily Mail* announced a breastfeeding boom among the wealthier: 'Middle-class mothers lead the charge with 90% rejecting formula milk.'[57] The push for increased breastfeeding is very much fuelled by the narratives around the superiority of breastfeeding for child development. With dwindling access to publicly funded resources, those who are better off can offset the shortfall by accessing expensive breastfeeding support, such as private lactation consultants.[58] But the reasoning might be somewhat misplaced. Research shows that the middle-class lifestyle and privilege, rather than breastfeeding, is by far the main driving factor behind a child's future prospects in life.[59]

The exclusive reliance on breast milk is not always the right approach to feeding newborns, something that Dr Christie del Castillo-Hegyi learned for herself, and with life-changing consequences for her and her child.[60] In 2009, Del Castillo-Hegyi gave birth to a healthy baby boy, following 'a healthy pregnancy and normal uneventful vaginal delivery', at Downtown Presbyterian Hospital in Albuquerque, New Mexico, where she was also an attending physician. He nursed immediately, latched without issue and was exclusively breastfed, just as Del Castillo-Hegyi intended, and with full encouragement from the paediatrics team.

Initially, all went well, and although her son developed jaundice – common in newborns – he and his mother were deemed well enough to be discharged. At home, however, her son wouldn't settle, cried through the night and would not stop nursing. On his third day at home, he became strangely quiet. Del Castillo-Hegyi also noticed that he had lost weight – again, something that is hardly unusual for newborns. Still, Del Castillo-Hegyi suspected something was wrong. She continued to breastfeed, desperate to improve his health through this method of feeding, and convinced by her medical colleagues that this was the right approach. At some point, her conviction wavered. She became concerned that her son might be losing weight due to inadequate milk supply, and so visited a lactation consultant the following day. There, a shocking discovery was made. Del Castillo-Hegyi was not producing *any* milk at all. Her child was starving, and no one in her medical team had noticed. Immediately, he was given formula milk and finally fell asleep. Three hours later he was found unresponsive, and when he was given a little bit more milk, he developed a seizure. Rushed into an emergency room, it was found that he was severely dehydrated and jaundiced and had critically low blood-glucose levels. Del Castillo-Hegyi was reassured that all was going to be well, but she feared the worst. And she had good grounds to be afraid, for she had spent years researching brain injury in newborns.

In the tragic case of her son, the emergency medical help came too late. Dehydrated and starved, neurons in his brain started to die. He was subsequently diagnosed with severe language impairment, sensory processing disorder, low IQ, fine and gross motor delays, and a seizure disorder, as well as autism and ADHD.

Over the years that followed, Del Castillo-Hegyi collected thousands of similar stories from women who got in touch with her through social media to share how their experiences of being pushed to breastfeed, even when they had reservations themselves, led to their children acquiring brain injuries and disabilities due to inadequate milk supply in the first few days of their lives. She now runs a charity called the 'Fed is Best Foundation', whose mission is to challenge the indiscriminate promotion of breastfeeding over ensuring adequate nutrition of the newborn baby.

Though research showing unambiguous benefits of breastfeeding is inconclusive at best, this does not dissuade the breast-milk campaigners from stating them in no uncertain terms in maternity brochures, on websites, on posters in hospitals, at antenatal classes and in the popular media in general. But sometimes, even a total lack of any scientific evidence (or even common sense) is not a reason to hold back from making a claim about breast milk. The 'Mothers & Others Guide', distributed to expectant parents across the NHS, offers the following advice in a section on smoking and breastfeeding: 'if you can't give up smoking it is still better than giving your baby formula milk'.[61] This claim, painting formula milk as *worse* than carcinogenic breast milk, is not only scientifically illiterate, but also plainly wrong and grossly irresponsible.

Unfortunately, 'breast is best' thinking continues unchecked and new parents find themselves pushed, pressured, and even economically coerced into making it work.

Rose Stokes, a British mother from Bath, found herself in a position similar to Del Castillo-Hegyi and thousands of other women: she was not producing enough milk, but she was determined to see it through.[62] Eleven days postpartum her milk supply still hadn't properly 'kicked in'. She was following the midwives' advice religiously, feeding on demand, pumping when she could, and topping up with formula as was necessary. She found a private lactation consultant online, who suggested that she try to use a special medication – domperidone – to stimulate milk production. Domperidone is normally used as an anti-sickness drug and works by blocking receptors in the brain that are responsible for vomiting.

But domperidone also finds its way to another brain region: the pituitary gland. The pituitary gland secretes a hormone called prolactin, responsible for causing lactation. Normally, dopamine in the brain stops prolactin from being produced, but domperidone blocks dopamine-signalling in the brain. The drug is sometimes prescribed to people with Parkinson's disease, and has a side effect in men and women alike: lactation.

This side effect led to increased off-label use of domperidone to stimulate milk production in breastfeeding women. However, it is not commonly prescribed for this purpose, and Stokes needed a letter from the lactation consultant to convince her GP to give her the drug. The consultant swore by domperidone, saying it was the silver bullet that allowed her to exclusively breastfeed her twins.

Stokes took the maximum recommended dose of domperidone: 10 mg, three times a day for seven days. But her milk supply didn't budge. Her son's weight dropped further, and Stokes was now very anxious about his well-being. The health visitor warned her that he was at risk of 'falling off the charts'. The lactation consultant told Stokes that when she herself had been breastfeeding, she had taken 120 mg of domperidone a day – four times the maximum recommended dose – and Stokes felt obliged to follow suit. She found an online pharmacy which supplied her with more medication, after an online consultation for her non-existent travel sickness. She increased her dose, but it still was not enough, and she soon ran out of pills.

Knowing that she would need a doctor to prescribe her with the required amount of medication, she turned to a private specialist in London who, after a £170 phone conversation, gave her a prescription for a huge stash of domperidone. Her milk supply increased somewhat, but inconsistently, even though she was now on over five times the maximum dose of domperidone. She battled on for two more weeks with little success and decided to stop taking the drug. In the meantime, she had to have a private ECG, because the huge doses of the medication had started to affect her heart. Long-time domperidone use is associated with a 70 per cent increase of risk of sudden cardiac death.

Having received no advice on coming off domperidone, Stokes went cold turkey. This is when her mental health deteriorated. She started having panic attacks, and noticed that depression and anxiety were taking over her life. Worried about this, she phoned the private doctor who apologised to her and informed her that she was experiencing withdrawal symptoms. Stokes needed to immediately go back on the medication and taper it off slowly, in decreasing doses.

However, her mental health declined further. She experienced suicidal thoughts and was referred to a specialist psychiatrist through her perinatal support team. Her antidepressant medication, prescribed sometime earlier along the way, was increased in dose, and then again, and again, seven times in total. Stokes finally stopped taking domperidone just before her son's first birthday.

Despite the risks associated with the use of domperidone, thousands of people around the world are recommended the medication and take it to increase their milk supply. As Stokes herself found, many of these people swear by it. But few are warned of the potential serious side effects of taking large doses of the drug for prolonged periods. Sometime after her harrowing experience, Stokes wrote an article in the *Guardian* recounting her story. She ends it with the following note:

I am pregnant again. This time, I will establish boundaries about how I approach breastfeeding and when I will give up if it isn't working. It has taken a lot of hard work to get here, but I am confident that, whichever way I end up feeding my next baby, we will both be OK.[63]

Patients deserve to be given objective and substantiated advice from their healthcare professionals that is tailored to their needs. Use of domperidone carries a risk, and patients should be made aware of this to make their informed choices, free of bias and presumption.

It may not be ideal, but domperidone does have a place in support of breastfeeding patients. It is an integral part of the 'Goldfarb-Newman Protocol', which is recommended in Canada to adoptive and other non-gestational mothers who wish to stimulate their milk supply.[64]

The same protocol can also be used when it comes to trans women who wish to breastfeed. However, this use is far from ideal, as the protocol has been developed for cis women, and trans women's bodies present specific issues. For example, the supplementation of female hormones is needed to promote the development of milk-producing tissue in the body. Medical literature on lactation induction for transgender women is very sparse, but in 2024 doctors from a gender healthcare clinic in Amsterdam successfully deployed an adapted version of the Goldfarb-Newman Protocol to stimulate lactation in a 37-year-old patient, who then breastfed her newborn baby.[65]

Lack of appropriate guidance is by no means the biggest challenge faced by trans women when it comes to breastfeeding. These women face a huge perception barrier from people who simply do not want to see it happen, on the grounds that it is 'unnatural'. Such barriers are everywhere, from the very cisnormative language used itself. In February 2024, University Hospitals Sussex NHS Foundation Trust issued a letter to its staff highlighting new research that showed that milk produced by transgender women is as beneficial for infants as milk from cisgender individuals. An outcry followed, and the reaction by the then Labour MP Rosie Duffield perfectly encapsulates the stigma faced by trans women: 'When a man has not and cannot grow a baby, why on earth are we pandering to this? Who does it benefit? Not the children.'[66]

Quite the contrary: opening up different, more tailored methods for infant feeding is directly beneficial not just to children, but to the patients who feel coerced into feeding in ways that are rigid and harmful for them. I think of my own, miserable experiences with breastfeeding – unable ever to get in a comfortable position, hampered first by my episiotomy, and then by my prolapse; of my poor supply of milk, of guiltily topping up their feeds with quietly procured tubs of formula that I would hide in the cupboards before the health visitors arrived. I think of Andrzej, declaring on more than one occasion 'I wish I could breastfeed instead!' and not only desperate to help, but to experience everything that a new parent might want to experience too, irrelevant of gender. I think of the new, adoptive parents who wish to breastfeed, and what doing so can open up for them – or the women who want to stop having to wake up every other hour in the night to express, or those who want their partners to sit up with the baby and bottle feed them instead.

The term 'natural' often comes loaded with prejudice; be it for the 'normal' (read, most common), or the 'traditional' (read, outdated). It *could* mean to do something in the most comfortable and intuitive way, for you and your body alone. It may be natural for you to breastfeed, or to give birth vaginally, or to have an epidural – all because you want those things. Equally, formula milk, a C-section, and no pain relief at all may come as natural decisions for you too. It is important that what is natural is not confused with what is *ideologically* (and financially) preferred by the healthcare provider, institution, or even the dominant culture. When it is invoked to cause harm – to carry out an unwanted and/or clinically unnecessary symphysiotomy, for example – the effects are far from natural, in any sense of the term. We must be vigilant whenever 'nature' is used to justify a form of violence, and it is simply not *natural* for a patient to be unnecessarily harmed in any medical setting. Equally, it is not natural for a patient to be coerced into harmful or personally detrimental practices because of a supposedly superior form of having a baby, or being a patient, or, even, of being a woman. You are the first person to have ever lived in *your* body. Only you get to decide what is 'natural' for you.

5. Sacrifice Yourself

In my friendship group, we all have a 'first'. First to learn how to drive, to get a job, to go on holiday to Southeast Asia, to buy a house. I was the first one to get married; Jess was the first to have an abortion. She was in her mid twenties when she accidentally became pregnant.

Her first instinct was to ask: How? Jess had been on the contraceptive pill for years and was notoriously strict about taking it and at precisely the same time, every day. We might've just got in after a late night, still drunk and barely in bed, but at 6 a.m. her alarm would sound, and she'd be hauling herself towards her bag and digging out the blister pack. She is the kind of person who has to remind everyone else to attend their appointments, and to take their pills. It seemed unbelievable, now, that she would have forgotten to take her own.

She hadn't. About a week later, she learned that her new epilepsy medication had been the culprit. When Jess was prescribed it, she had been warned of how it might affect fertility, and could cause congenital anomalies in a child. No one had told her that it could decrease the efficacy of hormonal contraception.

'They told me it could make me infertile,' Jess later recalled, with bitterness. 'If only.'

She needed the abortion fast. She was about to begin PhD fieldwork that would take her out of the country for almost a year, and before that she had a busy few weeks filled with catch-ups, appointments, her sister's wedding in the Highlands; in short, all of the things you desperately need to cram in before taking a long trip.

To make matters worse, Jess learned that she was further along than first thought. She had long since experienced irregular periods, sometimes going months at a time without one. That, coupled with a lack of any other symptoms or reason to believe she was pregnant, meant that she was already twelve weeks pregnant before she first saw a doctor. This struck out the possibility of her using abortion pills, as ten weeks was the cut-off point for use in her region of the country.

There are two types of abortion. The first is known as medical abortion, which in the UK can take place at home. The patient takes two prescription pills: mifepristone and misoprostol, which cause the lining of the uterus to break down. The embryo is passed out of the vagina, together with blood and the uterine lining. Sometimes, medical abortion is unsuccessful, and the patient is then referred to surgery.

The second option is surgical abortion, involving a procedure to remove the developing embryo directly from the uterus. In England, Scotland and Wales the cut-off for surgical termination of pregnancy is twenty-four weeks, unless there is a risk to the life of the patient, or the child would be born with severe disability. Depending on the method and how far progressed the pregnancy is, the procedure is carried out under local anaesthetic, sedation, or general anaesthesia. Then, either vacuum aspiration or dilatation and evacuation are used to remove the foetus. For vacuum aspiration, a tube is inserted into the uterus through the cervix and a suction technique is employed. More progressed pregnancies, however – usually those beyond fourteen weeks – are terminated using dilatation and evacuation. Here, the cervix is dilated and forceps are used instead of suction. When carried out in a hospital setting, both of these types of surgical abortion are carried out as outpatient procedures. They are genuinely considered to be safe and quick. The most common side effects include pain, cramps and bleeding for a few days following the surgery.

Jess was not worried about the procedure itself; she was more concerned with the wait for the hospital appointment. An inveterate worrier, she could not relax until the abortion had been carried out. Strung out, a ball of anxiety, she ended up collapsing on the dancefloor at her sister's wedding, smacking her head on the flagstones, having the first epileptic seizure she'd had in years.

A cousin took her to A&E. No one knew that she was pregnant, and she prayed that it wouldn't come up. Of course, she was hardly through the door to the examination room when the doctor was asking her if there was 'any chance' she might be. Even though she had half-expected the question, she was still taken off guard by the doctor's reaction after she answered in the affirmative.

'Congratulations! You must be so excited? Is this your first?'

So at odds was this line of questioning with her experience of being pregnant so far, that she didn't know what to say. Instead, she simply smiled back and nodded along, not thinking ahead to the other, predictable questions that are always asked of someone with a head injury, the next of which being:

'Have you consumed any alcohol in the last twenty-four hours?'

'Yes,' she said automatically, being as honest as she is non-confrontational. 'About five or six glasses of wine.'

The doctor's face clouded over.

Hastily, and somewhat lamely, Jess said what she should've said moments before: 'I'm having an abortion.'

The air in the room seemed to thin in an instant. 'How far along are you?'

'Over three months.'

'You shouldn't drink in pregnancy . . .' said the doctor, slowly, didactically.

'I didn't think it would matter,' Jess countered.

She was sent off for a head scan and blood tests. Her cousin had fallen asleep in the waiting room, head unknowingly propped up against the shoulder of a stranger. Jess slyly took a photo and shared it in the family group chat. The party was still going strong, and everyone wanted to know when she'd be back. Just waiting to see the doctor, she told them. Everything's fine.

When she was called back in to discuss her results, she was met not just by the doctor from before, but by a consultant too.

This is it, she thought to herself. I'm having a brain haemorrhage. She was no stranger to falls after a lifetime of seizures, but they had been happening with far less frequency of late – probably because of the new medication – and she had thought she was out of the woods. The pain and fear of past hospital visits came rushing back to her. This dizziness she was feeling couldn't possibly be on account of her tiredness, or the wine, or even the pregnancy, but instead some catastrophic and life-altering head injury. Countless seizures in her teenage years had brought her up to the precipice, and this had been the one to finally tip her over the edge. She'd have to give up her PhD and move back in with her parents. The consultant had come to tell her all this. She felt tears springing to her eyes.

Jess was taken aback, then, when she was told that her skull and brain both were perfectly fine. She had had a small stitch to staunch the bleeding, but it was dissolvable, so she could leave straight away and wouldn't have to think of it again. But before you go . . .

'Now Jess,' began the consultant. 'I know that you are three months pregnant. I also know that you have been doing some heavy drinking tonight—'

'I'm having an abortion,' she interrupted. 'I didn't think drinking was a problem.'

'Is drinking a problem for you, do you think?'

'No. It's my sister's wedding . . . I'm having an abortion and I thought it would be okay—'

'We have no record here of you having taken legally obtained abortion pills?'

The way the consultant let the phrase 'legally obtained' hang, slightly, sent a wave of panic coursing through her. Her words jumbled up as she rushed to explain: 'I'm not having one right now! I mean, I'm going to have one. When I get home.'

'Do you feel like you need to have an abortion because of the drinking?'

'No, I'd already decided, so I thought it would be okay . . .'

She felt like the doctors were trying to catch her out. She didn't know what, exactly, they were trying to accuse her of lying about – her drinking, her intention to have an abortion, or whether she had procured illegal abortion pills online. Jess so desperately wanted to explain to them how none of this was her fault – for some reason, that seemed to matter at the time. *I'm a good person!* she wanted to shout at them. *Honestly!* But she also knew that they had already made up their minds about her. And presently, the consultant was segueing from her needs to those of her unborn child.

'Listen, Jess. We would like to refer you to our Alcohol Brief

Intervention programme. This is aimed at helping you to quit drinking in order to protect your baby. Drinking alcohol in pregnancy can cause your baby to develop Foetal Alcohol Syndrome. This can cause your baby—'

Your baby this . . . your baby that . . .

If she was someone else – someone, she later said, with a totally different personality from her own – she would've stood up and left. Instead, she began to cry.

'I don't need . . .'

She struggled to get out what she wanted to say through the tears. Although it didn't seem like the consultant cared to understand what she wanted to say, and was all too quick to take her emotional state for grudging admittance of a drinking problem.

'We know you're not resident here in Scotland,' he spoke over her, in a gentle, pitying voice. 'And this programme would only be applicable if you were to stay on here. Otherwise, we'd like to get in touch with your local surgery and refer you to a similar service for pregnant women with alcohol dependence . . .'

She wanted to get out of the room as quickly as possible. She couldn't talk, so she found herself nodding along – and hating herself for it. A leaflet was pushed across the table – one that she shoved in her bag and never looked at again – and she left the room as quickly, but as politely, as her acquiescence would allow. The last thing she remembers the consultant saying to her was, in a final mortal blow to her sense of self-esteem: 'In a strange way, it's a good thing that you had your seizure today. Otherwise we might never have caught this at all.'

And by 'this', Jess understood him to mean 'you'. That they had caught *her*.

Jess's experience in A&E that night did not prevent her from having an abortion. It did, however, require some long and difficult conversations with her own GP back home, in order to remove the referral to the alcohol-abuse-in-pregnancy clinic from her medical notes – something that she worried might come back to haunt her if she ever got pregnant again in future. It also brought home how abortion is not just a medical matter, but a legal one, too. She had made the error of thinking that abortion was a straightforward affair in the UK – something that many of us do. And yet this is far from the case.

Abortions in England, Wales and Scotland are regulated by the 1967 Abortion Act. It allows the procedure to be carried out up to twenty-four weeks, but it has to be approved by two independent physicians and performed only in an NHS hospital or another medical setting approved by the Secretary of State. Any abortion procedures that do not meet these conditions are treated as a criminal offence.[1]

It may seem that abortion in Britain can be obtained on demand with no questions asked, but it is not the case. Apart from needing the approval of two doctors, certain conditions need to be met. These are: risk to the life of the patient; risk of grave permanent injury to their physical or mental health; risk of injury to the physical or mental health of any existing children; or substantial risk that, if the child were born, they would be severely disabled. In the vast majority of cases – around 98 per cent – the main reason cited is the risk to the patient's mental health.[2]

Even though abortion in Britain is de facto elective, it is not a patient's choice, and procuring it without permission is a criminal offence. Not in theory, but in practice: women continue to be prosecuted for it. In June 2023, Carla Foster, a 45-year-old mother of three, was sentenced to over two years in prison for obtaining drugs to cause an abortion over the legal limit.[3] In some respects, she got off lightly. Illegal abortion carries a maximum sentence of life imprisonment.

Foster obtained the abortion medication mifepristone and misoprostol under the 'pills by post' scheme, which was instigated during the Covid-19 pandemic. This involved a remote consultation with the British Pregnancy Advisory Service (BPAS). She was around twenty-eight weeks pregnant at the time of consultation – eighteen weeks past the limit for accessing medication through this scheme, and four weeks past the legal abortion limit – but she lied in her remote consultation with BPAS and claimed to be seven weeks pregnant instead. Shortly after receiving the medication, she carried out the termination at home. Because she was already well into her pregnancy, the procedure was far from straightforward. Foster required urgent medical help. She called emergency services, claiming to have gone into premature labour. Medics arrived on the scene and immediately pronounced the newly born foetus dead. Foster admitted to police what she had done, and was charged with the offence of 'child destruction'.

During her sentencing, High Court judge Sir Edward Pepperall acknowledged that Foster felt 'very deep and genuine remorse' about what had happened. Justice Pepperall also noted that she 'had a very deep emotional attachment to [her] unborn child' and that she was 'plagued by nightmares and flashbacks to seeing [her] dead child's face'.[4] Nonetheless, she was handed an unsuspended custodial sentence and was set to go to prison. Over thirty-five days of incarceration, she was not permitted any contact with her three children.

Foster's case was highly publicised and caused widespread debate. The Court of Appeal subsequently reduced her sentence, arguing that there was no good reason for her to be in prison.[5] Nevertheless, on top of her fourteen-month suspended sentence, she still had to undertake fifty days of community service. Nearly a year later, six women in the UK are currently awaiting trial for abortion-related offences.

While some women are imprisoned for having abortions, others who are denied them are killed.

While legal access to abortion seemed to improve drastically in the twentieth century, that global wave of liberalisation has, in recent decades, experienced a sea change, and nowhere in the West is this regression more evident than in Poland.

In September 2021, Izabela Sajbor sent her final text message. To her mother, she wrote: 'The doctors can't help as long as the foetus is alive thanks to the anti-abortion law. A woman is like an incubator.' She was thirty years old, twenty-two weeks pregnant, and waiting to die.[6]

She had been admitted to hospital in her hometown of Pszczyna, southern Poland, after falling over when playing with her older daughter and injuring her nose. Her mother took her to A&E on account of the bleeding. Coincidentally, her waters broke on the way. But it was far too early, and Izabela was immediately admitted to the maternity ward. Strict Covid-19 restrictions forbade her mother from accompanying her, so she was on her own.

Izabela already knew that she was carrying a baby with potentially severe congenital anomalies. Despite her waters breaking, her labour failed to progress, and doctors decided to wait it out rather than intervene. Any labour up to and including the twenty-second week of pregnancy was treated as a miscarriage and could not, by law, be induced (anything later would be treated as premature birth).

Izabela was terrified. She messaged her mother: 'The child weighs 485 g. For the time being, thanks to the anti-abortion law, I have to be lying down. They can't do anything. They are waiting until it dies or something starts happening, if not, I can expect sepsis. They can't speed it up. Either the heart stops beating, or something has to start.'[7]

In the messages that followed, Izabela indicated that her health was beginning to fail. 'They gave me a drip, because I was shivering from the fever. It's good I brought a thermometer, because nobody took my temperature. I had 39.9.'[8]

Izabela suspected that she was developing sepsis. She continued to message her mother and inform staff, until she was too ill to communicate any more. At this point, upon examination, it was found that the foetus no longer had a heartbeat. Finally the go-ahead was given for an emergency C-section; but it was too late. Less than twenty-four hours after going to the hospital with a bleeding nose, Izabela died on the gurney, en route to the operating theatre.

Izabela's story joins that of Dr Savita Halappanavar's, who was denied an abortion in Ireland in 2012, which also led to her death;[9] of fifteen-year-old Mildred's, who died in a Kenyan hospital in 2021;[10] of Olga Reyes in Nicaragua, who was left to bleed to death and suffer multiple heart attacks after doctors refused to abort her ectopic pregnancy;[11] and many, many others.

Izabela had, shortly before her death, requested an abortion on medical grounds. When it was rejected, she had begun looking into procuring one abroad. Her efforts had been hampered by the pandemic – travelling out of Poland was difficult at the time – and, once her waters broke, it was only a matter of time before the sepsis set in. Facing near certain incarceration, few doctors in the country would take the risk of carrying out an abortion in a case such as hers.

And yet, a *century* earlier, Poland was one of the most progressive countries in the world when it came to legal abortion access.[12] With the exceptions of Romania, Albania and (for a while under Stalin) the Soviet Union, abortion was legal and freely accessible in most socialist countries in the twentieth century. Before the country came under the influence of communism, abortion had been completely illegal in Poland regardless of circumstance. The legal stance was similar to the rest of continental Europe at the time, heavily influenced by the Catholic Church. In the 1930s, public debate on the subject came to a head. Abortion was generally opposed by conservative politicians and Catholic elites in the country, and supported by left-leaning liberals who looked to the Soviet Union as a model for women's rights. Lenin had made abortion available on request in Soviet Russia in 1920, not long after the October Revolution.[13] The main motivating factor behind legalisation was to limit underground abortions that were causing the deaths of thousands of women every year.

Religious conservatives managed to block the legalisation of abortion in Poland, but in 1932 abortion was allowed on medical grounds or when the pregnancy was the result of a crime.[14] Poland became the third country in the world after the Soviet Union and Mexico to legalise it on such grounds. It was also no longer illegal for a woman, in any circumstance, to decide to have an abortion – only the person performing the procedure could be prosecuted.

However, Stalin made a U-turn in 1936, to encourage falling population growth. So when Poland became a satellite Soviet state in 1945, its previously relaxed abortion laws took a hit. After the death of Stalin in 1953 the country restored its abortion laws, with the added provision that women could now request abortion on the grounds of a 'difficult life situation'. In practice that meant that abortion in Poland was almost available on demand to anyone.[15]

After the fall of communism, the Church significantly consolidated its hold over Poland. Decades of economic hardship, political turmoil and martial law at the hands of the communists made the Church, and Catholic-leaning political parties, in contradistinction, very popular. Between 1990 and 1996 Poland saw *seven* different prime ministers – a record that could strike fear into the heart of even the British voting public. Amid this turmoil, people turned, irrevocably, to the country's one enduring constant: the Catholic Church.

Abortion legislation was rolled back once again in 1993, made only possible if the mother's health was in danger, the foetus had severe congenital problems, or – still – if the pregnancy was the result of a crime. The ruling party from 2005 to 2023 – *Prawo i Sprawiedliwość* (Law and Justice – often abbreviated to PiS, and known in our Poglish-speaking household as 'Piss') – tried to introduce mandatory prison sentences for physicians carrying out abortions and women receiving them. Thousands of people took to the streets in a mass organised protest known as 'Czarny Poniedziałek' (Black Monday).[16] The government argued that the termination of foetuses with a 'high probability of severe and irreversible disability or incurable and life-threatening disease' contravened the constitutional rule of protection of human life.[17] People argued that women would die as a direct consequence of this legislation. Nonetheless, it was codified into law in January 2021 – the same year that Izabela died.

Upon news of her death, mass protests erupted in the country: far bigger than any that had taken place before, far bigger than anything the government could have anticipated. Church windows were smashed, statues of Pope John Paul II graffitied. '*Morderca kobiet*' read the signs. 'Murderer of women.'[18]

Amid all this turmoil, and in an act of defiance against popular, progressive opinion, the Polish postal service issued a commemorative stamp featuring none other than Gianna Beretta Molla – a Catholic Saint made famous for dying in childbirth. Nowhere outside of her native country of Italy is Molla more venerated than in Poland. Two months pregnant when a tumour was discovered in her uterus, Molla – herself a physician – refused a life-saving hysterectomy in order to save the life of her unborn and fourth child.[19] She died in 1962, following the birth, and was canonised by Pope John Paul II.[20]

Although the Church condemns any abortion as 'moral evil', saving the mother's life falls into a permissible category under the 'Doctrine of Double Effect': when an act of good cancels an act of evil.[21] While it may be permissible, it does not quite fit into the *ideal* – which is a woman's total self-sacrifice to her unborn child. In choosing this particular moment to present Molla on a stamp, the Polish government – and Church – was advertising its endorsement of motherhood as absolute sacrifice. Effectively, it was legitimising Izabela's death on 'holy' grounds. The deputy head of the postal service stated their hope that 'the story of [this] hero will give courage to mothers, who, awaiting the arrival of their child, face great dilemmas and problems'.[22]

In other words, those mothers should follow Molla's example, and sacrifice themselves whenever and wherever possible. Izabela and Molla succeeded in reaching the highest ideal of womanhood: to be a dead mother. Self-sacrifice, essentially, was a woman's holiest purpose. The reflection of historian and philosopher René Girard comes to mind: 'The peoples of the world do not invent their gods. They deify their victims.'[23]

The global pro-choice movement took a major hit in 2022, when the US Supreme Court declared that abortion is not a constitutional right – overturning the famous *Roe* v. *Wade* ruling from 1973. In the six months following the Supreme Court's decision, twenty-four US states either banned abortion completely or declared their intention to do so.[24] The impact of this ruling in the US – the perceived 'leader of the free world' – refocused attention on how relatively insecure the access to reproductive rights is, even in those places where they are most taken for granted.

Abortion on demand, or elective abortion, is still illegal in over 130 countries – the majority of the world.[25] Seventy-four countries prohibit it even if the pregnancy is a result of rape or crime; fifty-five ban it even in cases when the mother's life is at risk; and in nine it is completely illegal in *all* cases. The New York-based Center for Reproductive Rights, a legal organisation that seeks to advance women's right to reproductive choices all over the world, estimates that only 34 per cent of the global female population has (legal) access to abortion on demand. This does not mean that everyone with legal access has *actual* access in practice, though, and the centre also estimates that around 39,000 women die annually from unsafe procedures – including in countries where it is legal, too.[26]

In spite of the troubling recent developments in the US, and the general poor provision of legal abortion around the world, there are some signs of positive change. In 2019 abortion was decriminalised in Northern Ireland, where previous laws were even more restrictive than in the rest of the UK – prohibiting abortion except when the mother's life was in direct danger.[27] Now, abortion up to twelve weeks is legal in all cases. The British Labour MP Stella Creasy, who was instrumental in changing the law in Northern Ireland, has led a cross-partisan initiative to bring forward similar legislation in England, Scotland and Wales.[28]

In the US in 2022, President Biden's government sued Idaho – a state with one of the strictest sets of abortion laws – for failing to carry out life-saving abortions. In Poland in April 2024, the right-wing PiS government was defeated at the polls by Donald Tusk's centrist party, who had campaigned on the explicit promise of liberalising abortion laws. Immediately after Izabela's death, the then Polish Secretary of State Marek Suski, when questioned on the cruelty of the law that had killed her, shrugged off public concern and stated that 'people die, and that's biology'.[29] At the following election he was voted out of power. And so, we have reason to hope – albeit with caution. The belief that women should sacrifice themselves is certainly not a given.

6. Choose Joy

Almost a year later, and nothing had changed. My mind was full of cusps, cliffs, voids and avalanches. And I was so tired. Tired of trying to hold myself in, tired of being exposed to the air. Tired of thinking about it and trying to describe it to people. Russian philosopher Mikhail Bakhtin said that: 'Stress is laid on those parts of the body that are open to the outside world, that is, the parts through which the world enters the body or emerges from it, or through which the body itself goes out to meet the world.'[1] I didn't want to meet the world any more. I wanted it to leave me alone.

I wanted surgery.

There are many different types of prolapse repair surgery. Most tend to be carried out under general anaesthetic and require six to twelve weeks of downtime, and most women undergoing the surgery will be advised to stave it off until they are sure they will not want to get pregnant again. The basic principle behind surgical prolapse repair is to move the prolapsed tissue to its original position and secure it in place, either by attaching it to other parts of the pelvis (this is known as native tissue repair) or supporting it with a sling made from plastic meshes, biological grafts, or donor tissue.

For uterine vaginal prolapse, the most common type of surgery is called sacral colpopexy. This involves the prolapsed tissue being lifted and attached to the sacrum – a triangular bone at the base of the spine – using a piece of mesh or a graft. Alternative procedures, called sacrospinous ligament fixation and uterosacral ligament fixation, mean suturing the prolapse to ligaments in the pelvis.[2] Bladder prolapse repair requires something slightly more elegant. This procedure is known as anterior colporrhaphy and it is carried out by tightening the layer of tissue that separates the bladder and the vagina, a bit like gathering fabric to make a pleat, and suturing it together. Sometimes a piece of mesh or a graft is added to the site of the operation.[3] The procedure for posterior prolapse (posterior colporrhaphy) is very similar, but performed on the opposite side of the vaginal wall.[4]

Three recent reviews of published data on prolapse surgical repair carried out by Cochrane revealed a lack of research into the effectiveness of individual procedures, and exposed a gap left behind by the withdrawal of the plastic mesh.[5] While these procedures are complicated and under-researched, they also do not guarantee recovery. For sacral colpopexy, it's estimated that 23 per cent of patients will experience the return of their prolapse. For other types of uterine prolapse repair this ratio is even higher (estimated to be as high as 63 per cent). The data for posterior colporrhaphy is less complete, but some studies cite a shocking failure rate of 100 per cent! Apart from the possibility of failure, all these procedures carry with them a risk of multiple complications, including urinary incontinence and chronic pelvic pain after surgery: the very symptoms the surgery is supposed to cure.

Perhaps I was lucky, then, that my GP didn't recommend surgery when I broached the topic.

'Two years you'll be waiting to see a surgeon on the NHS,' she told me. 'And that's just for a consultation. I don't know how long you'll be waiting after that for the surgery, if they even agree to do it at all . . .'

In two years' time I would be in my thirties. *Everything* could've fallen out by then. I was almost in tears. I said that I needed something *now*.

'I think we need to focus on your positivity,' she said bracingly. 'Maybe you'd like to join a group called Weeping Willows?'

As she opened a drawer in her desk and groped about for a leaflet, I had to marvel at how much my life now felt like a bad sitcom. Yes, I knew Weeping Willows. I had even been to a meeting of theirs.

At the beginning of my first pregnancy, I went mad. It didn't quite happen overnight, but came on as the weeks progressed in a series of panic attacks interspersed with disturbed, racing thoughts, all of which centred on death: Andrzej's, mine, that of our unborn child. And then it upped a notch: now I was obsessing over planetary heat death and the death of God. I couldn't sleep at night, for the backs of my eyelids seemed to be plastered with the blank space of the end of time. The panic attacks began blending together; one day they were coming every hour, the next they didn't seem to have any perceptible end. I went to the doctor and told him that I thought I was seeing things.

He recommended that I go to a group for anxious pregnant women and new mothers called Weeping Willows. I didn't have much time to register what was happening, really, because the group's next meeting was that very afternoon.

'Just pop along and see how it goes,' he said, cocking his head to the side in sympathy. 'And come back if you're still feeling a bit low next week.'

I'm not sure why my psychosis wasn't recognised straight away. Andrzej thinks it's because of how high-functioning I came across at the time; what was coming out of my mouth ('I'm mad') was completely at odds with my engaged and smiling face, my balanced speech, my well-dressed appearance. How I came across, though, might not have made any difference: research conducted by National Childbirth Trust (NCT) indicates that nearly half of new mothers' mental health problems fail to get picked up by health professionals.[6] In any case, off to Weeping Willows I went.

A group of women of varying ages were arranged in a circle, a tub of biscuits passing between them. I was late – probably because I'd been ranting manically down the phone to my best friend, as I would do when Andrzej was at work and couldn't distract me from my visions – and awkwardly dragged a chair from a stack in the corner. Despite everything, I remember trying to do this in the most natural-, least *mad*-looking way possible. I made sure to look everyone in the eye and smile at them as I passed. Old habits die hard.

I had never attended group therapy before. A woman who was indiscernible from the rest, if not slightly older, indicated that she was the facilitator. She kindly asked me my name, which I repeated (*don't sound mad, don't sound mad*), and then told me that I only had to speak if I wanted to.

Around the circle we went. Everyone would first introduce themselves – although from the encouraging smiles and laughs, I guessed that I was the only newcomer – and then shared something that had made them feel particularly negative that week. One person talked about how her partner was acting distant and hadn't invited her to a work function. She was worried he was embarrassed by her changed appearance after pregnancy. Another discussed how her near-constant morning sickness was getting her down. I remember that the person immediately before me talked about the difficulty of finding her daughter a government-funded nursery space. There was no availability in her area, and her boss was pressuring her to go back to work full-time.

I didn't have to talk, but out of some earnest desire to join in (once again, old habits die hard) I said what had made *me* feel negative that week.

'Yesterday morning, I think I saw a little Asian boy sitting on my bed.'

Even before I opened my mouth, I knew how surprising my answer would be, but nothing could prepare me for the stone-cold silence that met my words. I powered on.

'He didn't do anything, and then after a few minutes . . . he was gone. He wasn't real,' I added, somewhat unnecessarily. 'It was a hallucination.'

I received a few nods at that. I think the others were grateful for something to latch onto and agree with: that I was clearly unwell.

We moved on to the next person, and the next, and the next. No one was smiling at me now – instead they avoided looking in my direction, and quickly dropped eye contact whenever it was accidentally made. When the group ended, we were invited to stay on and chat in a more informal manner. I was ready to leave, but the facilitator caught me before I left. She took me by the arm – very *forward* of you, I remember thinking – and said to me, seriously: 'Emma, I think you need to see a psychiatrist as soon as possible.'

Perinatal psychosis is a rare condition that mostly affects women following delivery, but can also develop during pregnancy.[7] Its symptoms are varied but can include hallucinations, delusional thoughts and suspicions, and episodes of mania mixed with depression.

Patients often become disoriented, lose the sense of reality, and become a danger to themselves and those around them. There is no good explanation for what triggers perinatal psychosis and there is no way of knowing if someone is at risk of developing the condition. Monitoring during pregnancy and afterwards is crucial, for its onset and progression can be fast.

My perinatal psychosis was, thankfully, diagnosed and treated almost immediately after that, and I never saw the little Asian boy again. When I got pregnant for the second time, I was prescribed anti-psychosis medication immediately. No one treated me as flippantly as that first doctor had, and my condition was recognised for what it was: life-threatening.

Thankfully, in recent years more attention has been given to women's mental health in and around pregnancy, and perinatal psychosis is something that maternity teams are increasingly looking out to spot. In 2018 NHS England reported that access to specialist perinatal mental health services was limited, as only 40 per cent of the country had a dedicated specialist community team. In 2023 there were specialist services in all forty-four local NHS areas in England, with further developments planned for the future. This expansion enabled over 13,000 additional patients to receive dedicated perinatal mental health support.[8]

Yet where the link between pregnancy and severe mental illness has received recognition in everyday medical practice, the connection between mental illness and menopause is still broadly ignored. It was a sudden episode of psychosis brought about by menopause that led to the tragic death of Frances Wellburn in August 2020.[9]

Wellburn was a 56-year-old NHS worker from Fulford, North Yorkshire. In what were to be the last months of her life, she was diagnosed with psychotic depression. It appeared to have come out of nowhere. Wellburn's psychosis took the form of paranoia. Her sister described it as follows:

> She became convinced that people close to her were trying to harm her and she lost all trust in everything that had previously given her life meaning. This frightening world became her reality and she lost

the ability to see what was happening to her as an illness she could recover from.[10]

Wellburn started experiencing suicidal thoughts and was admitted to hospital. Frustratingly, she was hastily discharged and with only a prescription of antidepressants for help. This medication did not improve her condition, but she was not contacted by the mental health services again. She was not on their priority list and deemed to be at 'low risk of suicide'.[11] A few days after this assessment was made, Wellburn took her own life.

At the urging of Wellburn's family, her case was made a subject of inquiry by the Health Services Safety Investigations Body (HSSIB). They found that serious deficiencies in how Wellburn's mental health risk was assessed contributed to her death. Specifically, the HSSIB pointed out that nowhere in the process did anyone account for the fact that Wellburn was undergoing menopause, which was likely the main contributing factor to her psychotic episode.

People experiencing menopause can experience depression and psychosis, and some go on to kill themselves. Research across three separate studies in the US, UK and in Australia has shown that the incidence of suicide in women peaks between the ages of forty-five and fifty, with the second highest rates in the years following, up to the age of sixty-four.[12]

Women who experience mental health deterioration around the time of menopause often see better improvement with hormone replacement therapy (HRT) than regular antidepressant medication. Indeed, 2015 NICE guidelines for UK doctors state that: 'For low mood due to menopause, HRT should be considered rather than antidepressants.'[13] Research has also shown that hormonal treatment given early in menopause can prevent the patients from developing severe depression later.[14]

Is, then, HRT the magic cure-all for menopause symptoms? The answer is not that simple. Many women don't want to take hormones, and some simply cannot. Making matters worse is the murky history that hormonal therapy has been mired in.

★

For the better part of medical history, right up until the mid twentieth century, menopause was widely considered to be a natural stage of life; perhaps not the most pleasant one, but something to be endured and then ultimately forgotten. It was *just* a phase, and one that would soon pass anyway. The welfare of menopausal women, and their mental health, wasn't something that physicians troubled themselves with. From the 1930s to the 1950s, following the 'discovery' of female sexual hormones, doctors prescribed hormonal pills and injections for a variety of health problems, but menopause remained a relatively minor target for hormonal therapy. Instead, doctors took an approach based on reassurance, with a focus on healthy living – together with a healthy peppering of sedatives.[15]

Then came the British-born, New York-practising gynaecologist Robert Wilson.

In 1963, Wilson authored an article describing older women as 'castrates' who 'exist rather than live'.[16] The loss of oestrogen caused diseases such as hypertension and osteoporosis, and was the reason for depression and melancholia, which was vividly likened to a 'vapid cow-like feeling'. Finally, there was decline in sexuality, caused by atrophied genitals and general loss of physical attractiveness. His solution to all this was to replenish a woman's oestrogen store.

Wilson succeeded in reaching a larger audience in 1966, penning the bestselling *Feminine Forever*, in which he rhapsodised about the benefits of oestrogen therapy.[17] In its first year, the book sold over 140,000 copies. Wilson's success was not only of his making. It was in large part thanks to the promotional efforts of the Wilson Research Foundation, which he set up with the generous financial support of pharmaceutical companies.[18] The investment certainly paid off: between 1966 and 1975 the market value of oestrogen therapy nearly quadrupled, and prescriptions for it doubled.[19]

The success of HRT came after decades of concerted effort from the pharmaceutical industry to sell it. The key marketing strategy was to portray menopause as something worthy, and indeed in grave need, of a cure: hence, the medicalisation of menopause. The antidote was advertised aggressively, invoking the usual promises of prevention of the decrepitude of old age, preservation of femininity, the endless extension of sexual performance.

In her 2007 book *The Estrogen Elixir: A History of Hormone Replacement Therapy in America*, public health historian Elizabeth Siegel Watkins traces another big shift that helped pharmaceutical companies to convince women that menopause was a treatable condition for which hormone replacement therapy was the 'cure'.[20] This involved advertising not to physicians, but to the women themselves.

Pharma companies turned to the Wilson Research Foundation, who had already begun a media campaign for this work on a grand scale, to help promote oestrogen therapy. With the support of his sponsors, Robert Wilson was able to reach millions of readers. He was interviewed in *Vogue*, where he advocated his 'puberty-to-grave' scheme for hormone replacement therapy.[21] His foundation was able to promote this view, so much so that by the early 1970s, popular magazines were including HRT in their beauty and fashion advice columns. When *Harper's Bazaar* published its 'Over-40 Guide on Health, Looks, Sex' in 1973, hormone replacement therapy was presented as a necessary accessory of the modern woman.[22]

Popularity of HRT grew further in the 1980s and the 90s, on the back of the gradual relaxing of rules around advertising prescription drugs. The US Food and Drug Administration first allowed this in 1985, so long as sufficient information about the product's risks and benefits was provided to the consumer. This requirement made printed adverts more practicable, but in 1997 the rules were further relaxed and television adverts for specific products started featuring on televisions in the US. Pharma companies' budgets for direct consumer advertising blew up, from $12 million in 1989, to $1.58 billion in 1999. High advertising budgets indicate even higher revenues. HRT was a lucrative business indeed.[23]

The number of hormone prescriptions grew steadily in the second half of the twentieth century, but truly skyrocketed in the 1990s from $36.5 million in 1992 to $89.6 million in 1999.[24] The American College of Physicians (ACP) recommended in 1992 that 'all women, regardless of race, should consider preventive hormone therapy'.[25] American-Canadian gynaecologist Jen Gunter, in her book *The*

Menopause Manifesto, recalls when she was training as an OB-GYN between 1990 and 1995: 'In clinic it was typical to start three to four women a day on [HRT]. We were trained to discuss [it] in the same way we talk about other preventative therapy, like mammograms.'[26]

Suddenly, it all imploded. The meteoric rise of HRT was followed by a spectacular fall from grace. In July 2002, the Women's Health Initiative – a large-scale, long-time multicentre, and federally sponsored clinical trial of HRT – was abruptly terminated, three years before its scheduled completion. The WHI was the largest ever randomised controlled trial of HRT in women, involving over two hundred investigators, 161,809 participants and forty clinical centres in twenty-seven US states. It was budgeted for $625 million over fourteen years, with the final bill coming close to a billion dollars.[27]

What caused its termination? The body overseeing the WHI study announced, in a bombshell article, unacceptable risks to participants who were taking part in the trial. Early data had found that women taking HRT had a 29 per cent increased chance of heart attack, a 41 per cent increased risk of stroke, and a 29 per cent increased risk of breast cancer.[28] It seemed clear that HRT was extremely harmful to women, and the trial was immediately stopped.

The termination of the WHI trial was front-page news around the world. Wyeth, the maker of Premarin and Prempro (two drugs used in the study), immediately lost a quarter of its market value. Within a year, prescriptions for both drugs dropped by 66 per cent and 33 per cent respectively.[29] Million-dollar lawsuits followed rapidly, and the company had to sell up in 2009. Women were abandoning HRT in their droves, and doctors were refusing to prescribe it.

When the WHI result broke the news, it rode on the coattails of a more general, public suspicion of the pharmaceutical industry – and women had particular cause for concern. Women distrust pharma more than men. We know this because studies have shown that lack of trust in the pharmaceutical industry is a major reason for women refusing to take part in clinical trials.[30] Their fears are certainly not unsubstantiated, as this business is dogged with scandals around harmful medicine being marketed and sold to women.

First on the list is, perhaps unsurprisingly, thalidomide. Introduced in 1957 in West Germany, where it was sold over-the-counter for morning sickness, it was pulled off the market only four years later when it became apparent that it caused severe congenital anomalies and stillbirths. It is estimated that over 10,000 children worldwide have been affected by thalidomide.[31] Despite the fact that the drug was offered mainly to pregnant women, its producer only ever tested it on rats.[32]

Then there was the hormone-based pregnancy test Primodos. Manufactured by the German drug company Schering AG, and widely used throughout the 1960s and 1970s, Primodos combined two hormonal pills that were designed to artificially induce menstruation in women who were not pregnant, thereby acting as a pregnancy test. Prior to Primodos the only available means for detecting early pregnancy involved injecting (male!) toads with the patient's urine.[33] The medication was withdrawn from the market by Schering AG in 1978 over suspected association with congenital anomalies and miscarriages. The company has always denied that the drug was harmful, but patient advocacy groups campaigned for decades to recognise the catastrophe of what they call 'the forgotten thalidomide'.[34] A landmark 2018 study by scientists at the University of Oxford's Centre for Evidence-Based Medicine proved that Primodos posed a serious risk to pregnant women, prompting a parliamentary investigation in the UK.[35]

In 1971, a drug called diethylstilbestrol (DES) was found to cause cervical and vaginal cancers in the daughters of the mothers who had taken it. Since the 1940s DES had been widely prescribed to prevent miscarriage and premature labour. During the clinical test spurred by the scandal, it was found to be ineffective for its intended purpose.[36] It was quickly banned for pregnant women in the US but continued to be sold in Western Europe until 1978.

Sodium valproate, a popular and effective anti-epileptic medication, sold by the French pharmaceutical giant Sanofi since the 1970s, has been another source of controversy, which is ongoing. In the mid 2000s, its potential for causing congenital anomalies such as spina bifida was revealed, but despite numerous warnings from regulatory bodies, it continues to be marketed and prescribed.[37]

Oestrogen replacement therapy itself was at the centre of a health scandal many years before the Women's Health Initiative trial, when in the late 1970s researchers observed a spike in the number of cases of endometrial cancer in women who were taking certain types of oestrogen therapy.[38] The formulations were changed to rectify the problem, but doubts lingered.

So in 2002, the results of the prematurely halted WHI clinical study of HRT fell on fertile ground for distrust that mothers had passed on to daughters for decades. Hormone replacement therapy was not safe, and women, once again, were being sold a product that was harmful and untested. The effects of WHI were profound and long-lasting. In the US by 2021, only around 5 per cent of menopausal women were taking HRT – a significant decrease compared to the 26 per cent of women who were reported to be on HRT in the years immediately preceding the termination of the WHI trial.[39]

That fateful WHI paper has been referenced by over 12,000 scientific articles in twenty years; its results have been analysed, dissected and reassembled, spurring hundreds of research studies and reviews. But just five years after the original publication, a paper in the same journal, including a number of the same researchers, highlighted major flaws in the study design and the way it was reported at the time.[40] The harmful effect was proved to be a mere statistical fluke: HRT was safe to take after all. But its reputation never really recovered; its reserves of trust had become depleted.

Suspicion of big pharma is bigger today than ever before. Scandals such as thalidomide and mesh have greatly contributed to such mistrust. However, in the case of HRT, even when there wasn't actually a scandal to be uncovered, people were quick to believe that there was. The effects are far-reaching, spilling out of the realm of women's healthcare and feeding into other subjects too. Indeed, big pharma should take a long, hard look at itself when it comes to contemporary anti-vax movements. How much of the growing distrust of vaccinations can be attributed to years of shameful dealings and dodgy trials perpetrated by the industry?

All of this adds up to a fundamental issue of distrust in healthcare. People who need medical attention the most can find themselves turning away from what claims to be – what *should* be – the source of their help. And if these people – if women – turn away from healthcare for solutions to their medical problems, where do they go to instead . . . ?

Enter Gwyneth Paltrow.

The high priestess of 'vaginal wellness' – a sub-section of the broader global health and wellness industry that has an estimated global value of $5.6 trillion[41] – Paltrow is CEO and founder of arguably the most influential vaginal wellness business in the world: Goop. Goop has built its reputation in no small part on the shock value of its barefaced rejection of the medical status quo. It advertises products that have been roundly debunked as useless or harmful by established medical bodies, embraces practitioners and techniques shunned by science, and takes a generally irreverent approach to academic consensus. Indeed, Goop's very appeal seems to be its 'open-minded' approach to the new (or, conversely, 'traditional') technologies and medicines that medical bodies reject: an approach that garners trust among its subscribers, who otherwise distrust the very medical bodies and institutions that critique it.

The enemy of my enemy is my friend.

'Wellness' as a broader concept is almost impossible to define, but in general terms represents a globalised, unregulated industry encompassing fitness, nutrition, personal care and sexual health.[42] Wellness can become a moral imperative to the autonomous citizen: look after your body and your mind, seek constant self-improvement, and think holistically. Wellness aims to tackle often nebulous systems and elements of contemporary life – and faces broad criticism for lacking an evidence-based approach and for its use of pseudoscience.[43] Others argue that it co-opts and distorts traditional practices, in a form of 'Orientalism', largely for social control.[44]

Wellness permeates many areas of the media and healthcare itself, particularly in places where healthcare is increasingly privatised. It shares many elements with homoeopathy and alternative medicine, although often coming in at a far higher price-point.

Goop started life as an aspirational lifestyle mailing list.[45] In 2008,

Paltrow began sending out a newsletter to subscribers – then, mostly consisting of fans – making recommendations based on her own, rarefied, rich sources and resources. Think G. Label trench coats and Betony Vernon jewellery, interspersed with adages such as 'ban white from your food' and 'learn to control your thoughts'.[46]

None of this was particularly out of character. Paltrow had already established herself as something of an LA eccentric: turning up to the *Anchorman* premiere covered in cupping bruises, practising transcendental meditation . . .

As her subscriber base grew, and hawks began to realise the possibilities of what Paltrow was building, her recommendations began to broaden out from the largely aesthetic to more personal, sometimes even profound, advice. What exactly Paltrow wanted to do with Goop – then a not wholly unique form of celebrity-fronted lifestyle brand – began to crystallise and take shape. 'I want to help you solve problems,' is how she described it in a later interview. 'I want to be an additive to your life.'[47]

The more serious, or committed, the advice offered, the more attention it drew. People praised and disparaged her forthright tone in equal measure: *She isn't afraid to go there.* Unlike many celebrities of the age, trained by their PR teams into parroting asinine, risk-averse statements, Paltrow went where others feared to tread. She wasn't ashamed to be rich, and she wasn't ashamed to be perceived as a hypocrite either. On her smoking habit, seemingly at odds with her quest to rid the world of toxins, she said: 'It's what makes life interesting, finding the balance between cigarettes and tofu. My one light American Spirit that I smoke once a week, on Saturday night.'[48]

People found her approach refreshing. And those who found it clinical, *especially* those people, still clicked on the links.

In 2014, Goop moved into e-commerce. It no longer 'recommended' (or advertised) other products, but began to sell its own. These primarily consisted of vitamins, fashion, houseware products, and a non-toxic skincare line, all with ridiculously high price-points. One pair of pyjamas was being sold for $725.

Twenty-fourteen was a big year for Goop in more ways than one. It was the same year that Paltrow's infamous 'conscious uncoupling' post temporarily crashed the site in the wake of her separation from Chris Martin. Paltrow had been directing a lot of attention towards diet-based wellness products and concepts, and had published a few cookbooks. One, published in 2013, was dismissed by *The Atlantic* magazine as the 'Bible of laughable Hollywood neuroticism'[49] – further fuelling the fire of interest in Goop's endeavours. Such was the general media response to Goop at this time: light scorn.

Goop might never have made the transition from straightforward wellness brand to the entire face of vaginal wellness in the popular imagination, if it hadn't been for 'vaginal steaming'. In early 2015, Goop reviewed the LA-based spa Tikkun. So the website wrote: 'The real golden ticket here is the Mugwort V-Steam: You sit on what is essentially a mini-throne, and a combination of infrared and mugwort steam cleanses your uterus, et al. It is an energetic release. If you're in LA, you have to do it.'[50]

This simple recommendation caused a storm, even by Goop's standards. Vaginal steaming, then, was a not-so-well known practice outside of super-rich spa circles – yet another questionable, experimental option offered by the more expensive spas as an add-on to their other, more standard services. Goop's review raised the profile of 'V-steaming' almost overnight.

Vaginal steaming involves sitting over a pot of scalding hot water infused with herbs (most commonly mugwort) with a view to 'cleansing' the vagina and uterus to reduce premenstrual symptoms, alleviate pain during sex, and even, possibly, increase fertility. The claim that the vagina contains self-created impurities which hamper its functions is medically baseless; so too is the idea that steam is able to travel through the vagina and reach the uterus. In reality, the steam can travel no further than the vulva, posing a serious heat risk to the genitalia (indeed, in 2019 a Canadian woman reportedly suffered second-degree burns to the vulva after attempting to V-steam at home[51]). In addition to the risk of burns, the herbs involved pose the risk of allergic reaction – especially mugwort, which is closely related to the highly allergenic ragweed.

Following Goop's positive review of vaginal steaming, animated discussion online and in the press ensued. Journalists weren't so much as scornful now, but enraged. Gynaecologists were offered op-eds in abundance to give their opinions on the practice; some, such as Dr Jen Gunter, used their own platforms to vociferously debunk it. On her website's blog-post entitled 'Gwyneth Paltrow says steam your vagina, an OB/GYN says don't', Gunter is clear that – in her professional opinion as a gynaecologist – vaginal steaming is not only useless but potentially harmful: 'Mugwort or wormwood or whatever when steamed, either vaginally or on the vulva, can't possibly balance any reproductive hormones, regulate your menstrual cycle, treat depression, or cure infertility.'[52]

Vaginal steaming, if it doesn't burn you or give you an allergic reaction, can make your vaginal health *worse*. Raising the temperature of the vagina through the introduction of steam will cultivate the perfect environment for the proliferation of pathogenic bacteria and harmful yeasts, such as candida. Harmful microorganisms are potentially the cause of infertility and menstrual cramping, so creating an environment where they can multiply makes no sense.[53] For Goop's audience, it doesn't perhaps matter. The established tenets of science aren't to be trusted; this is instead about taking control.

Taking control is a common subject in vaginal wellness: particularly regarding one's lifestyle, diet, and – most crucially – mindset. Our mental state is framed as largely being shaped by the choices that we make. In a somewhat blatant rebuttal to accusations of materialism levelled against the field of vaginal wellness, Goop published a podcast interview entitled 'Finding Joy Again' with writer Ingrid Fetell Lee, author of the 2018 book *Joyful: The Surprising Power of Ordinary Things to Create Extraordinary Happiness*. Fetell Lee opens with the question: 'When you put on your clothes, how do you feel?'[54] The subtext here being: You can justify buying nice clothes if they make you *feel* good. Materialism is acceptable so long as it alters your mindset. All of this – this whole industry of wellness – is really beyond reproach, if it serves to help people 'feel good'. Feeling good – or, more importantly, *choosing* to feel good – is central to our health and well-being, so the logic goes.

In Goop's guide to menopause, it lists the main symptoms. The risks to one's mental health are greatly underplayed: 'Emotional symptoms may include mild depression, anxiety, mood swings, and irritability. Be sure to talk to your doctor about other possible reasons for depression, such as low thyroid hormone.'[55]

Mild depression. Irritability. These are a far cry from the suicidal thoughts of Frances Wellburn. And then 'be sure to talk to your doctor about *other* possible reasons for depression'. So that depression, then, is probably *not* related to the menopause?

The guide briefly mentions HRT in its treatments section, but is quick to remind us that

> there are still questions about the safety of using hormones like oestrogen for long periods of time. After the potential dangers of oral hormone replacement therapy (HRT) were reported in 2002, most research has been directed at finding safer forms and doses of hormones (and not focused on alternative treatment modalities).'[56]

As we know, the 2002 research was not fit for purpose. And yet Goop cites it here, because – of course – stoking distrust of pharmaceutical science is its principal strategy. You do not need to take HRT for menopause; you can merely *choose joy* instead (by buying one of their products).

After being told that I would have to wait two years for surgery, I briefly became convinced that I might catch an infection or be rendered permanently immobile. I was starting to feel like a hypochondriac. Every day I had a new theory, entirely contra to what the doctors were telling me, legitimised by endless googling. What if, instead of a prolapse, it was really a tumour pushing itself out of my vagina? Or, what if it was actually a swelling, and I had some life-altering infection instead?

My friends, gripped with worry, would call and ask: 'Have you slept?', 'How are you feeling?' All *I* wanted to talk about was my most recent hypothesis. In their voices I heard their uncertainty and scepticism: 'Are you *sure* this time?'

Downstairs, I could hear my children screaming and my husband struggling to manage. In moments of particular crescendo, it'd all get too much, and I'd be overcome with guilt. I would swing my legs out of the bed and heave myself onto the floor only to feel that treacherous pulsing pressure in my nethers, and sullenly return to bed, feeling worse than before. I'd slide the lock off my phone and start typing. It's *got* to be an undiagnosed kidney infection. And then what if it leads to blood poisoning? Or scarring? Or total organ failure . . .

Around 45 per cent of people who give birth globally are reported to experience psychological birth trauma, although given that this statistic is based on self-declaration, the true number is likely to be higher. It's 'an international public health problem', write researchers in *The Journal of Perinatal Education*.[57] Psychological trauma can have far-reaching consequences for a person's life and mental health. It can interfere with breastfeeding, subsequent childbirths, baby bonding, other interpersonal relationships. The psychological effects of birth trauma have for so long gone under-studied, and only in recent years have postnatal PTSD, and postnatal and perinatal depression begun to be commonly diagnosed in women experiencing symptoms such as flashbacks, intrusive thoughts, nightmares, mood swings and physical symptoms.[58] This indicates a marked turn in the serious attention given to perinatal mental health, where for so long women have been expected to simply put up with the so-called 'baby blues'. Nevertheless, there is still a distinction made between PTSD and what are supposedly acceptable levels of perinatal depression and mood disturbance. While hormonal fluctuations will influence mood, damaging and traumatic birth experiences – and their anticipation – have a profound effect on an individual's mental health.

Women in general have been found to have higher levels of 'health anxiety' and are more likely than men to be diagnosed with SSD (somatic symptom syndrome), a condition characterised by experiencing symptoms that do not exist, or 'excessive thoughts' about those that do.[59] Women suffer more medical trauma than men, which has an impact on their mental health, and this includes many obstacles to diagnosis that ultimately delay or prevent treatment. There is currently what feels like an epidemic of women's conditions going underdiagnosed. This is not just the case with gynaecological issues: in 700 diseases, researchers found women are diagnosed on average four years later than men.[60]

Take endometriosis – a condition that approximately 190 million people in the world suffer from (that's a staggering 10 per cent of all women and girls) – which can be left untreated for years before being diagnosed.

Endometriosis happens when endometrium – tissue similar to the lining of the uterus – starts growing elsewhere in the body.[61] Most commonly, this occurs in the ovaries, the fallopian tubes, and around the uterus and the ligaments surrounding it, but is also commonly found elsewhere, in the vagina, cervix, bowel, bladder and rectum. Less commonly, it has been discovered outside of the pelvic region: in the lungs, in the brain, and on the skin. This tissue responds to the same hormones that govern the menstrual cycle, and so can swell, shed and bleed on a monthly or regular basis. Unlike the lining of the uterus, however, this blood and other cell debris has nowhere to drain away to, and it instead accumulates inside the body. Eventually, immune cells will digest and disperse the excess, shed blood, but great pain – and inflammation – can be caused in the interim. So-called endometriosis adhesions, a product of the inflammation, can produce scar tissue around the site of the endometriosis. As scar tissue is more rigid than the softer, often pelvic, organs around it, it can end up binding the organs – gluing them together like duct tape. This causes a very specific, and severe, pain: a pulling and tugging sensation exacerbated by increased body movement. Around half of all people affected by it experience chronic pelvic pain and extremely painful periods, sometimes to a disabling degree. Pain during sex, painful and frequent urination and bowel movements, chronic back pain and generally reduced mobility consequently are all other common symptoms of the condition.

Over 75 per cent of patients with endometriosis report being misdiagnosed with another condition first, and almost 50 per cent have been misdiagnosed with a mental health disorder (such as hypochondria).[62] Many report being made to feel as though their symptoms are 'all in [their] head' prior to diagnosis. Many of those will suffer psychologically alongside their endometriosis and because of it, only to have their mental health problems diagnosed in its place. A Brazilian study in 2009 found that over 86 per cent of endometriosis sufferers show signs of anxiety and depression, which is hardly surprising.[63]

Until the 1990s, medical textbooks and clinical literature would commonly describe endometriosis as 'the career woman's disease':[64] it was thought to affect women who, instead of getting pregnant, had chosen to pursue their careers. By failing to get pregnant, these women had let their periods *run riot*, which in turn had led to them developing endometriosis

Despite this having been irrefutably disproven, some doctors will *still* posit pregnancy as a viable cure for the condition. A 2018 review by Swiss and New Zealand researchers found that: 'It is not uncommon for women with endometriosis to be advised that becoming pregnant might be a useful strategy to manage their symptoms and reduce disease progression.'[65] The same article confirms that this advice is not based on reliable scientific data:

> Few studies of very limited quality are available to evaluate the effect of pregnancy and the postnatal period on the development of endometriosis. The development of endometriosis is variable and there is no evidence that pregnancy can be expected to generally reduce the size and number of endometriotic lesions.[66]

The authors then go on to suggest that recommending pregnancy to sufferers can be *harmful* to them, due to the fact that endometriosis can negatively interfere with pregnancy outcomes. Pregnant women with endometriosis have an increased risk of ectopic pregnancy, which can prove to be fatal.

Ironically, while pregnancy is being offered as a cure to endometriosis, the condition is the leading cause of infertility in women. The WHO defines infertility as the inability to get pregnant after one year or longer of trying. Up to 50 per cent of infertile women are estimated to suffer from endometriosis.[67]

Furthermore, women experiencing infertility are likely to be told, either implicitly or explicitly, that their mental state may be a contributing factor. On its website, Mayo Clinic – the world-leading academic medical centre – states that, while it is 'unlikely that stress alone can cause infertility, [it does interfere] with a woman's ability to get pregnant.' It goes on to state that women with depression are twice as likely to experience infertility.[68] While a correlation between the two can be proven, a causal link cannot. In cases such as endometriosis, treatment is dependent on persistence; a persistence that may instead be diagnosed as depression or anxiety.

In the cases where women *are* experiencing anxiety — likely exacerbated by the long and agonising fight for diagnosis — it can be weaponised against them. How often are we told that anxiety is deleterious to our health? Time and time again, I was advised by my doctors not to be stressed about the thing they couldn't at first even name, and then never precisely, because stress would likely make it worse. The worse my prolapse got, the more I worried about it. The more I worried about it, the more I thought I was making it worse. Ridiculous, of course — but don't underestimate the power of blame.

Imagine if instead of attempting to guilt-trip women out of their health anxiety (as if telling someone not to be anxious has ever worked in the history of the world) we could get to the bottom of what's causing it. What's *really* causing it.

Feelings of self-blame after pregnancy loss are a common experience. Clinical guidance for practitioners on how to combat this advises focusing the patients' attention on the fact that they could not have done anything to prevent it from happening. This contradicts most advice given to pregnant women, however, which implies that every move made during pregnancy — every feeling experienced and every thought — will have a profound impact on the unborn child. This harks back to the medieval concept of 'maternal imagination', where a woman's body is seen as so susceptible to external events that merely looking at a frog in pregnancy, say, might cause her baby to have webbed fingers; or too long a glance at a portrait of Christ might give her newborn baby a beard.[69] This not only served as yet another mode of policing women's actions and thoughts; it also squarely blamed them for any congenital anomalies in their newborns. Men, on the other hand, were entirely relieved of their genetic (or otherwise psychological) responsibility for the health of their children. The consequence of this thinking was expressly material: women were made accountable for the care of their disabled children while men were not compelled to contribute any care whatsoever.

Today, women continue to bear the burden of responsibility for childrearing, reproduction, and fertility in ways that *far* outstrip their power and control. In a moving article in the *Guardian* written in 2010, British poet Joanne Limburg shares how she blamed herself — and her anxious thinking — for her miscarriage.

> The miscarriage took several weeks, and in that time I saw no fewer than five scans of a vital, kicking baby. The last of these had been ordered to confirm what everyone thought would be bad news; instead, the radiographer turned the screen to show me the heart, still beating after a month of blood loss and three days of contractions. 'This baby is a survivor,' she said, and I believed her, so when I finally lost the pregnancy only hours later, I knew which one of us was at fault. It was not, as one doctor put it, that my body had been 'making sure that it has a perfect baby', because the baby had been perfect — perfect, and innocent, and blameless. Only its mother had let it down. Perhaps I was bad; perhaps I was being punished; perhaps my fears about something bad happening had themselves made the bad thing happen.[70]

Limburg's anxiety did not cause her miscarriage, but it is understandable that she should feel like this when a woman is taught to understand that even *thinking* the 'wrong' way can have dire consequences for her health.

Attempts are increasingly being made to remove stigma around miscarriage, but for women to stop blaming themselves for negative health outcomes, healthcare providers need to consider the harmful effects that unsubstantiated, impossible-to-follow advice — such as 'having a positive mindset' — can cause. It is also deeply reductive, if not outright dangerous, to flippantly append mental health to the poorly understood root causes of miscarriage. More broadly it belies a lack of interest, or care, in getting to the bottom of a whole host of gynaecological and women's health issues when 'just stop worrying' is prescribed as a legitimate treatment for physical disease. All the while, a patient's mental health is assumed to be purely within their own control – allowing mental ill health to go undiagnosed and untreated.

Deep down, many women know that worry during pregnancy cannot cause miscarriage, just like postnatal depression and perinatal psychosis are not merely 'worry' either.

It is this denial of the reality of their experience by medical systems that can amount to the perception of gaslighting, which in turn can result in a profound, if unacknowledged, distrust of the very healthcare systems that are supposed to help them. Distrust in healthcare can have disastrous consequences for women's public health, and the vaginal wellness industry is but the latest manifestation of centuries' worth of medically gaslighting unwell women.

7. Stop Complaining

Pregnancy is supposed to be a time of making new friends: at all those NCT meetings and antenatal classes, pregnancy yoga sessions and second-hand baby clothes sales. But I only made one friend when I was pregnant: Grace. We met in the doctor's waiting room, sometime after I began treatment for perinatal psychosis and just as my mood and anxiety were stabilising. She was sitting on the bench opposite me, visibly pregnant too, and reading a copy of Donald Winnicott's *Babies and Their Mothers*. I had read something by Winnicott once before, and even though I couldn't remember the title of it, motivated by my pathological need to *get involved*, I told her that her book was interesting. She smiled and, setting it down upon the mound of her belly, asked me what I thought about it. I don't know, I replied. At that, her smile broke into a laugh.

Grace and I instantly clicked. She, too, was feeling sensitive about her lack of engagement with the pregnancy sphere of influence. We were both on the young side; not for the rest of the world, but for Cambridge, where I hadn't met anyone so far with a baby who was under the age of thirty. Crucially, we shared a similar world view – although mine was much more naive than hers, as I was soon to learn.

We began going on walks through the city together. I'd collect her from her house on the one side of the river, and she'd walk me back to mine across the bridge. Standing upright for long periods of time was good for us, as we were both suffering from pregnancy-related heartburn. When I finally remembered to mention this to my GP, she gave me a prescription for Gaviscon – no questions asked. In passing, I suggested to Grace that she should do the same. She simply rolled her eyes.

'I already told her about my heartburn, and she told me to change my diet.'

We shared a doctor's surgery, but not a doctor. I urged her to switch to mine instead, who I got on with immensely. She did and all seemed well, for a while. Until something similar happened again.

'You know you were telling me about getting a blood test for anaemia . . .' Grace began.

'Mmm.'

'The doctor wouldn't give me one.'

'Why not?'

'She told me that I'm just tired from the pregnancy and probably pushing myself too hard.'

I scrunched up my face and started to protest. 'But we have exactly the same symptoms and she didn't say that to *me*—'

'Emma,' said Grace lightly. 'You're white.'

Grace was used to being dismissed when it came to her health on account of her being Black. This hadn't started in pregnancy, and she doubted it would end with it either. But she was really beginning to worry about childbirth, and the impact this implicit (and, sometimes, explicit) racism might have on her and her baby – although as Grace's partner was white, she felt, she said, that she had 'the best chance possible'. Whether or not his race had made a difference in the end, her positive prediction came true, and she did, thankfully, go on to have as smooth a labour as can be hoped for, and delivered a healthy baby boy.

She could have had a very different birth outcome. Despite the fact that Grace and I come from similar backgrounds – we're two working-class British women who grew up in the countryside, were born in the 1990s, and were the first in our families to go to university – we also represent two vastly different demographics: Black and white. Nowhere is the difference between these groups starker than when it comes to healthcare outcomes – and *especially* what it means for pregnant women. Black women in the UK are an appalling 3.7 times more likely to die in the perinatal period than white women.[1] In the US, a country which many in the UK perceive to be marked by racism as if our own is not, has a roughly similar rate.[2]

Rianna Cleary, a Black British teenager, discovered that she was pregnant at a police station in North London in February 2019.[3] She was barely eighteen, and a recent care-leaver with a difficult past. Her mother, who suffered from drug addiction, had been largely absent from her life and, from the age of four, she had been cared for by her father and paternal grandmother. Cleary was very close to her grandmother but, at the age of fourteen, she passed away. The loss hit Cleary hard: she was soon excluded from school and subsequently placed in a care home in Wales by Social Services.

In 2016, still a teenager, she was sentenced to a period of confinement in a secure unit in Bristol following a number of minor offences. When she was released, she suddenly found herself homeless. Her father had been sent to prison in the intervening period and, as Cleary later put it: 'Everything continued to snowball very badly for me. I didn't have anywhere to live permanently and I kept getting arrested.'[4]

When she became pregnant, she had no permanent residence and was living in and out of a hostel. Later that year, she pleaded guilty to a robbery charge and asked to be moved to a prison while she waited for sentencing. Her hope was that support would be more easily available to her there. Social Services in Camden, where she'd ended up, had already informed her that her child would likely be taken away from her soon after birth, and she would have to go to court to fight for the child's custody. It would be a lengthy, costly, and deeply upsetting process. Cleary needed all the help she could get.

In prison, however, she *did* in fact find the support she sought. Cleary encountered other women in similar situations, but felt that they were receiving better treatment from the authorities than she was on account of race. They were not being presented with threats of having their children taken away from them like she was, despite having near identical criminal histories to them. Cleary said that she 'wondered at that time if I was being treated differently from them because of my race, because I was young or because of my past. I felt like I was trapped and had nowhere to go.'[5] She actively wanted to be a mother, and looked forward to the birth of her child, but she was afraid and despondent all the same.

Cleary was remanded in HMP Bronzefield just outside of Ashford, Surrey, when on 26 September she went into labour. Only she wasn't sure about it at the time. She had been given vastly different due dates for any point between August and November. She was experiencing strong cramps but, never having been through childbirth before and having had inadequate preparation for this moment, she couldn't be sure.

She eventually managed to fall asleep in her cell that afternoon, but was woken by agonising pain at around 8 p.m. She rang a buzzer in a call for help. An officer answered this at 8.07 pm and Cleary, in so much pain that she could barely speak, managed to plead to the officer for medical assistance. The officer, however, became distracted by another call. Half an hour passed, and Cleary had not been attended to. She made another call but this time there was no answer. Several *hours* later, a different officer passed by her cell and shone a torch into it. Cleary, on all fours, was in acute distress. Later, the officer would contest that 'nothing caught my attention, so I moved on'.[6]

She passed out at some point in the middle of the night. All she remembers is that the film *Killer Joe* was playing on the television in the corner of her room. When she regained consciousness, she found her baby – Aisha – lying on the floor. Thinking quickly, and despite her own dire physical state, Cleary bit through the umbilical cord attaching Aisha to her and wrapped the small baby in a towel. Everything from the floor to the walls of the cell as well as Cleary's bed and sink was covered in blood.

It wasn't until 8.30 a.m. the next day that the door was finally opened again to her room. Officers had somehow failed to notice the carnage inside – it was other inmates who had raised the alarm.

Staff attempted to resuscitate Aisha but, with no neonatal oxygen masks available in the prison, they had to use an adult mask. In any case, it was far too late, and the baby was pronounced dead at 9.03 a.m. Only then was Cleary taken to hospital.

The inquest following Aisha's death took nearly four years. The coroner established that the baby was either stillborn or had died shortly after birth. Cleary had discovered her unmoving with blue lips and covered in meconium – newborn faeces that is a sign of neonatal distress experienced in the womb during birth.

Evidence was heard from nearly fifty people – prison officers,

Camden Council officials, and staff at the Ashford and St Peter's Hospitals NHS Trust who had been formally responsible for providing maternal care to inmates. Testifying were also the representatives of Sodexo, a multibillion-pound international company who had won a contract to run HMP Bronzefield from the UK Department of Justice. Multiple systemic failures were identified and guilt apportioned: Rianna and Aisha Cleary had been failed by everyone around them. In a moving testimony before the inquest panel, Cleary described her ordeal as 'the worst and most terrifying and degrading experience of my life. I am still struggling to come to terms with what happened.'[7] Strong words from someone who had, by all accounts, already struggled through a particularly difficult childhood and early adult life.

Cleary wondered whether race had been a factor in her poor care and Aisha's death. Given the overwhelming statistics — that Black women are almost four times more likely to die in childbirth than white women — I think it is safe to assume that it likely was.

A landmark 2019 study of some 2,700 mothers in the US, titled 'Giving Voice to the Mothers', has shown that Black (but also Indigenous and Hispanic) women reported significantly higher rates of mistreatment during their pregnancy. This included instances of verbal abuse, scolding, and dismissive attitudes, as well as ignoring or refusing requests for help.[8]

A 2020 survey by the California-based charity Kaiser Family Foundation found that most Black adults believe the healthcare system treats people unfairly based on their race, with one in five Black and Hispanic adults reporting that they were personally treated unfairly in the past year.[9] The share of Black mothers reporting unfair treatment was one of the highest. Black women were also more likely to report that they weren't believed and that they were being refused a treatment, test, or pain medication they thought they needed.

When I told the doctor that I had heartburn, I was given medication. When Grace told the doctor that she had heartburn, she was told it was down to the food she was eating (even though she knew that wasn't true). When she was experiencing tiredness and lethargy, she was told she was probably overexerting herself (even though she knew that wasn't true). I, on the other hand, was whisked away for a blood test to confirm my underlying anaemia, commonly experienced in pregnancy.

Black people are consistently gaslighted into thinking that what they are experiencing is not real, that they are not really in that much pain, or rather that the pain they are experiencing is something that simply can be put up with.

In Toni Morrison's novel *The Bluest Eye*, set during the Great Depression, Pauline Breedlove – a working-class, physically disabled Black woman – describes her experience of giving birth in hospital for the first time:

> They put me in a big room with a whole mess of women. The pains was coming, but not too bad. A little old doctor come to examine me. He had all sorts of stuff. He gloved his hand and put some kind of jelly on it and rammed it up between my legs. When he left off, some more doctors come. One old one and some young ones. The old one was learning the young ones about babies. Showing them how to do. When he got to me he said now these here women you don't have any trouble with. They deliver right away and with no pain. Just like horses. The young ones smiled a little. They looked at my stomach and between my legs. They never said nothing to me. Only one looked at me. Looked at my face, I mean. I looked right back at him. He dropped his eyes and turned red. He knowed, I reckon, that maybe I weren't no horse foaling. But them others. They didn't know. They went on. I seed them talking to them white women: 'How you feel? Gonna have twins?' Just shucking them, of course, but nice talk. Nice friendly talk. I got edgy, and when them pains got harder, I was glad. Glad to have something else to think about. I moaned something awful. The pains wasn't as bad as I let on, but I had to let them people know having a baby was more than a bowel movement. I hurt just like them white women.[10]

The fallacy that Black women experience pain differently from white women neither began, nor ended, with the Great Depression. A 2016 study in the *Proceedings of the National Academy of Sciences* reported that nearly half of first- and second-year students at the University of Virginia Medical School were found to believe that Black people's skin is physically thicker than white people's and that Black people experienced less pain than white people.[11] This idea is a product of nineteenth-century experiments that were conducted by Georgia enslaver and 'physician' Thomas Hamilton.[12] Hamilton regularly inflicted torture on enslaved Black people in the name of medical experiment. One man in particular, John Brown, suffered acutely: Hamilton would create blisters all over his body while trying to prove that Black people's skin 'went deeper' than white skin. Brown was forced to endure these experiments, which left him covered in scars, until he escaped to England and recorded his experiences in a memoir. He described how Hamilton applied 'blisters to my hands, legs and feet, which bear the scars to this day. He continued until he drew up the dark skin from between the upper and the under one. He used to blister me at intervals of about two weeks.'[13]

It was Hamilton's intention to prove that the difference between Black and white people was more than skin deep. He wanted to show that a higher pain tolerance in Black people – along with an assumed lower intelligence – further legitimised the abuse of their enslavement; it being 'all they were good for'.[14] Around the same time, John Marion Sims had drawn on thinking circulated in medical journals at the time that biological differences meant that Black women were able to take pain better than white women to justify his experiments on enslaved women with vesicovaginal fistula.[15]

Today, the pain tolerance of Black people in medical settings continues to be treated differently from that of white people. Studies show that Black patients in the US, when exhibiting the same symptoms, receive fewer treatments and fewer diagnostic interventions. Physicians prescribe less pain medication to Black people than white people – they are 40 per cent less likely than white people to be prescribed medication for acute pain, and 34 per cent less likely to receive opiates.[16]

Grace thought that her partner being white meant that she might have a higher likelihood of a safe and healthy birth, where in fact research suggests it is the race of the doctor that most affects healthcare outcomes for Black people. Black patients experience better healthcare outcomes when they are being treated by Black doctors. Black people in counties with more Black primary care physicians live longer, and areas with a higher prevalence of Black doctors have longer life expectancy and lower mortality in Black populations.[17]

Other studies have shown that when Black patients encounter Black doctors, they are more satisfied with their care, more likely to receive preventive care, and are more likely to agree to the doctors' recommendations, including blood tests and flu jabs.[18] In 2020, a study of 1.8 million hospital births in Florida found that Black newborn babies cared for by Black doctors had twice the chance of survival of those cared for by white doctors.[19]

In 2000, perhaps the world's most decorated living scientist, James Watson – one half of Watson and Crick, the British–American pair who famously won the Nobel Prize for discovering DNA (off the back of the largely unacknowledged Rosalind Franklin) – presented to a crowd of scientists at the University of California, Berkeley, a paper entitled 'Sun and Sex'.[20] Its central claim was that skin colour directly affects libido, and that people with higher levels of melanin in their skin have a higher sex drive. While his research was never published (and thus rendered subject to rigorous academic criticism), academics at the presentation immediately condemned it as baseless and unscientific. Watson was merely parroting a deeply racist stereotype about Black people: that they were more sexually active than white people. The idea of the hypersexual Black woman, in particular, has long been a cause of panic in the white, Western imagination – a form of society-wide projection given how Black women were raped and sexually abused by their enslavers. In white supremacist fearmongering, they are both hypersexual and hyperfertile – firing out babies left, right and centre, in an effort to 'replace' the white race with Black people. In other forms of white supremacism masquerading as conservatism, they may be presented as the vessels of venereal disease, tempting innocent white men into sex in order to contaminate them with sexual diseases, which may, in turn, cause infertility.

In reality, Black women in the US are twice as likely as white women to experience infertility, while being half as likely to receive medical help for it.[21] There is no biological reason for this, and neither is it on account of lifestyle factors – which tend to be overplayed when it comes to discussions on infertility anyway.

The leading global cause of infertility in women is endometriosis. As noted in the last chapter, it takes, on average, eight years to diagnose (and even longer to treat), and is exceptionally painful. The cause of endometriosis remains unknown, even though the condition is by no means a recent discovery. Lesions like endometriosis were reported in medical literature as early as 1898, and the disease was first described in 1927 by the American gynaecologist John A. Sampson, who also coined the term.[22]

For a long time, the most widely accepted theory of the cause of endometriosis was known as 'retrograde menstruation', also due to Sampson. Retrograde menstruation attributes the growth of endometrial tissue outside of the uterus to the backward movement of the menstrual flow. Fragments of the endometrium from menstruation are said to move up the fallopian tubes instead of down it, and into the lining of the abdominal cavity, where they lodge themselves among the healthy tissue and transform into endometriosis. This theory, however, has mostly been debunked, and the condition remains as much of a mystery as ever.[23]

A 2019 medical review published in the *British Journal of Obstetrics and Gynaecology* found that Black women were half as likely to be diagnosed with endometriosis than white women.[24] There is no biological reason to believe that Black women are less likely to *have* the condition, which suggests that they are instead being routinely and massively underdiagnosed for it. A study of African American women in urban Detroit, published in 2012, concluded that these women, in fact, often show more severe growth of endometrial tissue and at completely different places in their bodies than white women; evidence that they have suffered with it for longer (i.e. it has had longer to develop), but also further complicating diagnosis – as it doesn't always present as expected, being more advanced – and hindering subsequent management of the condition too.[25]

The relationship linking race and ethnicity to endometriosis diagnosis and treatment went for a long time ignored and, up until the

1970s, it was considered to be a 'White woman's disease'. Of course: if it was seen as the plight of career women who failed to have sex and get pregnant on account of their busy lives, this is *not* something that Black women would've been accused of.

American gynaecologist Donald Chatman, who set out to disprove that endometriosis was a 'White woman's disease', found that Black women were being commonly misdiagnosed with pelvic inflammatory disease instead.[26] Pelvic inflammatory disease (PID) is a common complication of sexually transmitted infections. In the US, Black women are more likely to be diagnosed with STIs than all other groups of women.[27] Researchers fall over themselves to link this to socioeconomic and lifestyle factors – others use this data to prop up the racist stereotype of the hypersexual Black woman – but the *real* reason for the disparity lies with the simple fact that Black women get tested far more often. Studies conducted in emergency departments in US hospitals have shown that Black women are four times more likely to be tested for STIs than women of other racial groups.[28] This testing is largely justified as only taking place when a patient shows symptoms of STIs, but STI symptoms are similar to those in most other pelvic conditions and it will come down to assumptions made about the patient by their attending practitioner. When a Black woman presents with the symptom of pain during sex, for example, it will likely be seen as a sign of an STI – and she will subsequently be tested for one. Whereas when a white woman presents with the same symptom, it is far more likely to be thought that she is suffering from something else – and she will not be tested for an STI. This commonplace discrepancy in testing vastly skews data for the relationship between STIs and race.

Pre-eclampsia, a serious and potentially lethal medical condition occurring in pregnancy, is 60 per cent more likely to occur in Black women than white women. Black women are also five times more likely to die from pre-eclampsia and its complications, making it a leading cause of maternal death for Black women.[29] Many reasons have been proposed to explain this. We know that Black women are not monitored as carefully as white women during pregnancy, and when they present with symptoms they are far more likely to be dismissed.[30] This indicates that Black women miss out on vital care at the level of diagnosis, slipping through the net due to lack of adequate attention from practitioners.

But is this the full picture? Is there perhaps something more pervasive at play? Black women in the US have worse general health than white women due to economic disadvantage and reduced access to medical care.[31] Then there are possible environmental factors which are linked to the increased probability of the condition for women who live in more polluted areas, as is often the case for Black people in the US. But simply being rich does not prevent a Black woman from developing pre-eclampsia. Beyoncé revealed that she experienced the condition while she was pregnant with her twins Rumi and Sir Carter. The condition left her body swollen and painful and she was bedridden for more than a month.[32] The most seemingly privileged Black women are also vulnerable to the Black maternal mortality rate. In the case of thirty-year-old Chaniece B. Wallace, a Black doctor can die of it too.[33]

Wallace wasn't just any doctor: she was a highly decorated paediatrician. She had completed her medical degree at her home state university and then moved to Indianapolis, where she was Pediatric Chief Resident at Indiana University School of Medicine. In October 2022, she and her husband Anthony were awaiting the birth of their first daughter. Wallace was four weeks away from her due date when she was admitted to the emergency department of the hospital she worked for. She had been experiencing steadily worsening headaches for the past month or so. Earlier in the day of her hospital admittance, she had a routine prenatal appointment. This picked up dangerously high blood pressure. Her hypertension was a sign of developing pre-eclampsia. She was rushed into the operating theatre for an emergency C-section. Two days later, she was dead.

Pre-eclampsia is a complex disorder, affecting 2–8 per cent of all pregnancies and leading to over 50,000 deaths each year globally.[34] Like many of the conditions mostly affecting women that we have discussed so far, its causes are not fully understood, but its primary symptom is universally recognised: a sudden increase in blood pressure. So sudden that its name derives from the Greek word for a strike of lightning, *eklampsis*.

In later stages, the condition can lead to kidney and liver failure, pulmonary oedema (fluid in the lungs), and the loss of vision. At this point, pre-eclampsia can quickly develop into eclampsia, which is characterised by whole-body seizures and violent convulsions. Without immediate medical intervention, and often despite it, the risk of death to the woman and unborn baby is very high.

However, the risks that come with pre-eclampsia don't simply disappear upon delivery. By the time Wallace's newborn daughter, Charlotte, was delivered, her pre-eclampsia was so progressed that it led to kidney damage and rupture of the liver. Wallace underwent multiple operations to repair her damaged organs, but her doctors were not able to save her.

Wallace's death was entirely preventable. Her headaches were a well-known early sign of elevated blood pressure, which would have marked her pregnancy as high risk and required her to be given close monitoring. Lindsey Carr, associate editor of the journal *Contemporary OB/GYN*, wrote in Wallace's obituary that her death 'highlights the glaring racial disparities in maternal mortality and morbidity for Black women in the US'.[35] Eclampsia and pre-eclampsia in Black women are a leading cause of death in pregnancy.[36] These conditions should be taken very seriously. Doctors should be on high alert for signs of them in pregnant Black women at all times.

As with other conditions, the risk of pre-eclampsia in Black pregnant people is often linked to socioeconomic factors – but socioeconomic causes here are unconvincing and Wallace's case highlights the fact that simply being affluent does not mitigate the costs of racist disparities in healthcare. Wallace was highly educated, surrounded by a supportive network of family and friends, had ready access to medical treatment, and was herself a healthcare specialist, *and* in a discipline that often dealt with the condition. Even so, she was not offered closer pregnancy monitoring, and her doctors had not taken her symptoms seriously enough.

There are other high-profile African American victims of pre-eclampsia too. Tori Bowie, a highly successful track and field athlete and Olympic gold medallist, was found dead at her home in Florida in May 2023.[37] She had not been seen by friends and family for several days prior, prompting a panicked wellness check from authorities. Her autopsy showed that she had died of eclampsia, and her premature baby was found lying stillborn next to her. Even the richest Black women, and even the healthiest of Black athletes, are not safe from unequal healthcare treatment.

This is by no means a US-only issue. And it's also a frustratingly ongoing one. The 'MBRRACE-UK' report, a major research project investigating maternal deaths, stillbirths, and infant deaths in the UK, found that while there has been a small decline in the maternal mortality rate for Black women in recent years, the overall disparity has remained largely unchanged for over a decade.[38]

Blame continually gets shifted onto the shoulders of Black women. One academic paper in 2000 even linked increased Black maternal mortality from pre-eclampsia and other conditions to 'lifestyle factors'.[39] This drips with presuppositions and value judgements, but if that wasn't bad enough, one of those very lifestyle factors explicitly given is 'unsafe sex practices'. Sexual practices, unsafe or otherwise, cannot cause pre-eclampsia: this is a wildly egregious, unsubstantiated claim, and says more about the racism of researchers than the actual subject of their research. This link also echoes the earlier misdiagnoses of Black women with endometriosis. Black women are being blamed for their own and their babies' deaths. The article advises better education among Black women in healthy lifestyle practices in pregnancy, and the importance of early access to prenatal care.

Grace gave birth to her second child a week after I gave birth to my daughter; despite only a few days' difference in age, there will be a whole school year between them. My daughter was unlucky, born on 31 August – the cut-off point for the school year, destined always to be the youngest one. She'll be the last one in her class eligible for a provisional licence, the last one to (legally) get drunk in a club. She started school recently, head and shoulders smaller than the rest. Grace's son, on the other hand, towers above the children in his nursery group. Where my daughter is quiet and cautious, hidden at the back of the class, he is confident and rambunctious – a natural-born leader. Everyone tells Grace they expect great things from him. Outwardly, she agrees. In private she's not so sure. We talk about the negative perception of Black boys in the UK, and how they bear the brunt of some of the worst education statistics. She lives in fear of the day that both he and his older brother begin to come under police scrutiny, for the mere fact of the colour of their skin. She doesn't know how to tell her bright, smiling, optimistic boys what exactly the world has in store for them.

'But at least they're not girls,' she says, shamed by her own relief.

This comes, of course, from a place of painful knowledge. However bad it may be for my daughter, growing up as a woman in the world, and however bad it may be for her sons, growing up as Black men in the world, nothing quite compares to the experience of a Black girl: having to field negative perceptions, stereotypes, and physical and institutional violence from every direction.

Despite such hurdles, Black women continue to fight tirelessly against oppression. They advocate for real change, and in the UK today their work is having a very material effect, especially on Black maternity and perinatal healthcare.

In 2017, Tinuke Awe was diagnosed late into her pregnancy with pre-eclampsia.[40] Because it had not been picked up soon enough to be adequately treated, it meant that her labour had to be induced. The labour progressed quickly. Her midwives didn't believe that she was as progressed as she was; once they finally checked how dilated she was, she was told that she had missed the window for pain relief. On top of this, she also had to have an instrumental delivery. None of this was what Awe had planned for, and yet it was all easily preventable – if only she had been *listened to* by her medical practitioners.

After giving birth, she soon realised that her story was not uncommon. So many other Black people were birthing in similar contexts; essentially, she realised, preventable trauma was being caused by a failure to listen. 'I was hearing the same thing over and over again, that Black women don't feel listened to,' she told *Vogue*, 'that their pain is not taken seriously, and that they just feel like they're being dismissed all the time.'[41]

In 2019, Awe connected over Instagram with Clotilde Rebecca Abe, a healthcare professional with experience in campaigning for better maternal outcomes for Black patients. Together they founded the organisation Five X More. One of the first things they did was to launch a petition demanding the government improve Black maternal healthcare. The petition received over 100,000 signatures and the subject was subsequently debated in the House of Commons.

Further afield, and around the same time as Five X More was created, the US-based Black Mamas Matter Alliance (BMMA) launched the Black Maternal Health Week.[42] This aims to strengthen cross-sector activism and amplify specific issues faced by pregnant Black patients all around the world. In 2024, the theme focused on reproductive justice – acknowledging how the lack of equitable access to reproductive healthcare (from abortion care to fertility treatments) intimately intersects with maternity needs.

And there *is* evidence that change is slowly coming. Take 'Five X More', which was named after the shocking rate at which Black women were dying in childbirth in the UK, compared with white women.[43] This statistic came from the 2019 MBRRACE report. The 2024 statistic is that Black women are 3.7 times more likely to die in childbirth than white women: a small improvement, though there is a long way to go.

Before their 2024 general election win, the Labour Party pledged in their manifesto to improve the safety of maternity services in the UK, and set an explicit target to close the Black and Asian maternal mortality gap. This is a huge improvement on their predecessors, the Sunak government, which repeatedly blamed poor maternity healthcare on 'bad apple' hospitals and refused to meaningfully acknowledge the disproportionate harm being done to Black patients and those from other ethnic minorities.[44]

Acknowledgement of the problem is only the first step. Better awareness of poor birth outcomes for Black patients must not be seen as an end in itself. While the subject makes its way increasingly into the mainstream, healthcare providers have to look at what they can do to implement positive change beyond simply raising public perception of the issue.

In a report giving practical recommendations to the UK government, Five X More suggested better training for healthcare providers in medical conditions that disproportionately affect Black women, such as sickle cell anaemia, hypertension, keloid scarring and pre-eclampsia.[45] They also recommend increased diversity in medical textbooks so that students can better diagnose conditions presenting in those who do not have white skin. It is now of utmost importance for the current UK government, along with all governments, to put into action these recommendations and make NO MORE a reality.

8. You Had a Baby

Somewhere between the first and the second bottle of wine I decided that I wanted to have sex. It was my twenty-ninth birthday and, prompted by the inevitable slew of thoughts about the coming year – the last one of my twenties – and fuelled by a deep-rooted desire to return to some semblance of my old self again, I thought: *Maybe it'll be fine.* Maybe it'll be *good*? Jean Garnett described sex in her open marriage as 'romantic in a way that culturally under-scripted moments often are'[1] – and God knows we didn't have a script for *this*, with not a single mention of sex and 'prolapse' on the NHS website, and not a word from any of the countless practitioners I'd seen about it either. Surely it couldn't be so bad?

The children aren't home, I pointed out. They were staying the night with my mum. The timing couldn't be better. The generally recommended six-week postpartum wait had *long* since passed and we had to try at some point, didn't we? Andrzej was hesitant. It's up to you. Are you *sure*?

The bedroom was spinning so we turned off the lights. I don't remember anything of the lead up, only the jarring realisation with penetration that I couldn't feel a thing. I was numb from the entrance inwards. It was as though someone was rearranging the furniture, and then, with that, came the intense desire to urinate. In my drunken state, I foolishly thought that this was the coming of a strong orgasm. That if I only let my guard down, all the old feelings would come flooding back. Maybe I was about to have a *squirting* orgasm: didn't they say that was always preceded by the urge to pee? It's important to let go, the sex columnists advised. For the first time in my life, I took their advice and did just that: I let go.

Like the breaching of a dam, warm liquid began to pour out of me. It was like when my waters had broken in childbirth: the sheer volume and power was like nothing I had ever known. This was no squirting orgasm; there was no accompanying pleasure, only the sensation of extreme painful fullness followed by an immediate, dragging deflation. *Wet and gushy*, but in a bad way.

Andrzej screamed and pulled away from me in horror. He thought that I was bleeding, that he'd caused me to violently haemorrhage. Leaping across the room, he threw on the light. The room was suddenly blinding. My body looked long and white and very far away, legs akimbo, atop a fast-spreading pool of straw-yellow piss. Andrzej was standing at the bottom of the bed, naked, thighs and belly dripping wet.

I expected to see some relief in his face, knowing that it wasn't blood but only, thankfully – *thankfully!* – piss. But his eyes were full of concern, glued to the space between my legs. If I had been sober, I wouldn't have looked. Yet now, weak with drink, my eyes trailed inexorably downward. A small red tip jutting out from my vagina. Cylindrical and long enough to count. A penis.

The next day I learned that it was my bladder – apparently it can do that. At the time, I could only laugh. Andrzej didn't, and when my laughter turned to tears, he cradled me on the bed – the two of us entwined in the piss-soaked sheets – and told me that it would all be alright.

In the days and weeks that followed I found my thoughts constantly returning to Knuddelbär.

One summer when I was a student, I made the reckless decision to au pair in Austria. I lived for eight weeks in a remote mountain town where I was put in sole charge of four young children, even though I had never so much as babysat a child before. I knew nothing of toilet-training or weaning or tooth-brushing – or even first-aid, as it turned out, when the oldest one broke his arm in the park, and I cried as much as he did. The days were long and exhausting. I lived in the basement alone but for the family hound, a beautiful Hungarian Vizsla. His name was Knuddelbär, and he was still only a puppy. Paws as long as his legs, rusty red forehead all furrowed like a brain. When my au pair mother wasn't looking, I'd let Knuddelbär share my bed. One night I was woken by the feel of something small and wet slopped on my ankle. I pulled aside the duvet and Knuddelbär, still fast asleep, was lying sprawled across my legs. He had an erection, and it was pasted to my foot; like a sticky toy that you throw at the wall, only hard and secreting mucus. It made my stomach turn. Before my eyes, as he began to rouse from sleep, it sunk back down into its furry, hidden sheath, revolving like a lipstick back into its casing. It was red, too. *As red as licked red candy.*

I loved Knuddelbär, but that night I kicked him out of my bed and never let him back in. I knew it wasn't his fault that he had an organ that he couldn't control and that disgusted me so deeply. He'd stand at the end of the bed and look up at me with big baleful eyes and whine quietly, willing me to accept him back into the fold. I felt sorry for him, I really did. But I didn't want him anywhere near me.

Now, I didn't want to be anywhere near me. I didn't recognise what I had become. I didn't even feel as though I passed as human any more. If an alien race came down to earth and discovered an anatomy textbook it simply wouldn't know what to do with me. Human bodies are supposed to have bounds; our skin and our membranes the borders of our inner, intimate landscapes. There is supposed to be a distinction between inside and out. Now that my walls had fallen I wasn't sure what I was any more. I felt like a jellyfish – all gelatinous membrane, slick with the fluids lining my cavities, wicked out of me like piss from a baby's nappy. Some of it was piss. Some of it something worse. Like a Sainsbury's bag-for-life filled with offal: you can't close me; anyone can take a peek inside, but *God knows* they'll regret it. Like broken bones that breach the skin or deep-sea creatures washed up among the shoreline debris after tsunami. *Offal* things: disgusting, displaced, the opposite of sex.

I'm not sure I conveyed all of this to my GP exactly when I visited her soon after, but I managed to get out the fact that sex was *bad* now. I should have been able to predict her answer – should've known that it would be contrary to the one I was given when I visited another GP before I was pregnant, briefly suffering from pain during sex. Then, he told me that pain during sex was *normal* for young women. He'd read on my notes that I had just come off the pill. *Have a baby*, he advised; *that'll make it better.*

'You had a baby,' the GP said to me now, slowly, placatingly. 'You can hardly expect things to be like they were.'

At some point between January and March 1989, Janet Phillips, a middle-aged, married, working woman living on the outskirts of Dayton, Ohio, illegally entered a house not far from her own. A soft-spoken woman in her early forties, with a delicate face framed by a cloud of permed hair and a pair of lightly drawn eyebrows that painted permanent surprise, Phillips had a clean criminal record and no evident financial need for home burglary. Indeed, the only thing that she was later found to have taken from the house was a small lapel-pin.[2]

Number 7152 Paragon Road sat empty that spring. It had been recently repossessed and sold off at sheriff's auction – an ignoble fate for the Colonial Revival, 3,000-square-foot, 2.2-acre property that had once played host to the crème de la crème of Dayton society. Think California-style pool parties on the lawn (swimsuits discouraged) and late-night dinners that overflowed into morning; bronze sculptures over the hearth, and original paintings on the walls; diamond necklaces coiled on the vanity.

By 1989, nothing of any real value remained in the house. The lapel-pin was relatively worthless, and Phillips wasn't there for that anyway. What she sought was something else, something dumped in the bags of garbage piled up on the property. Whether or not she found what she was looking for in those bags, we will never know. What we *do* know is that they contained thousands of pages of medical documents – patients' notes – which had, originally, belonged to the owner of the house: Dr James C. Burt – Janet Phillips's gynaecologist.

Dr Burt called himself the 'Love Surgeon'. In 1975 he co-published with his wife Joan – the owner of the lapel-pin – a book called *Surgery of Love*, detailing his own unique brand of gynaecological surgery.[3] Phillips didn't know any of this when she first visited him in 1981. All she knew was that he was a registered OB-GYN based nearby, in Centerville, the south suburb of Dayton where she lived, and that he held late hours – two things she was after. Those, and another doctor's opinion. She had already seen two other gynaecologists for her painful cramping, and both had suggested that she *may* need to have a hysterectomy. She was hopeful that Burt would advise otherwise. Quite the contrary. Burt diagnosed her with aggressive ovarian cancer and told her that she would need a full hysterectomy *as soon as possible*. In November that year, she was admitted to hospital.[4]

However, in addition to performing a hysterectomy, Burt operated extensively on Phillips's vagina and vulva. He removed her labia minora completely and circumcised her clitoris. The clitoris was re-angled downward by about one centimetre towards the opening of her vagina, and her perineum was restructured so that it now overlapped with the bottom of the vaginal opening with a small fold of skin.[5]

Phillips had, unbeknown to her, been treated to a form of Burt's 'love surgery'. He had initially developed this procedure as a form of episiotomy repair – repair of the perineum following surgical cutting during childbirth – but it deviated from accepted practice so much that it bore no resemblance to anything that could be classed as simple episiotomy repair. Burt's surgery fundamentally changed the angle and axis of the vagina, the location of the clitoris, and did away with large parts of the vulva. All of this followed from his fundamental tenet: that women's bodies were not anatomically suited for penetrative sex. He believed that women could not enjoy satisfactory sex (meaning: were less likely to have penetrative orgasms) due to the body's naturally poor structure – something worsened still by the effects of childbirth.[6]

The first step in the love surgery's development was the addition of a few extra stitches during normal episiotomy repair, thereby making the vaginal opening 'tighter'. This was with a view to making sex better for the patient, and for the patient's partner. Soon, Burt decided to go further than adding a few extra stitches and began experimenting with the clitoris too. From the mid 1960s onwards, he started working on the skin tissue around the clitoris and, in doing so, found that he had moved the vaginal opening closer to it – something that would, he thought, improve sexual response during penetrative sex. To complement this, he began tightening and lifting the tissues around the perineum. In Burt's reasoning, this meant that during sex in the missionary position the changed vaginal angle now forced the penis to hit the clitoris during penetration. However, due to this extensive rearrangement of tissue and skin of the vulva, a significant portion of the labia minora was now in the way – blocking the entrance to the vagina. Burt's solution was to simply cut it off.[7]

While the newly fashioned gradient of the vagina was supposed to make for more pleasurable penetration, it also meant that the penis could collide with the vaginal wall rather than sliding into the vaginal canal. This could be uncomfortable and/or painful for both partners. By the mid 1970s, Burt had added an extra component to address this: he would cut through the pubococcygeus muscle. This muscle, part of the larger group of tissues that make up the pelvic floor, is more commonly known as the 'Kegel muscle'. Cutting through it loosens the tension in the rear vaginal wall, making it easier for a penis to push against it. As a final flourish, Burt decided to circumcise the clitoris by removing the clitoral hood. This was supposed to increase the stimulation of the organ, making orgasm a doddle.[8]

This extensive and damaging surgery was performed widely in its many variations over time, on almost all women whose babies he delivered. He would sometimes perform it in the delivery room of the maternity ward, immediately after labour, when his patients were sedated for what he would describe to them as 'episiotomy repair'. As was the case with Phillips, he also performed the surgery during hysterectomies, and often while carrying out uterine prolapse repair. In other words, whenever Burt had a patient anaesthetised on the surgical table, he would proceed with the surgery – with or without their consent.

In his patient notes for Phillips, Burt tells the story quite differently. According to him, she agreed to a total hysterectomy *and* 'vaginal reconstruction'. He states that he informed her of what that would entail, in some detail, and even goes so far as to say that she brought the subject of vaginal reconstruction up first *and* explicitly requested it.[9] The evidence is weighted heavily against him. Many other women came forward with similar, if not virtually identical, accounts.

At first, Phillips thought that the complications she was experiencing after surgery were due to the hysterectomy. At least that's what Burt told her, when she came to him with a plethora of problems. Among them was bladder incontinence, and the fact that she could not entirely void her vagina of urine. By reangling her clitoris downward, Burt had effectively pulled the urethra into her vagina. Whenever Phillips urinated, the liquid collected in a small pocket that had been newly created inside her vaginal cavity. She often had to stand to urinate, and even then was left with wet underwear afterwards. Recurring urinary tract and kidney infections naturally followed.[10] These led to such bad back pain that she even sought help from a chiropractor. Burt told her that these bladder complications were par for the course.

Phillips was also experiencing bleeding and pain during sex. This Burt took more seriously. In his patient notes, he describes talking with Phillips at length about her sexual difficulties after surgery. He doesn't note the fact that he warned her not to see another gynaecologist about it, though.[11] When she finally did, years later, the doctor – upon examination of her butchered vulva and vagina – told her that he had no idea where to even begin in treating her.[12]

Other patients of Burt experienced similar issues. Numerous underwent subsequent surgeries in the hope of rectifying them, only causing yet further scarring and injury. Vaginal and abdominal pain, pain and bleeding during sex, repeated infections and difficulties walking were all listed as examples of the ways Burt had harmed them. By removing the clitoral hood, even the slightest chaffing from clothing, let alone constant rubbing during sex, could be excruciatingly painful on the overexposed clitoris. Cutting through and loosening the pubococcygeus muscle limited a patient's ability to control urine flow and defecation – rendering them potentially both bladder and faecally incontinent. One patient, Barbra Roberts, reported problems with her intestinal muscles.[13] Another, Jimmie Dean Browning, had to have a catheter inserted for six months following surgery.[14] And contrary to what Burt supposedly set out to facilitate, many reported being unable to have penetrative sex with their male partners ever again.

★

In January 1989, Burt was forced to surrender his licence following a string of lawsuits that would eventually cost him over $21 million.[15] It was found that Burt hadn't forewarned many of his patients about what he was going to do to them, and when he had given *some* indication, he vastly over-promised what he was surgically able to achieve. His patients had mostly come to him for hysterectomies or routine post-pregnancy repair, but what they were left with was extensive scarring, chronic infection and pain, and often the need for corrective surgery. One woman's subsequent surgeon described her genitals as looking like a 'filleted fish'.[16] Another claimed that Burt had talked her into a hysterectomy simply so that he could 'improve' her sex life.

Burt always maintained his innocence and claimed that he had acted in the best interests of his patients. '[My medical practice] has been conducted with great concern for the welfare of women,' said Burt when interviewed. 'There are a lot of women with problems involving vaginal intercourse that are either not being adequately addressed or not being addressed at all.'[17]

This might have been true; it indeed may still be true today. However, American writer and academic Alice E. Adams compares Burt to the notorious John Marion Sims in this defence – of showing a wholesale disregard for their patients' autonomy and well-being, and masking it with 'the expression of compassion'.[18] Where Burt never sought meaningful consent from his patients, Sims' patients were enslaved women with no power of consent from the outset. As the so-called 'father of modern gynaecology', Alabama surgeon Sims experimented on enslaved Black women in the 1840s to develop his techniques of vesicovaginal fistula repair – without anaesthesia.[19] Unlike Burt, Sims admitted that his patients experienced great pain. 'Lucy's agony was extreme,' he said after accidentally leaving a sponge meant to soak up urine in the woman's urethra, that caused her to contract sepsis and almost die.[20] Like Burt, Sims argued that what he did was in the best interests of his patients and, in the absence of their consent, we are expected to take both men's word for it. Neither one acknowledged how these procedures were most clearly in their *own* best interests, financially and reputationally (at least for a time). While Sims' legacy may be contested in some circles, it is praised in others, and many of his innovations continue to be employed to this day, including 'Sims' Speculum', which is used in gynaecological surgery.[21]

Neither Burt nor Sims' thinking came out of a vacuum of course. Burt had developed his surgery in the years following the publication of a ground-breaking and controversial report titled *Human Sexual Response*, by sexologists William H. Masters and Virginia E. Johnson in 1966.[22] The pair changed the way sex was viewed by scientists and the general public alike. Female sexual response, and in particular the orgasm, received unprecedented attention. Masters and Johnson reaffirmed the clitoris' pivotal role in female sexual arousal, dispensing with the myth that there was such a thing as separate vaginal and clitoral orgasms. This division was one of Sigmund Freud's central psychoanalytical tenets. He regarded clitoral orgasm as infantile, and clitoral masturbation as essentially a masculine activity that was slowly repressed during puberty.[23] Driven by the adolescent woman's burgeoning penis-envy, the vaginal orgasm took centre stage, as the main erotogenic zone transitioned from the clitoris to the vagina.

But not all followers of Freud took his theories and reached the same conclusion. The nineteenth-century psychoanalyst Marie Bonaparte thought that women's bodies were poorly arranged for sex. Writing under the pseudonym A. E. Narjani, Bonaparte asserted that the reason why some women, herself included, couldn't reach vaginal orgasm was down to the distance between the clitoris and vagina. When the two are too far apart (more than 2.5 cm, she determined) vaginal orgasm was rendered more difficult, if not impossible. Reaching vaginal orgasm became something of both a personal and professional crusade for Bonaparte, leading her to develop a procedure – along with the surgeon Josef Halban – to move the clitoris closer to the vagina: a procedure she underwent herself – twice – to no avail.[24]

Burt read Masters and Johnson and recognised the central importance of the clitoris and the regressive view of Freud. But he was not a progressive either. He was also not the first surgeon to turn his attention to the clitoris. A hundred years prior to Burt, British surgeon Isaac Baker Brown advocated and widely performed clitoridectomy (surgical removal of the clitoris) as a cure for 'female hysteria' and what he viewed as 'excessive masturbation'. Baker Brown's career ended in ignominy – not because of his views on the causes of insanity in women (his colleagues were largely in agreement), but because he was found to be operating on them without their consent or through coercion. In 1867, he was expelled from the Obstetrical Society of London and headed to the US, where he spent the last few years of his life popularising his treatment.[25]

The attitudes of society and the medical establishment at the time of Baker Brown and Burt, over a century apart, were different, but their practices complemented each other. Where Baker Brown sought to cure women of clitoral stimulation, Burt wanted to cure them because their clitorises prevented them from enjoying intercourse. In her essay in the book *Bodily Discursions*, Adams writes that both Burt and Baker Brown 'operated to make women conform to traditional heterosexual values and both believed that women suffer from natural sexual pathology'.[26] Ultimately, both frame the vagina as an illness in need of cure.

From a surgical point of view, Burt had been performing a unique form of female genital cosmetic surgery (FGCS) on his patients. What started off as a form of post-childbirth corrective surgery quickly morphed into something less corrective and more constructive.

Nowadays, there are a whole host of FGCS techniques available. Labiaplasty, clitoral hood reduction and vaginal 'tightening' are the most popular, globally. There is a loose consensus that these procedures are not generally undertaken for 'medical' reasons, thus distinguishing them from gender affirmation and reconstructive surgeries, although the distinctions made are sometimes hazy, as we shall see.

Labiaplasty, the most sought-after form of FGCS, involves the removal of tissue from the inner labia (the labia minora) which is perceived by the patient to be too big or long.[27] There are a number of different techniques employed by surgeons to achieve this, the most common being the wedge and the trim. When undertaking the trim method, the surgeon removes the outer edge of the inner labia, making them flush with the outer labia. If not performed carefully, the trim can produce an uneven look around the clitoris. The wedge technique was developed in response to this problem. Here, a 'wedge' of tissue is cut out from either side of the labia and the remainder are stitched back together, often resulting in what some practitioners describe as a 'cleaner' look.

These may be the most common techniques, but the labiaplasty universe is ever expanding. Plastic surgeons with a flair for innovation (and a nose for potential demand) constantly experiment with new methods, resulting in different looks, all starting around the $5,000 price-point. A surgeon particularly famous for his contributions to the field is Californian doctor Red Alinsod. Alinsod claims to have invented the 'Barbie' style of labiaplasty in his Laguna Beach practice in 2005.[28] This involves trimming the labia down so that they ultimately resemble the doll's smooth, clamshell-like crotch. Described on Alinsod's website as 'a more aggressive reduction of the labia minora to the point of complete excision', it is one of the most requested forms of FGCS available at his clinic.[29]

The concepts behind some of Alinsod's procedures veer between the absurd and the tragicomic. Labia majora augmentation is called the 'vampire wing lift', and it is claimed to combat labial laxity in the 'gaping' and 'flapping' labia majora (you get the picture).[30]

Perusing Alinsod's website, 'labial laxity' is a term commonly employed – presented as a medically acknowledged condition of the labial tissue (implying, of course, that it is something in need of medical correction). If you consult a gynaecological textbook, you will find no mention of this so-called condition. A search for the term 'labial laxity' on the world's largest online database of medical literature, PubMed, retrieves precisely zero results from scientific articles published from 1879 onwards. It simply is not a recognised medical condition. Another such term is 'labial hypertrophy', which Alinsod uses to describe enlarged labia, again presenting it as a medically recognised condition. Slightly better represented in the literature, this term retrieves thirty-five results from PubMed. Most of these references pertain to cases and treatment of hypertrophy caused by underlying conditions such as tumours or genetic disorders. It's a symptom rather than a condition in and of itself.

What exactly constitutes a medical condition? There's no straightforward answer to this question. A vague, minimal requirement is recognition from a medical establishment but beyond that, things can get a little messy. In her book *Doing Harm*, Maya Dusenbery writes about 'contested' conditions, where usually 'the 'contest' is between, on the one hand, mostly women patients who believe their condition to be an organic one and, on the other hand, a medical establishment that assumes their '"medically unexplained symptoms" are all in their heads'.[31] These conditions can be widely known (examples include chronic fatigue syndrome, fibromyalgia and chronic Lyme disease, all of which, as Dusenbery assumes, disproportionately affect women), but not universally accepted. Equally, there will be little-known conditions that are well described in medical literature. Doctors will often rely on international and national reference works to diagnose patients. Efforts to standardise medical treatment worldwide necessarily involve identifying and classifying disease and, to that effect, the WHO publishes the International Classification of Diseases (ICD). The ICD is recognised as a standard reference for medical diagnosis in all 194 WHO member states.[32]

The ICD is regularly revised and is currently in its eleventh edition. Alinsod's term 'labial hypertrophy' doesn't feature in ICD-11, or any of the earlier editions. However, it does crop up in the section on 'Acquired abnormalities of vulva or perineum', as 'hypertrophy of the vulva'. This is described as an 'enlargement or thickening of the tissues of all or part of the female external genitalia, such as the clitoris, labia, vestibule, or glands'.[33] With his use of 'labial hypertrophy', Alinsod is playing fast and loose with the medical terminology, exploiting the fact that the initial condition it loosely derives from is vague. Hypertrophy of the vulva can *technically* include the hypertrophy of the labia also, and there is also no mention of an underlying cause. There is no standard and nothing to relate it to; the ICD-11 does not mention labia that are 'too long', 'overlarge', 'drooping', or any of the other terms Alinsod uses to diagnose it. But this 'official' medical language can be easily manipulated to make it seem so.

You would be hard pressed to find a health insurance provider in the world who would reimburse FGCS for the reasons Alinsod diagnoses labial hypertrophy. The NHS website states that 'labiaplasty is not usually available on the NHS. But it may be offered in some circumstances – for example, if the vaginal lips are abnormal, to repair tears after childbirth, or to remove cancerous tissue if a woman has vulval cancer.'[34]

Medical historian Sarah B. Rodriguez recognises a notable shift in how labial normality has been understood over the years. When describing the rise of FGCS in the US, she shows how, long before the boom in procedures around 2008, patients who presented with concerns about their labia would not be offered surgical intervention but were instead reassured by their surgeons that their labia were normal.[35] There was, and still is, no agreement on the criteria for normal-sized labia. Even though there was no clinical consensus for what was normal, women would be informed, at the discretion and personal choice of their physicians, what was considered normal. Still to this day, clear guidelines defining 'abnormal' labia do not exist. Some give anything below 5 cm in length, or anything below 10 cm; others say anything more than a 3–4 cm discrepancy in lip size, or 5 cm upwards.[36] In contrast, guidelines for the 'normal' size of male genitalia exist in abundance. Medical papers on the subject began to be published as early as 1899,[37] and a study in 1996 stated that 'only men with a flaccid length of less than 4 centimetres (1.6 inches), or a stretched or erect length of less than 7.5 centimetres (3 inches) should be considered candidates for penile lengthening'.[38] There are no such similar recommendations for people seeking labiaplasty.

Rodriguez notes that the trend of reassuring patients in the US began to cease around the 1980s, even though it continued long after in other countries and is often employed by doctors treating patients presenting with labial abnormalities today. The entire patient–physician relationship in the US was altered during this time, firstly due to changes made to medical advertising rules (ushering in the era of the marketisation of medicine), but also off the back of the patient advocacy movement of the 1970s that pushed for greater autonomy and decision-making power for patients. Physicians became less didactic in their approach to healthcare, letting women decide for themselves what they regarded as normal or otherwise in terms of labia size. Normal became more about how a patient *feels* rather than telling them what they are. This moment of greater patient autonomy just happened to coincide with the moment where it became financially beneficial to physicians for patients to judge their labia as in need of surgical intervention.[39]

In 1982, there was a significant alteration made to medical advertising law. The Supreme Court ruled that physicians were now permitted to advertise beyond their own field of practice. This allowed for the direct solicitation of patients, namely through placing adverts on billboards, television, and in local and national print media. Physicians were encouraged and sometimes forced to compete for trade, and to offer glitzier, less strictly 'medical' promises in their adverts to the public. Cosmetic surgery became an increasingly appealing field for surgeons. As Rodriguez points out, 'cosmetic surgery is a specialty defined by skill and not by anatomical location or disease state', which opened the doors for what was possible and where.[40] It is also a field in need of constant innovation, due to changes in body norms and aesthetic fashions.

Between 1970 and 1996, the US saw a 269 per cent rise in the number of cosmetic surgeons.[41] During the same period, the need for many traditional reconstructive surgical procedures waned as a consequence first of the introduction of car seat belts, and later on of airbags. Market demand for non-clinically indicated procedures made up for this deficit, and then far outstripped it.

Aside from these structural factors shaping the way medicine operated, many attribute the general growth of cosmetic surgery to its increased visibility. With the loosening of laws around advertising in the US and elsewhere, the media became saturated with images and information about procedures, which led, in turn, to higher requests.

The FGCS boom came at the tail end of the cosmetic surgery explosion, and it hasn't yet reached the popularity of other cosmetic procedures, like breast implants. In 2019, there were 1,795,551 cosmetic breast implantations worldwide, compared to 164,667 labiaplasties in the same year.[42] While markedly fewer labiaplasties than breast implantations take place every year, the trend for labiaplasty is certainly growing. There was a 73.3 per cent increase in the global number of labiaplasty procedures between 2015 and 2019.[43]

This boom may well be happening as social taboos around discussing female genitalia begin to fall away. Patients who may have traditionally harboured distress about their labia, but had been conditioned not to discuss it, now find themselves more empowered to speak up and seek medical intervention. Indeed, Rodriguez reports surgeons wondering in 1989 whether there were women, 'not being helped as much as they could be because they are too uncomfortable to voice their concerns' about their labia.[44]

Some believe that pornography has a central role in peddling a particularly narrow image of the diversity of female genitalia. Labia types that stray from a single, unrepresentative view can be perceived as in need of medical intervention. In some ways, it is empowering that physicians want women to make up their own minds about what they consider normal, but in others it merely enables different, more pernicious sources to determine the criteria, ones that do not necessarily have the well-being of individuals in mind.

Pornography is not the only origin of unrepresentative images of female genitalia. Few medical textbooks include images of vulva at all, and where they do, they most often feature small, non-protruding, symmetrical labia.[45] Medical literature has a history of negatively shaping perceptions of what female genitalia ought to look like. The 1948 edition of *Gray's Anatomy* famously excised the clitoris entirely. A recent survey of medical textbooks published between 2007 and 2021 found that less than half included photographs of the clitoris.[46] Only one presented photographs of different clitorises, showing their variation, and only one depicted the clitoris of a woman of colour.

For a doctor to reassure a patient that their labia are normal is to assume that this is what the patient wants their labia to *look like*, and that their motivation in pursuing surgery is purely aesthetic. Separating the different motivations behind this surgery, however, is not so straightforward.

For some, it is related to pain and discomfort. Eighteen per cent of respondents in one study requested FGCS for reasons relating to 'discomfort', as did 26–64 per cent in another study.[47] Gynaecologist

Jen Gunter talks of women tucking their oversized labia into their underwear 'like a Dumbo ear', and their labia being dragged into the vagina painfully during sex.[48] Surgeons describe patients complaining of them 'pinching or chafing when walking or sitting' and of painful sex. In the NHS guidelines on FGCS, the surgery is generally not recommended except for: 'Where the labia are directly contributing to recurrent disease or infection.'[49] In this regard, FGCS may not be so far from other surgical procedures to the vulva that seek to stop discomfort and pain. In certain cases of vulvodynia – unexplained pain in the vulva – that are localised to the opening of the vagina, (the vestibule) a procedure called vestibulectomy may be performed. Vestibulectomy is the surgical removal of the part of the vulva that is painfully affected. It is usually only recommended to women where all other attempts at treatment have failed. The same procedure is also used to treat a condition called lichen sclerosus, a chronic disease that causes painful, itchy white patches to appear on the skin of the vulva. Although there is currently no cure for lichen sclerosus, surgical excision of affected tissue is the last resort for many patients.

For some, labiaplasty may be sought in the pursuit of better sex. Surgeons certainly advertise it heavily with increased sexual pleasure in mind. On her website Alexandra Runnels, a gynaecological surgeon practising in San Antonio, Texas, gives the following account for the rise of FGCS:

> Women did not want to live with unflattering, sagging, and large labia, nor did they want to live with gaping open vaginas and lack of sensation when having sexual relations. Both young women wanting a sleeker appearance of their genitals and older women wanting to repair the ravages of childbirth and time are at the forefront of demand to look and feel young again. Southern California became the birthplace of this movement.[50]

From this, we can deduce that vaginas 'ravaged' by childbirth and time – essentially, 'bigger' vaginas – make for less satisfying sex, in and of themselves. This claim is greatly debated. In fact, there is much evidence to show that cosmetic surgical intervention reduces sexual pleasure, but this is mainly through complications that arise from surgery (such as the creation of scar tissue, chronic pain, the need for reoperation). Surgeons such as Alinsod and Runnels respond that *their* surgery is better than others, thus the likelihood of complication is far lower. And anyway, it's not just the *patient's* sexual pleasure Runnels has in mind. Elsewhere on her website she writes:

> Due to the effects of childbirth, ageing, trauma, and/or genetics, the vaginal tissue and surrounding muscles can become stretched and lose their strength and tone. The loose and unsatisfying feeling that many women feel can also be felt by their male partner during intercourse. Labial enlargement, unevenness, or traumatic tears from childbirth can also affect the labia to make it look unappealing.[51]

Runnels does not sound like someone who wants the patient to decide on their own idea of a normal labia. She sounds more like someone who wants any woman who has given birth, been traumatised, or even merely aged, to deem their labia in need of medical intervention – and not just for their own sake, but for their male sexual partner's benefit too. Here, we see the concept of informed consent being pushed to its very limit. She's not breaking any rules, though. She's just doing what she must do as a doctor and a businessperson. Dr Business.

FGCS has a bad reputation. 'Labiaplasty is a procedure whose time for popular acceptance has not yet come,' write a group of plastic surgeons from Northwestern University in *Aesthetic Surgery Journal*.[52] The stigma surrounding it comes from all sides: some argue that women seeking it are merely tools of the patriarchy (without autonomy of thought), others that they are vain, too rich, and perhaps deserving of their delusions.

Further complicating matters is the almost unavoidable comparison with female genital mutilation (FGM). Bioethics lecturer Arianne Shahvisi argues that the two sets of overlapping procedures are falsely distinguished based on racist presuppositions about women and consent; while white women are fundamentally emancipated, they are free to give informed consent for FGCS; women of colour, on the other hand, are by definition unable to give informed consent, and so suffer FGM.⁵³ Shahvisi proposes that we make a distinction between female genital cosmetic procedures not based on who they are being carried out on (working-class Muslim women, say, instead of middle-class Christians) but based on if and how consent is given for them.

The fact that we have two distinct terms – FGCS and FGM – for sometimes identical surgical practices is in itself questionable. In her book *Vagina Obscura*, American science journalist Rachel E. Gross identifies three main issues with using 'FGM'. Firstly, the term with relation to its definition by the WHO ('all procedures involving partial or total removal of the external female genitalia or other injury to the female genital organs for non-medical reasons') is inconsistent, as it doesn't exclude labiaplasty and other forms of FCGS, or even genital piercings. Secondly, it is imprecise, as it covers everything from small cuts to the clitoral hood, to infibulation (the removal of the vulva and suturing it over). Lastly, many who have undergone such procedures can find the term 'mutilation' stigmatising. In response to these criticisms, scholars have suggested that we refer to such surgery as 'genital cutting' instead.⁵⁴

It is certainly worth asking why we consider some female genital cutting barbaric when it happens in non-Western cultures, and as acceptable when it involves white Western women instead. However, I'm not sure that FGCS *is* considered broadly acceptable. It would be naive to mistake the fact that it does happen for it being culturally embraced. Similarly, the fact there may be an emerging 'ideal' vulval appearance – maybe influenced by pornography, maybe by other factors – does not mean that the means of procuring that look are accepted either. Reduction of breasts or other unspecified organs is met with much greater acceptance than labia reduction, and patients may find themselves overemphasising their physical complaints, likely as a tool to better justify the surgery.⁵⁵

When critics compare FGCS to genital cutting, it is often not to better understand stigma surrounding it, or to critique the colonial lens through which it is often reported and judged, but usually to further condemn both sets of practices. All forms of female genital cutting come under the same suspicion no matter what context they are taking place in, or the autonomy or agency of the patients involved. It is important to note that the international legal response to genital cutting is to criminalise it when it is carried out on minors. Of course, what constitutes a 'minor' differs from country to country. In British law, genital cutting constitutes an offence when it involves a 'girl' (sic) under the age of sixteen.[56] Health and social care professionals, as well as teachers, have a duty to report it when it is indicated in girls under the age of eighteen. A significant statutory component in determining genital cutting is consent. If we take genital cutting to mean the non-consensual cutting of a woman's genitals, then – unless you hold that Alinsod's adult female patients do not have the mental capacity to consent – FGCS and genital cutting are markedly dissimilar procedures.

Meanwhile, where FGCS is compared to genital cutting, it is held as strictly distinct from another set of procedures that involve female genital cutting: vaginal reconstructive surgery. These procedures, in contrast, are considered to be 'clinically indicated' and medically founded, as opposed to the merely aesthetically indicated (supposedly) desire for FGCS. As Australian anthropologist Lindy McDougall points out: 'Western medicine has a long history of gynaecological intervention after childbirth, including procedures to correct fistulas, tears, prolapses, and incontinence,' and not all of that is strictly medically indicated. 'After childbirth, it is not unusual for doctors to insert an extra stitch into a woman's vagina,' she continues.[57]

Episiotomy is the term used to describe surgical cuts made to the vagina and perineum during labour. These cuts are made with the aim of preventing serious tearing. It may seem like a paradoxical procedure, as to perform it guarantees trauma to the area and the subsequent need for repair. The argument for it has long since been that cutting, unlike tearing, leaves a cleaner cut – clinically cleaner (so easier to fix and with less likelihood of causing complications) and aesthetically cleaner too. A slew of studies have investigated whether a policy of routine episiotomy, offered as part of normal labour management, is better for the patient (compared to a selective approach where it is only performed when absolutely necessary). The results all clearly indicate that offering women episiotomy as a standard does not reduce overall vaginal and perineal trauma.[58]

Sometimes an episiotomy can make matters worse. One of the two commonly used types of episiotomy – a cut straight down the middle of the perineum – puts women at increased risk of fourth-degree tearing. This is when the vagina tears all the way to the rectum, causing very serious health problems, including faecal incontinence. The alternative – a diagonal cut – tends to be more painful and more difficult to repair.[59]

On the Mayo Clinic website, recovery from episiotomy is described as 'uncomfortable'.[60] This may be something of an understatement. Following the birth of my first child, I was unable to move for weeks without the sensation of a blade slicing my vagina in two. If I stretched my legs too far apart, I could feel my stitches beginning to tug at the seams, and they would open again, weeping clear sera mixed with blood. When I peed, I had to pour lavender water over the wound to dilute the urine, and in my weaker moments would take a swig of wine to steel my nerves ahead of my bowels betraying me. Once the cut itself had healed, the sharpness of the pain gave way to a sort of blunt numbness in the broad region of my seat. That lasted almost a year before petering away into weak, electric, pins-and-needles-like twinges running down the curve of my buttock and into my vagina. Only then could I physically discern where precisely the scar sat. Before, it felt like I had been maimed just about *everywhere*.

All of this and more (pain and numbness during sex; infection) can be intensified by poor technique and bad stitching on the part of the practitioner. Later surgical episiotomy repair, carried out by plastic surgeons, is not uncommon. On its website, the British Association of Plastic Reconstructive and Aesthetic Surgeons lists birth trauma surgery (including episiotomy repair) together with labiaplasty and vaginal tightening, all under the collective term 'Female Genital Tract Surgery'.[61] There is also a significant overlap with urogynaecological surgery, as one of the procedures offered for vaginal tightening is posterior repair, which is also used to correct prolapse.

The lines between these procedures are blurred. Not only are they performed by the same specialists, but they are developed by the same people too. What works well in one procedure may be incorporated into another, and in this manner, techniques – and priorities – blend. Episiotomy repair is often undertaken with aesthetic concerns in mind. Sometimes, elements of vaginal tightening will be utilised for better sexual function (and pleasure). The so-called 'husband stitch' – the act of putting in an 'extra' stitch to better tighten the vagina supposedly for the male partner's pleasure – has been discussed extensively in popular media. In 2014, a gynaecologist in Rio de Janeiro was recorded asking a patient's partner if he would like it 'small, medium or large'.[62]

Alinsod doesn't just carry out FGCS. In addition to his labiaplasty and vampire wing lift, he performs other urogynaecological procedures such as prolapse repair, endometrial ablation and uterine suspension. A list of inventions on his website feature several unique mesh devices, supposed to aid incontinence and support prolapsed organs. There are radiofrequency devices for faecal incontinence repair right next to radiofrequency devices for labial laxity repair. The gun-shaped apparatus purports to use radio waves to induce 'tightening of the affected area'.[63] Needless to say the evidence for its effectiveness is scant.[64] Alinsod is not unique in his field; he isn't even unique in the US context. Urogynaecologists all over the world partake in private practice, where they will develop and invent treatments across the spectrum of vulvo-vaginal health and well-being.

Stigma surrounding FGCS is not only misplaced (based on false dichotomies between medically indicated and otherwise; overly concerned with and critical of the motivations of the women who seek it) but it can also achieve the opposite effect of what it usually intends. The whiff of judgement and bias can drive seekers of important information away, leading them to other, less trustworthy sources. In *The Perfect Vagina*, Lindy McDougall talks of how some people refer to plastic surgeon's websites for medical information pertaining to their vulvo-vaginal region.[65] Unable to find concrete information elsewhere – firm indicators of what constitutes 'normal', for example – they may turn up on the page of a plastic surgeon who presents comparison 'before and after' images. On such websites they may find their concerns accepted and legitimised, and thus the source feels more trustworthy.

Take the NHS webpage on labiaplasty, for example. It introduces the subject with the following:

> Some women want a labiaplasty because they do not like the look of their labia. But it's completely normal to have noticeable skin folds around the opening of your vagina. In most cases, it does not cause any problems, which is why labiaplasty is rarely available on the NHS.[66]

A norm is asserted here, and yet no clarifying information is given. The phrase 'do not like the look of' comes across as childish, and demeaning of an adult's self-perception. It is stated that labia do not usually cause problems. But what about when they *do* cause women problems? Beneath these words, one senses the message that labiaplasty is not an acceptable course of action (and that one's concerns about one's labia are not acceptable, or real).

Another researcher sums up the 'problem' of FGCS perfectly:

> While the psychological underpinnings of genital anxiety as well as its origins as a cultural production and social construction must not be ignored, it is similarly problematic to universally admonish as disingenuous a woman's newfound sexual and personal self-confidence and experience of pleasure as a result of FGCS.[67]

Much of what can be said here applies to cosmetic surgery, and indeed most aesthetic bodily modification, more broadly. The reason why this is such a thorny area is because the battle for autonomy over women's bodies – and over our vulvas, and vaginas – is still so hotly contested. As we have seen elsewhere in this book, women expend *so* much energy – if not whole lives – attempting to wrestle back control of their own bodies: from doctors, from abusers, from medical institutions, and from society at large. In this context, it's no doubt healthy that we treat any pressures for us to change our bodies with suspicion – equally, we must think about what it means when society *doesn't* want us to change, either.

★

There is no strong consensus among medical regulatory agencies over how gender-affirmation surgical procedures ought to be best carried out. The UK's executive body in setting healthcare standards, NICE, offers no guidelines for gender affirmation surgery (or, in fact, for any other aspects of trans medical healthcare). And while the situation differs from country to country, there is a huge variation in the techniques. When it comes to male-to-female gender affirmation surgery, the only constant elements are the removal of the testicles (orchidectomy) and the penis (penectomy). The specific methods for using the patient's tissues to create the vagina, labia and clitoris vary considerably, and entirely depend on the skills and preferences of the surgeon.

As the vaginal cavity needs to be created anew (the specific procedure known as vaginoplasty), tissues need to be found to form it.[68] This can be skin derived from the penis and scrotum, segments of the gut, lining of the abdominal cavity (peritoneum), or skin grafts from other parts of the body (such as the abdomen). There are advantages and disadvantages to each approach and no single one emerges as a far superior gold-standard, according to the latest guidelines by World Professional Association for Transgender Health (WPATH).[69] However, the penile inversion approach remains most popular.[70]

Penile skin is considered well suited to vaginoplasty as it is smooth, hairless, elastic, and has only thin connective tissue. But unlike the interior of the vagina, it is dry and does not self-lubricate to the same degree.[71] Scrotal skin has the advantage of geography in that it's already in the right place and can be inverted and fashioned into the vaginal cavity more easily. The disadvantage is that it contains hair follicles, making hair growth inside the vagina a common complication. Physicians can later use tweezers to remove these hairs, or cauterise them if they are extensive. Scrotal skin also has a layer of muscle underneath (the dartos muscle, which causes the scrotum to contract in response to temperature) which must be removed. Sometimes, the scrotum does not provide enough tissue material for creating the vagina and has to be augmented with penile skin anyway. Skin grafts from elsewhere in the body are an option but, as with scrotal skin, they also bear the problem of hair growth, and can leave light scarring at the site of the removed skin. The main advantage of using pieces of tissue collected from the gut (usually the bowel) or the peritoneum is that these tissues produce mucus and therefore can be self-lubricating to some degree. This can ultimately give the vagina a more comfortable feel, especially during sex.

How and whether the clitoris and the labia are reconstructed (clitoroplasty and labiaplasty respectively) is even more variable. The glans of the penis can be used to make a neoclitoris and the parts of the shaft can be separated and placed around the opening of the neovagina to provide additional sensation. The reconstruction of labia minora is not always performed but where it is, it usually uses penile or scrotal skin, though the amount of material may be scarce if the tissues were used to make the neovagina. There are *no* guidelines to date on how to best construct the labia or the clitoral hood, and the choice of technique is wholly up to the surgeon.

Due to the lack of guidelines, and a lack of consensus over best techniques in the field, trans women seeking this surgery must grant their surgeons an exceptional level of trust. In *Vagina Obscura*, Gross interviews male-to-female gender affirmation surgeons and discusses with them the different techniques employed.[72] Each will bring a unique interpretation to their creation of a vagina. Where the earliest neovaginas were formed with heterosexual penetrative sex in mind, better technologies – and a better understanding of the body itself – means that surgeons can consider various other factors such as external and internal aesthetics, lubrication, protective bacterial flora, structural integrity, and increased female sexual pleasure. Balancing these concerns is up to the surgeon, and some may focus more or less on any given element.

These procedures have come a long way – in most cases, they are now relatively safe and successful. One recent study of a Brazilian clinic found that in 214 instances of penile inversion vaginoplasty, only 16 per cent – 34 people, but this is still an improvement on years past – underwent some form of reoperation, and there were no recorded cases of regret among any of the patients.[73]

Access to these procedures is still, however, a hurdle. In her book *The Transgender Issue*, Shon Faye describes trans healthcare in the UK as largely 'unreformed, anachronistic and unfit for purpose'.[74] Care is accessed through one of only a few specialist gender clinics, to which prospective patients must first be referred by their GP. The average wait time for a first appointment is three years. Subsequent appointments may take months to come through, if not longer. Unsurprisingly, many people turn elsewhere for their gender-affirming care, either via unregulated channels, or the private sector. This can be financially ruinous. Seeking to curb the costs (or wait), some opt to travel abroad for procedures. This comes with its own logistical problems, such as hidden costs, the major time investment, and a significant upheaval to one's life. Outside of the UK, others may travel abroad because care isn't provided in their own country at all. Georgia, Russia, Slovakia and Poland are all examples of states with no provision at all for trans healthcare. Compounding these issues is a global lack of surgeons specialising in gender-affirming surgery. In the US, only twenty states have surgeons who specialise in gender-affirming vaginoplasty procedures.[75]

All in all, trans people find themselves consistently blocked from accessing care. Care that is, in many ways, impressively advanced on account of the dedicated development and global collaboration of specialists. The problem here isn't the surgery, but the system.

Meanwhile, I found myself being encouraged into having a form of genital surgery that I had no interest in having whatsoever.

I didn't *want* to go private, but piss-gate was the final straw. I couldn't face the prospect of entering my thirties like my elderly grandmother: incontinent, unable to have sex, and crying about it all in the theatre.

I visited two private gynaecologists: one in Cambridge, one in London. The first was recommended to me by a friend who happens to be a midwife, and the second by my straight-talking GP. I decided to visit two, just in case they gave me conflicting information – something that my friends who were used to visiting private doctors had warned me about.

Of course, that is exactly what happened.

The first told me I needed a cube pessary, a die-shaped rubber device recommended for patients with progressed prolapse. The second told me that I needed a hysterectomy. The first one told me that I should not, under any circumstances, get a hysterectomy; it would likely lead to 'vault prolapse', and I was too young to even contemplate that outcome. I should use a cube pessary instead, and he could even offer me the newest model (the one that they use in Hollywood). The second gynaecologist told me that I should not, under any circumstances, accept a pessary. It would only make my SUI worse and could leave me incontinent. Seeing as I had already been told I shouldn't get pregnant again, I might as well get a hysterectomy now – because I'd definitely need one in the future.

I asked both for their opinion on surgical prolapse repair as a middle way: neither surgeon offered them and, coincidently, neither thought they were all they were cracked up to be, in any case.

Friends offered me more names, more numbers. I had wasted a significant chunk of money by this point on introductory appointments that I had, in my naivety, assumed would be complimentary. I decided to let one final doctor break the tie – best of three, right?

This one was based in London. Andrzej had accompanied me to the previous two appointments, but he couldn't make this one, so I went alone. Is that why it happened?

The surgeon seemed nice. We had a chat at his desk – dark mahogany with a green leather top, significantly better than the one my GP had – and he sat quiet and attentive while I explained to him the current, unfavourable assemblage of my genitalia and within. He gave the impression of having heard it all before, but being no less empathetic for it. This was reassuring.

He led me to the examination table and, unlike my previous experiences, didn't draw a curtain for me to undress behind but rather turned his back on me instead. I didn't make much of it – he was going to see me naked in a moment anyway – and I got up onto the bed which, like the desk, was yet another visible upgrade. The examination went much like any other, if a little longer than my NHS ones had been – just like the two other private appointments I'd attended. I'm not sure what the extra length added, in terms of his observations, but it made me feel as though I was getting my money's worth, at least.

When we were back at the desk, he pronounced his findings. I'd need an operation, he said. *Yes!* I thought. Just what I wanted. And then he asked me how much I wanted him to take off the lips.

I was stunned.

'No, I . . .'

'It's nothing serious,' he said, smiling his calm smile. 'But after childbirth we always see *some* sign of elongation to the lips, and I really think you'd benefit from just a little . . .'

'No,' I said firmly. 'No thank you.'

He put up his hands in apology, sensing my horror. 'I'm not saying it looks bad,' he said quickly. 'I'm just thinking of your sex life.'

I got out of there as fast as I could. Turns out I didn't want surgery after all.

9. Which Box Do I Tick?

Two weeks after our daughter was born, she developed a fever.

I was lying in the bath when I heard a commotion downstairs; and then Andrzej was barging through the bathroom door and rifling through the cupboard under the sink.

'The baby's really hot. Where's the thermometer?'

When I went down the stairs moments later, hastily thrown-on clothes sticking to my wet body and bubbles of unrinsed shampoo popping in my hair, it was to find my husband and mother huddled in council. I approached the bassinet perched on the sofa. Swaddled up tight in a blanket, my daughter lay stone-still and fast asleep. The skin on her face was blotched yellow and red. Beside her head lay the digital thermometer. It read 41 degrees.

'You need to call 999,' said my mum, approaching me – the family's designated call handler – with her phone.

I hesitated, thinking of the angry 'DON'T WASTE NHS TIME!' posters plastered all over my GP's surgery.

'*Do* I call 999 for this? Is it serious enough? What about 111?'

'It says on the website not to use 111 for children under five,' explained Andrzej. 'Just call 999.'

I did as he said and was put through to an operator. After taking my daughter's information, she explained that she would need to ask me a further series of questions to establish the exact nature of the situation. Great, I replied. Let's go.

First up: 'Is she conscious?'

I looked down at my heavily sleeping newborn. 'Well, she's asleep.'

The operator persisted. 'But is she conscious?'

'I don't know what the difference is?' I said.

'*Can* she wake up?'

'Can she wake up?' I mouthed to Andrzej. Looking a bit

bewildered, he began to gently shake the baby. She remained resolutely asleep, but grimaced in discomfort.

'She's pulling a face?' I answered uncertainly.

'Okay,' said the operator. 'Has she vomited?'

Yes, she had vomited. A pile of dirty white muslin cloths sat scrunched up on the table, and fresh ones floated over the radiators like ghosts. The whole house *stank* of vomit. It had done so since we'd returned from hospital.

'Well, yes,' I replied, exasperated. 'But she's a *baby*.'

The operator sounded equally short when she said: 'Look, I just need to know which box to tick . . . Let's try another one. Does she seem confused?'

I ended the call.

'Fuck this,' I announced, tossing the phone towards my mum and casting about for the car keys. 'We're going to the hospital.'

Science likes a binary; if we think of binary sets as taxonomies, then no one does it better than the scientists. Taxonomy establishes hard borders, distinguishes groups and classifies their members based on predetermined criteria. Their validity is, in reality, easily threatened, and the criteria most catastrophically fail when applied to those who cannot be put into either box. Christiane Völling, the first intersex person to ever win a case against non-consensual surgical sex reassignment, proves that powerfully.

Völling was born in 1959, and grew up in the small town of Kalkar, in what was then West Germany. In her early years, Völling's life was not yet marked by ambiguity and confusion surrounding her sex. Völling was assigned male at birth and raised as such: an identity that would later prove to be in stark contrast with what she considered to be her biological and psychological self. She was designated as male because the midwife who delivered her took a quick glance at the newborn's genitals and decided that who she saw was clearly a male baby.[1]

Unbeknown to Völling until many years later, she was born with two X chromosomes, typically associated with being female. She also had a genetic condition called congenital adrenal hyperplasia (CAH), which in persons who have the XX chromosome pair can lead to excess production of androgens, male sex hormones. The symptoms of CAH vary greatly, but some individuals with CAH possess what is medically termed as 'ambiguous genitalia'. This happens when external and internal sex organs combine both male and female characteristics, making the person intersex.[2] In Völling's case, what was female was mostly hidden from sight, buried inside her abdomen.

During puberty, as expected of a growing teenage boy, Völling's hair grew in a typical male pattern and her voice deepened. Maybe she did not shoot up as much as her peers, but her parents consoled her by saying she was a 'late bloomer'.[3] The first sign that something was unusual about her body was a chance discovery during a routine operation. In 1976, at the age of fourteen, she underwent an emergency appendectomy, to treat acute appendicitis. During the operation, the surgeon noted the presence of what seemed to him to be internal female reproductive organs.[4] (The appendicitis, caused by bacterial infection, was unrelated. In her early life, Völling, like many intersex people, had no physical problems or discomfort due to her condition.)

The surprising discovery during Völling's appendectomy was the start of a series of both wilful and unthinking omissions and misinformation that were to mar her life forever. Völling's family were informed that young Thomas (as Christiane was known at the time) was suspected to have double cryptorchidism, commonly referred to as 'undescended testicles'. She was admitted to hospital again, a few months later, for an exploratory operation.[5] The surgeon opened up her groin all the way to the bladder, but found no sign of testicles or the spermatic cords that connect them to blood supply and provide a route for the sperm. Suspecting that the testicles were hidden even deeper in Völling's body, her abdominal cavity was cut and exposed.

There were no testicles inside Völling's abdomen either. What the surgeon did find was a pair of perfectly well-developed ovaries, correctly connected to two fallopian tubes. An unidentified mass of tissue next to the ovaries was also found, so a biopsy was taken and sent to a histologist, who two days later confirmed that the mass contained epididymis, a structure whose main function is to store and transport sperm from the testicles.

Following the operation, Völling, who believed herself to be male at the time, was informed that a pair of ovaries had been found inside her abdomen and that she was '60% female'.[6] A severe mental health crisis ensued, and Völling started having recurring thoughts of suicide. In desperation, her older sister wrote a letter to a senior physician professor at a university clinic in the area, asking him for help.[7]

In December 1976 Völling finally received a consultation with a urologist, with the intention to discuss her 'ambiguous genitalia'. In the meeting, they also addressed the treatment options for hypospadias, a condition where the opening of the urethra does not align with the tip of the penis, but rather comes out on the underside of the shaft. By now, Völling was seriously questioning her identity, and this was recorded in her hospital notes: Völling 'personally feels neither male nor female'. Overall, it was recommended that, should she feel a tendency either way, a suitable operation should be offered to her.

Later that month, Völling's tissue samples were sent for a chromosome analysis, which yielded female chromosome make-up of forty-four autosomes (non-sex chromosomes) and two X sex chromosomes. This finding was never shared with Völling by the medical staff. By March 1977, Völling's mental health had deteriorated even further and her sister penned another letter to the same doctor, asking him if it were possible 'to make a man or a woman' out of her sibling.[8] In July 1977, Völling was admitted to hospital with the diagnosis of suspected 'female pseudo-hermaphroditism', and a referral to undergo 'a hormonal examination and surgical removal [of the female reproductive tissues]'.

To the medical staff of the time, Völling was a hermaphrodite. This term, rooted in the Ancient Greek *mythos*, is now considered obsolete, inaccurate, and even offensive. In her book *Intersex*, the British critical writer and visual artist Catherine Harper notes how the word hermaphrodite 'arguably carries the mythological and fetishistic associations that serve to dehumanise and stigmatise the living individual to whom the term is applied'.[9] But offensive language is just the tip of the iceberg when it comes to how medical professionals have historically treated (and often still treat) intersex people.

Intersex variations such as Völling's fly in the face of rigid Western societal concepts of sexual duality. Sigmund Freud wrote: 'When you meet a human being, the first distinction you make is "male or female?" and you are accustomed to make the distinction with unhesitating certainty.'[10] For Freud, and generations of physician-scientists before and after him, sex was a fact of biology: immutable, stable and binary. As Harper points out, people with intersex varieties challenged this 'unhesitating certainty'.[11] The only way to dispel this challenge was to correct the ambiguity.

At the hospital, Völling was assessed to be 'psychologically stable', which was attributed by the doctor to the prospect of a corrective surgery following the earlier urological consultation. The professor whom Völling's sister had originally reached out to disclosed Völling's chromosomal analysis to the medical staff at the hospital, but the information was again withheld from Völling, as it 'could have possibly confused him'. Despite the hospital's earlier record of Völling 'feeling neither male nor female', according to the registrar's assessment, there was no evidence of Völling's questioning 'his male sexual consciousness, his male gender role and his male sexual orientation'.[12] Any doubts and hesitations were dismissed at the stroke of a doctor's pen.

Völling's body and life changed irreversibly on 12 August 1977. A full official record of the operation that was performed on her that day has never been found, but a short anaesthesia report survives, specifying the purpose of the surgery as 'testovarectomy', or surgical removal of testicles and ovaries. The details of what happened can be further reconstructed from a personal diary entry of a physician who attended the operation, written two days later. He reported 'a normal female anatomy with pre-puberal uterus, normal sized ovaries, blindly ending vagina',[13] all sighted upon the opening of the abdomen. This physician attributed the external masculine development in Völling's body to either CAH or an adrenal gland tumour, correctly diagnosing Christiane Völling for the first time.

A histological analysis of the tissues cut out from Völling's abdomen, from the hospital's records, provides what is probably the most accurate description of her physical condition: 'Rudimentary atrophic uterus with flat regular myometrium and sparse portions of epithelium of the vaginal portion of the cervix. Ovarian tissue with cystic follicles, primary and secondary vesicular follicles as well as scattered *corpora albicantia*. Male germ plasm in the form of a testovar cannot be detected.'[14]

During the operation, the surgeon removed Völling's uterus and her ovaries, which could support the development of eggs. There was no sign of tissue capable of producing sperm cells.

Völling was not told any of this. Following the operation, she says that she was led to believe that 'degenerative genital tissue or some sort of tumour'[15] had been removed from her body.

Having lived as a male for eighteen years, Völling was trying to hold onto her 'masculine' identity, but it was slipping away. A year later, she underwent the first in a series of procedures aimed at reconstructing the urethra and improving the 'male' sexual functions of her body. These left her with persistent kidney infections and a urinary dysfunction.[16] Her GP declined to talk to her about her condition following the operation, and when she finally confronted him, he replied: 'People like you have been in the past shown at travelling shows.'[17]

In the Western world in particular, intersex people have been variously labelled as mythical or unnatural, circus freaks, or scientific curiosities. It has suited both the cultural and the medical establishments to paint their condition as something elusive, mysterious, rare and ephemeral, but this is simply not true.

The Intersex Society of North America and its successor, interACT, estimate the prevalence of intersex conditions to be in the region of 1 in 1,500–2,000 live births.[18] Given that 605,479 babies were born in England and Wales in 2022, we can therefore presume that between 900 and 1,200 of them were intersex: the metric here being presence of 'atypical' genitalia that necessitated the attention of a specialist in sex differentiation.[19]

How rare is 1 in 1,500–2,000 people? To make a fair comparison, let us consider another congenital anatomical condition: cleft palate. Recent available data reliably puts the prevalence of cleft palate at 1 in 1,700 births.[20] This means that in 2022 just over 1,000 children with the condition were born in England and Wales. We all likely know people who were born with a cleft palate: there are a number of public figures who have the condition and are vocal about it. For those with access to basic medical care, it is usually dealt with swiftly and efficiently in infancy, with little or no medical consequences for later life. Is being born with cleft palate considered rare, exceptional or mythic? No. It is as common as being intersex.

'Intersex' as a medical term first appeared in the early twentieth century, but its widespread use follows the pioneering work of intersex activists, such as Bo Laurent,[21] and the academic studies of American sexologist Anne Fausto-Sterling, who popularised it in the early 1990s, noting the problems with the term 'hermaphrodite'.[22] Intersex is not a single medical condition, but an umbrella term used to describe 'people [who] are born with sex characteristics (including genitals, gonads and chromosome patterns) that do not fit typical binary notions of male or female bodies'.[23] Some forty different medical conditions can cause a person to be regarded as having intersex variations, although clinicians often disagree which conditions should be included in that list.[24]

In effect, such discussions are often used to marginalise people with intersex characteristics. Intersex activists have been proposing a shift towards definitions of intersex that are more respective of social and historical contexts, rather than just based on medical taxonomy.[25]

Christiane Völling's condition, congenital adrenal hyperplasia (CAH), is the most common cause for intersex characteristics. In CAH, genetic mutations alter the production of sex hormones, androgens or oestrogens, making too many or too few. In the first case, individuals who have XX chromosomes (usually associated with being female), experience what is termed as 'virilisation' of genitalia, for example an elongated clitoris, but may also have genitals indistinguishable from that of 'typical male', especially in early childhood. Chromosomal men (XY) with excess androgens are usually only mildly affected, for example with early onset puberty.

For individuals with insufficient production of both androgens and oestrogens, regardless of their chromosomal makeup, the condition leads to underdeveloped, or intersex, genitalia.[26]

Other intersex conditions might be caused by the body's inability to respond to sex hormones, an example being androgen insensitivity syndrome (AIS). Here, the sensors in the reproductive cells are 'deaf' to the testosterone, which would ordinarily signal them to grow into a testicle. Children with XY chromosomes (usually associated with being male) can then develop feminised genitalia and secondary female characteristics, such as breasts or bigger hips.[27]

Then there are conditions which affect the chromosomal 'sex' of the individual. Two of the most common are Turner and Klinefelter syndromes. People with Turner syndrome have only one sex chromosome, the X chromosome (sometimes written as Xo, in distinction to XX or XY for typical female and male). With one X chromosome only, ovaries cannot form, growth is affected, and secondary sex characteristics are absent. In Klinefelter syndrome an XY chromosome pair is accompanied by an additional X chromosome (XXY). Individuals have 'male' genitalia, but are infertile and develop 'female' secondary sexual characteristics.[28]

Rarer conditions which lead to intersex characteristics are Mayer-Rokitansky-Küster-Hauser (MRKH) syndrome, vaginal atresia, ovotesticular syndrome, XX male syndrome, XY gonadal dysgenesis, Xo/XY mosaicism and aromatase excess syndrome.[29] Each condition can present differently, and affect individuals to a varying degree. The understanding of the causes and these conditions is relatively new to medicine, having been reached in the latter half of the twentieth century.[30] Before then, cultural and societal attitudes, rather than scientific knowledge, led the doctors' approach to intersex people, with little or no concern for their welfare.

In early modern America, medical practitioners, influenced by the teachings of puritan ministers, regarded 'monstrous births' as a sign of divine providence.[31] Mothers and their overactive, impure imaginations were blamed for birth anomalies. Medical ignorance also informed legal proceedings: intersex babies were used as evidence of out-of-wedlock liaisons, impotence, rape, and to substantiate divorce claims. Many intersex women were misdiagnosed as simply having enlarged clitorises, which was seen as a sign of sexual vice, making heterosexual sex impossible and being a sure path to lesbianism.[32]

As medicine in the US (and in most of the Western world) became professionalised in the nineteenth century, doctors started imposing their traditionalist views of marriage on intersex people.[33] Medical practitioners, now largely recruited from the respectable middle classes, made the first incursions to 'normalise' the intersex genitals and thus facilitate lawful heterosexual relations. With little to go on in terms of knowledge of anatomy or physiology, let alone genetics, doctors made completely subjective decisions forcing patients to conform to their ideals of heteronormative duality.

Around the same time, medical sexism and misogyny collided with the racism of the colonial West. Historian and professor of gender and medical ethics Elizabeth Reis traces the changing landscape of prejudice about intersex and ethnic minority people in her book *Bodies in Doubt*. As the medical profession sought to establish itself on a more scientific basis, doctors began regarding marginalised populations as objects of their research and evidence for their theories. The nineteenth century saw a proliferation of scholarly articles on 'malformations' in African Americans. As Reis notes: 'monstrosity [. . .] and blackness went hand in hand'.[34] The fear of sexual ambiguity found a perfect corollary in ideas about racial purity.

The early nineteenth century brought a new theory: sexual inversion as an explanation of homosexuality.[35] 'Inverts' were sexual perverts, who were attracted to the same sex against the natural order of things. It was only a matter of time before hermaphrodites were thrown into that category. Physicians were confounded by their ambiguous genitalia and terrified of the possibility that intersex individuals could be attracted to the 'wrong' sex. Doctors began interrogating intersex people about their sexual proclivities, choosing a label of 'man' or 'woman' in order to prevent homosexuality.

This new paradigm collided with the first serious forays into surgical intervention, in the early decades of the twentieth century. Development of genital surgery was fuelled by the introduction of general anaesthesia and improvement in surgical techniques in general. Doctors developed new methods to cut up intersex bodies, but the dogma at the time was still to facilitate the only 'lawful' sex: penetrative intercourse between a vagina and a penis.[36] An intersex patient who was attracted to women would be given a penis (with the aim of getting an erection). A patient who preferred men would be given a vagina. And where there was no sexual desire: a vagina. Sexual impulses were a male thing after all.[37]

In the 1920s and 30s, a crisis ensued, caused by the medical establishment's adoption of the so-called 'gonadal' standard of sex determination.[38] Gonads are specialised body organs that can produce reproductive cells: sperm and eggs. So the presence of testicles or ovaries was taken as the evidence of the patient's 'true' sex, superficially resolving the conundrum of 'ambiguous' genitalia. But, as we have seen, nature still could confound doctors' neat taxonomies, as this did not solve the questions of intersex patients with mixed gonads. In any case, old modes of decision-making persisted, and doctors still insisted on taking heterosexual marriage as the ideal outcome of their medical treatment.

By the mid twentieth century, doctors were focusing their attention on producing 'mentally healthy' individuals, who would be well equipped to perform their adult 'gender role'.[39] Needless to say, the tacit precondition of this was heterosexuality. This new approach found its most vocal proponent in the figure of Dr John Money, a prominent sexologist, whose work defined the medical treatment of intersex people, and continues to wield influence to this day.

Money was a New Zealand-born American professor of paediatrics and psychology at Johns Hopkins University, and a founder of the first sex and gender identity clinic in the US. A prolific author of academic publications, during his lifetime Money monopolised the approach to medical care of intersex people.[40]

Money's treatment protocols relied heavily on early surgical intervention in infants born with ambiguous genitalia. For Money, sex assignment was an arbitrary decision which could be taken irrespective of chromosomal sex, presence of gonads, hormone exposure, and internal and external genitalia. Crucially, parents were advised not to inform their children about their condition, because of the possibility of 'interfering' with the process.⁴¹ Tens of thousands of children around the world were treated according to Money's recommendations.

In 2004, UK public broadcaster Channel 4 aired a two-part documentary series titled *Secret Intersex*.⁴² A ground-breaking endeavour, the programme focused on the actual, lived experiences of intersex individuals and their families, but also, crucially, the impact that the medical treatment of intersexuality has had on their lives. One of the persons interviewed was Louise Thompson, who was twenty-nine years old at the time of airing.

Thompson was born with a typically male XY chromosome set, but her body was 'profoundly sex ambiguous'.⁴³ She had a part of one testicle, one complete ovary, and a vagina, but no uterus. When she was born, Thompson's parents were told they had a boy, which they promptly announced in a local newspaper. Afterwards, the doctors changed their mind and informed the parents that their newborn was in fact a girl. Finally, the third time round, the doctors settled on intersex. Alice Dreger, professor of clinical medical humanities and bioethics at Northwestern University, writes how intersex birth creates a 'social emergency'⁴⁴ – reflected here in the haste with which Louise was labelled and mislabelled by the paediatric staff.

Thompson was treated for her intersex condition at Middlesex Hospital in London (now part of University College London Hospitals). Following Money's guidelines, the doctors successfully persuaded her parents to consent to genital surgery on their child. An arbitrary decision was made to surgically assign Thompson as female. Her consultant surgeon, Christopher Woodhouse, acknowledged that she 'might well have been assigned male if she had been born today'. Woodhouse also noted with candour that surgeons often 'make it up as [they] go along', a statement which belies the certainty of John Money's lancet.⁴⁵

Louise's body bears marks of surgeons' attempts to 'correct' it. Her ovary and partial testicle were removed early in infancy, followed by years of reconstructive surgery. Interviewed by Catherine Harper in *Intersex*, Thompson describes that she 'found her childhood genital surgeries difficult to remember'. But the ordeal she went through was impossible to forget. The surgeries were unsuccessful: she did not get a 'satisfactory vagina' and suffered from incontinence which required permanent artificial drainage.[46]

Passing from childhood to adulthood, Thompson was in and out of the surgical ward. She recollects how, at the age of twenty and following yet another surgery, she repeatedly asked for a mirror, only to be repeatedly refused. When she was finally allowed to glance at her groin, she discovered a severely swollen and bruised mass of tissue. It took four months to heal. Finally, at the age of twenty-nine, she underwent her last vaginoplasty. Louise reached some form of emotional closure, but her mood was that of resignation: 'there is nothing else for them to do'.[47]

Louise Thompson now feels female, and was raised as a woman by her parents, who had acted on the explicit orders of her physicians. Her being intersex, however, was kept completely quiet from friends and family and, most crucially, Thompson herself. This is the experience of most intersex people. Thompson describes herself as 'a sad and lonely child', who grew up unsure about her gender role.[48]

Her teenage years were marked by trouble and tension, which culminated in her being sent to a residential care school. There, she experienced the shock of discovery. In conversation with the school matron, she confessed her dream of settling down with a husband and kids. She recollects how the matron's 'face dropped'. She informed Thompson that she would never be able to have children. This was the moment that Thompson described as her 'world ending'. She shut down and refused to hear any more explanation from the matron. A time of immense anguish ensued for her, and she contemplated suicide. She directed her anger at her parents. In a letter to her mother she wrote: 'You lied to me . . . why did you keep me alive to go through all this?'[49]

Medics act as gatekeepers to knowledge and are ultimately responsible for opening the space for informed consent. When the child is too young, their parents and guardians provide consent, but they frequently feel lost and in pain themselves. Louise Thompson's mother recalls how she couldn't talk to her daughter because she felt she couldn't herself understand anything that was happening. This secrecy erodes the bond between the child and their carers. Allison, a mother of another intersex child interviewed by Catherine Harper, speaks about this damage: 'I felt very lonely and frightened by what I didn't understand. My husband felt so angry at the doctors. I just felt they wanted to say [my son] wasn't natural and to tidy him away. Our happiness at becoming mum and dad was totally ruined, we nearly fell apart.'[50]

When Thompson was old enough to be able to understand – and question – what had happened to her in infancy, it was far too late to reverse any of the medical decisions made about her. The anger she felt is certainly something experienced by many intersex people who have been treated similarly by those around them. Morgan Holmes, Canadian sociologist, activist and an intersex person herself, describes her feelings in a way which resonates with others: 'Knowledge of myself and where I fit in is what was stolen from me by being medicalised and by having my body altered against my will.'[51] Intersex people often feel suspended between identities and expectations put on them by society. Holmes was fortunate enough to be able to grasp onto the one and only constant she had and felt sure of: 'Having my genitals mutilated has made me no less intersexual; it has merely made me a mutilated intersexual.'[52]

The vows of silence binding the parents of intersex children and the medical staff are a prescription of John Money's treatment protocols. He believed that truth would threaten the attempt at socialising the child to their assigned sex and interfere with the treatment. This tenet came from Money's early research and a specific experiment he conducted in the 1960s and 70s. Subsequently, it proved to be Money's most notorious case, and a shocking example of child abuse in the name of medicine: the story of David Reimer.

David Reimer was assigned male at birth and was not intersex. But he attracted Money's attention when he was referred to his clinic following a botched circumcision at the age of around eight months. Crucially, for Money, he was one of two identical male twins – his brother was to serve as the basis for comparison in the experiment.[53]

Reimer's penis was severely burned following a non-standard procedure performed by the family GP to address phimosis – a fairly common and benign condition in which the foreskin fails to fully retract. The damage was so extensive that it could not be repaired surgically and Reimer was effectively left without a penis. His parents were advised to take him to Johns Hopkins University Hospital and seek help from Dr John Money, a rising star in his field.[54]

Money claimed to have believed at the time that to assure Reimer's future happiness, he should be reassigned as female. His parents were persuaded to follow Money's advice.[55] So, Reimer underwent bilateral orchidectomy – a medical term for surgical castration – and his scrotum was altered to resemble a vulva. He was renamed Brenda, raised as a girl and encouraged to 'behave' like one. During puberty, he was given hormone therapy to stimulate breast growth. Money regarded this case as a huge success. It spurred a series of research papers and conference appearances that brought Money fame and attention. For the purpose of publication, Reimer was anonymised, and the 'John/Joan case', became a celebrated experiment in sexology.[56]

David Reimer was brought up according to Money's 'optimum gender rearing model', which, although ahead of its time in proposing that gender was learned rather than innate, was also sexist in the old-fashioned way, enforcing a strict gender binary that dictated which behaviours were male and which were female.[57] Moreover, it was also based on the fallacy that sexual binary corresponded to the gender binary. Money's intersex patients were encouraged to behave in ways that were stereotypically male or female, according to the sex to which they had been assigned by doctors. Details of how Money achieved this with Reimer were conspicuously absent from his published accounts.

Throughout his childhood, Money observed how Reimer and his brother Brian were brought up: he wanted to ensure that the brothers were growing up as 'normal' girl and boy siblings. Brian was the 'control' part of the experiment: assigned male at birth, according to his chromosomal and physical characteristics, and brought up as one, a typical boy, and encouraged to follow what Money took to be typical boy interests and behaviours.[58] To ensure that his guidance was adhered to, Money held regular private psychological sessions with the twins. What these meetings involved became public knowledge only following the release of *The New York Times* bestselling biography of Reimer: *As Nature Made Him: The Boy Who Was Raised as a Girl*, by Canadian journalist John Colapinto.

When the brothers were six years old, Money decided to introduce the children to 'sexual rehearsal play', which he believed was part of forming 'healthy adult gender identity'. As part of this process, he showed the two brothers pornography. Reimer later recalled: 'He'd say to us, "I want to show you pictures of things that moms and dads do."'[59]

Then, he forced Reimer and his brother to replicate the acts they saw in these images. He would make David go on all fours on the sofa in his office and instruct Brian to come up from behind, place his crotch against David's buttocks and 'play at thrusting movements and copulation'. At another session, he ordered David to lie on his back with his legs spread apart and have Brian lying on top of him. Brian also recalls that Money would take Polaroid photographs of the twins during these meetings.

Money, who was usually mild-mannered and avuncular around Brian and David's parents, would turn irascible and aggressive when left alone with the twins. He did not respond well to defiance. As part of his routine, he would order the brothers to perform 'genital inspections' on each other. The brothers resisted Money's 'treatment', which only provoked his anger. Reimer recalls how on one occasion Money 'told me to take my clothes off and I just did not do it. I just stood there. And he screamed, "Now!" [. . .] I thought he was going to give me a whupping. So I took my clothes off and stood there, shaking.'[60]

The trauma and the ongoing ordeal left the Reimers in deep turmoil, even though they were not at the time fully aware of Money's abuse. The family broke off all contact with Money and, when David Reimer was fourteen years old, his parents told him the truth about his birth, circumcision, and subsequent sex reassignment.[61] Money continued touring lecture halls and conference venues speaking of his success with the John/Joan case.[62] In the meantime, David Reimer began living as a man. He underwent a double mastectomy to remove breasts that had grown following female hormone treatment, and took testosterone to masculinise his body. He also had a series of (largely unsuccessful) surgical procedures aimed at constructing male genitalia and undoing some of the damage done in his early years.

When David Reimer's story became public knowledge, he turned into a vocal advocate and activist in the burgeoning intersex rights movement. Although he was not intersex, he identified strongly with the cause. He would speak frequently of his deep sense of unease as a child, of an internal knowledge of sorts, which was always there, telling him that he was not really a girl.[63] His and his brother's treatment at the hands of Money and his colleagues was deliberately designed to allow them to 'test' their theories about intersex people. But Reimer also suffered at the hands of medicine, which acted with all its power to enforce the rigid sex binary, ignoring the inconveniences of informed consent and research ethics, and allowing a sexual abuser unchecked access to vulnerable children.

Ultimately, it claimed the lives of both David Reimer and his brother Brian. Brian took a fatal overdose of antidepressants in 2002. Two years later, Reimer, riddled with grief and remorse, and plagued by the trauma of his childhood, took his own life.[64] Reimer's mother believed 'her son would still be here if he had not been subjected to the gender experiment'.[65] She directly blamed Money for the deaths of her children. Dr John Money died in 2006, never having publicly commented on what happened to his most famous research subjects.[66] By then, the tide had turned on his practices.

In 2008, Christiane Völling emerged victorious from a Cologne courtroom, a landmark ruling in her hands. Her surgeon was found guilty of unlawfully operating on Völling without her informed consent. In the judge's opinion, 'this invasive procedure should not have been performed without a full explanation'.[67] The surgeon, whose identity is protected by German law, subsequently fought against the ruling, but the verdict was upheld in courts of higher instance and Völling was eventually awarded €100,000 in damages.[68]

Alongside reparations, Völling also petitioned the court for legal recognition of her sexual identity and name. By the time the trial finished, Völling was living as a woman and identified as such. Her road has been far from easy.

Following the operation in the summer of 1977, Völling trained as a nurse and found work in a hospital in Düsseldorf, where she remained for the rest of her professional career.[69] Adulthood was marked by Völling's struggling to grapple with her identity. Over the years, she found support in her older sister: 'Without her, I would have long taken my own life.'[70] It was Völling's sister who encouraged her to understand and piece together the truth about the fateful events of her early life.

Völling spent months sending requests to hospitals, scouring through archives and searching for medical notes and documents, all to get some clarity about treatment she received in the 1970s. Though many of her records were lost, destroyed or misplaced, she eventually learned exactly what she was not told by medical professionals.[71] She discovered not only that she had been robbed of her internal organs, but also that she had two X chromosomes. Völling decided to start her life as a woman and fight the legal battle over what happened to her when she was a teenager.

When Völling was awarded damages by the German court, it was in large part because she successfully argued that the treatment she was subjected to left her unable to live her life as a woman. Evidence presented by one of the medical experts called to testify on behalf of Völling was clear and convincing. Had Christiane Völling not been reassigned as male, it would have been possible for her to get pregnant.[72] She was born with a uterus and functioning ovaries, which were removed without her fully informed consent. With proper hormone replacement therapy and reconstructive surgery on her vulva and vagina, she would have been able to conceive and give birth.

The personal life stories of these three people, Christiane Völling, Louise Thompson, and David Reimer, though different in detail, at heart show the consequences of the same tension between medicine and societal norms. Their bodies were perceived as an affront to the pre-existing categories of what a person *should* be. And thus decisions were made, with no or limited consent, to surgically and irreversibly alter them, in the hope of fitting them into a box. This had profound, and sometimes tragic, consequences for how they perceived themselves in the world and how the world perceived them.

In her adulthood, Thompson fully embraced her identity as a woman. She made conscious decisions to undergo surgeries that would change her body in ways that involve proper informed consent. She wishes to live as a 'normal' woman and knows that this is the best path for her: 'I'd like for the right man to come along – like most people would.'[73] She can reflect on what happened to her: '[it] would be a bit unfair to say whether it was right or wrong [. . .]', adding, as a warning, 'but it shouldn't be done'.[74] And she is also fully aware, just as Völling is, that she will not be able to lead the life of womanhood she would want for herself.

In her autobiography, *Ich war Mann und Frau* ('I Was Man and Woman'), Völling recalls sleepless nights as a child when she would repeat to herself: 'I am a girl, I must not forget that I am a girl.' This knowledge felt natural to her and constant, but also hidden from view, 'like a small, underground river'.[75]

Reimer, Völling and Thompson have all been damaged by healthcare's drive to box them in through medical violence. But even when consent became available for them, choice was not. Medical events in their childhoods had already closed off some paths and avenues that their lives could have taken. But then again, was there ever any choice anyway? Only two options were on the table: woman, man – and nothing else, and certainly nothing in between. Intersexual identity did not even emerge as a possibility in the minds of the doctors who treated their intersexual patients.

It was the rise of the intersex rights movement in the 1990s that began slowly shifting this narrative. Judith Butler, the American critical and gender theorist, writes how: 'the intersex movement has been galvanised by the Brenda/David case, able now to bring to public attention the brutality, coerciveness and lasting harm of the unwanted surgeries performed on intersexed infants'.[76]

Butler also addresses the ultimate goal of the intersex movement – intersex liberation:

> The point is to try to imagine a world in which individuals with mixed genital attributes might be accepted and loved without having to transform them into a more socially coherent or normative version

of gender. In this sense, the intersex movement has sought to question why society maintains the ideal of gender dimorphism when a significant percentage of children are chromosomally various, and a continuum exists between male and female that suggests the arbitrariness and falsity of the gender dimorphism as a prerequisite of human development. There are humans, in other words, who live and breathe in the interstices of this binary relation, showing that it is not exhaustive; it is not necessary.[77]

In 2013, the Third International Intersex Forum, a meeting of intersex activists and intersex organisations from around the world, convened in Valletta, Malta. One of the results of the meeting was the 'Malta Declaration' – a profound affirmation of intersex rights: 'Intersex people must be empowered to make their own decisions affecting own bodily integrity, physical autonomy and self-determination.'[78] In 2015, Malta became the first country in the world to enshrine protection of intersex children from non-consensual medical interventions into its law.[79]

Societies around the world are grudgingly, but steadily, accepting that people's sexuality and gender fluidly exist on a spectrum. The right of people to question their gender, to change it, and to even physically change their sex – born out of the struggle for LGBT recognition in the latter part of the twentieth century – is being entrenched in legislation, despite repeated and vicious attacks from people who are desperate to uphold the status quo. The world is beginning to acknowledge that the categories that we have, since time immemorial, conformed to aren't any real indication of who and what we really are.

Intersex rights are intimately bound with trans rights and, as the fight for trans justice moves increasingly into the mainstream, so too do intersex issues – but not always in the most helpful ways. Some opponents of trans rights strive to downplay the rate of intersex conditions to further solidify the gender binary: intersex people become framed as rare anomalies, in no way able to meaningfully trouble the clear distinction between man and woman. Where in reality, being intersex is as common as having cleft palate, or red hair, or being a twin. Others still may compare non-consensual surgical procedures carried out on intersex children to young people accessing trans healthcare, grossly misrepresenting the nature of both in the process.

In such debates, intersex becomes portrayed more like a metaphor rather than the lived identity of real people. Their pain is consigned to the footnote of other, seemingly more important, conversations. Intersex people deserve so much more than this. And if protecting intersex children means having to dismantle a medical establishment based on an outdated gender binary, then what are we waiting for . . . ?

Andrzej shouted at me for hanging up on the emergency services. He thought it was rude and uncalled for. But once we got to the hospital, and our daughter was rushed to the front of a twelve-hour-long queue, her small body put through the pain of lumbar puncture, and the results confirmed that she had sepsis, he took it all back.

My daughter's story is an imperfect allegory for the position that intersex people and their parents are put in by a box-ticking system. The questions that the call handler had asked me over the phone weren't fit for purpose and the boxes that she needed to fit our daughter into hadn't been made with her in mind at all. Any attempt to make her fit the criteria – yes she is conscious; no she isn't vomiting; yes she's acting normal – might have caused her untold harm. Instead, my daughter was administered with life-saving antibiotics and was out of hospital two weeks later. In the days following her admission to hospital, doctors informed us that her infection marker level had been shockingly high and even a delay in her treatment of an hour could've severely impacted her health outcome. It is fortunate that I was able to hang up on the 999 call and circumnavigate it by going to the hospital directly; intersex people, however, often can't just tell someone to fuck off and then make it on their own. They require the solidarity of all of us to make the world a better fit for them, and not the other way around.

Conclusion

Cause of Death: Woman

The day that my daughter was born was the worst day of my life until, three and a half years later, it was replaced by my son's fifth birthday. After school we had driven to a nondescript carvery pub in Bedford that happened to have a children's play area inside. He had insisted that this was the place he wanted to go to for his birthday treat – the shabby pub with sticky tables and perpetually enraged staff at which we'd randomly stopped one time in passing. I had packed all of his presents in the car, and he opened them at the table, to the eye-popping envy of the surrounding children and the evident chagrin of their parents. He was so delighted with the Lego Maersk container ship that he demanded my phone so that he could take a shaky video of it to send to his 'Gaga', my mum. She'd only recently left and was back home in Shropshire recuperating after helping us over half-term. Practically the moment I sent her the video, I noticed that she had seen it. She called me immediately after.

'That's so lovely! Can I wish him a happy birthday?'

I tried to lure my son away from the presents and over to the phone, but he was too distracted and couldn't settle. He expressed fear that his little sister would manhandle them. My mum agreed that it was a likely outcome, and said she'd call him first thing the next morning instead.

While the children dragged themselves about on broken plastic ride-ons, Andrzej and I reminisced on my son's birth. In some ways, it had been even worse than my daughter's one – and I didn't have to crouch over a mirror to see the wounds either, but only had to look into my baby's small newborn face: two deep welts lined his cheeks, a blue circle crowned his head. The bruises from the forceps blades and vacuum machine made him look like a boxer, and he wore on his face the same colours hidden beneath my paper knickers. Andrzej took out his phone and found the very first photograph he'd taken of us – mother and child huddled together on the birth-room gurney, shellshocked, survivors of a storm. We both welled up with happy tears, then laughed at how old and cliched we had become.

We also talked about how I was coping much better with my prolapse – it had become less of a mental burden, even if the physical effects were still largely the same, and how I had finally, if reluctantly, come to terms with my now altered state of being. I had another glass of the house wine (and then probably another).

We didn't know until later that my mum died that night. She died of untreated coronary heart disease, despite having presented with every major symptom of it for over a decade. Each ailment had been wrongly diagnosed as something else: diseases typically associated with women and, therefore, of less consequence. She was told that her stiff and painful shoulder was arthritis. Her shortness of breath was misdiagnosed as asthma. Her tight chest was attributed to panic attacks, and her sore neck to indigestion. The nausea and dizziness were linked to the menopause, and so she was prescribed HRT – something you should not be taking if you have coronary heart disease. Every month she would traipse to the pharmacy and collect two bags full of medication: inhalers, steroids, anti-anxiety tablets, anti-inflammatories, acid reflux relief; all padded out with the necessary drugs to manage the side effects of this veritable cocktail – bloating from the HRT, insomnia from the steroids, migraines from the SSRIs. And finally, enough pain relief to knock out a horse; tacit allowance that none of the rest were working. When my uncle found her body, well preserved because she couldn't afford to heat the house, her bed was a nest of hot water bottles, wheat bags and heat pads – and not just because of the cold. They were the talismans she was never without, a desperate bid to take the edge off the pain – and hopelessness.

When I got there the next day, I couldn't bear to disturb them – such was their magical hold over me, even after their betrayal – and I lowered myself onto the bed ever so gently before calling someone off the dark web to come and crack her passwords. I needn't have bothered; they were all simple combinations of my birthday, my husband's, her grandchildren's, the cat's. I looked at her browsing history and found her final searches: 'Fast heart rate in asthma', 'asthma attack with chest pain', 'fast heart rate with asthma', 'pain in arm with asthma'. I wept for a while and then laughed like a drain. It had been there right in front of us all along: her broken heart. Had it not written the story of our lives? Being kicked out of the house she had bought jointly with her husband when I was a baby; he then resurfaced periodically in our lives, like unbanishable mould, blooming in the worst moments, half-choking us to death. Her long-absent father who'd peek in when he was 'about', who wouldn't go near the fridge because he knew its emptiness tasted of guilt. In that house these men had left her to spoil, with rotten window frames they only had to rattle to get in through. Toilet-water leaking into the kitchen walls below; blending together the bright suns and moons she'd stencilled onto the cornices. The slumlord who threatened to kick her out the one month in twenty-four years she was a day late paying the rent because of a mistake made on a housing benefit form by an overworked bureaucrat who wouldn't say sorry. Mum sobbing down the phone to me: *This is it, Emma, I'm finally homeless.* Getting myself into debt to pay the bastard; him telling me, after she'd died, that I had a week to empty the house and *don't forget to re-carpet the hallway* – so I opened the taps and flooded the place. I listened to the messages on her answerphone as the house groaned like the sinking *Titanic* and the big light flickered overhead like a flame. Even through the tinny speaker on the handset, I could hear the remorse in her GP's voice – I can't believe what's happened, I am so sorry, so terribly sorry, for not booking in an ECG – I should've known, she was so *young* – always in so much pain – I know Ann-Marie has a daughter, I think she should get her own heart checked out now because, well, you never *know . . .*

In my mother's inquest notes, her cause of death should not have been given as coronary heart disease, but rather: Woman. Being a woman had killed her; if she had been a man, she would probably still be alive today. She'd have been taken seriously, sent for tests, given a stent. I'd have had her for another twenty years, maybe. Even another year and she might've been remembered by her grandson, but five is too young. The same day of the year I became a mother, I lost a mother. The anniversary of my own induction into the much-vaunted Motherhood Hall of Fame was the same day as her graduation from it. One in, one out.

Coronary heart disease is the leading cause of death globally, in both men and women.[1] Despite this, it is still perceived as a disease that predominantly affects men. While it is true that men are more likely to suffer from it, women are much more likely to die of it.[2] Misdiagnosis, treatment delays and poor aftercare for women with the disease are rife. Coronary heart disease is the most common cause of heart attack – when a blockage prevents the supply of blood to the heart. You are likely to be conscious during a heart attack (as opposed to cardiac arrest, a term which is often conflated with heart attack). Quick diagnosis and treatment are key, but women are 50 per cent more likely than men to get a wrong initial diagnosis.[3] A 2017 US study found that doctors more often prescribed angiograms to men – a specialised X-ray of the blood vessels in and around the heart which have been injected with dye – even when women presented with the same symptoms: chest pain followed by an unsuccessful treadmill test.[4] Coronary angiograms are considered 'the best method of diagnosing coronary heart disease', yet doctors consistently recommend that women do not need them. Similarly, after suffering from a heart attack, women are less likely to be prescribed with statins or beta blockers[5] – both of which have been proven to reduce the risk of a subsequent heart attack.

It isn't just practitioners who are affected by this gender bias when it comes to heart disease: women *themselves* are less likely to think that they are having a heart attack.[6] A systematic review of global clinical records found that, on average, the delay between the onset of heart attack symptoms and the arrival at A&E for men is up to three and a half hours, as opposed to over seven hours for women.[7] This is in stark contrast to the general trend of women going to the hospital more often, and more immediately, than men for almost all other conditions.[8]

The myth that coronary heart disease is a men's health issue is compounded by another, equally pervasive misconception: that women experience the symptoms of heart attack differently from men, on account of biological sex difference. This is untrue, and yet the idea has been difficult to shrug off and you are likely to encounter it in even the most well-meaning contemporary medical literature. The British Heart Foundation recently attempted to put this falsehood to bed once and for all by funding a study to disprove it.[9] Nearly 2,000 people were enlisted who, between 2013 and 2017, had been admitted to the A&E department of Edinburgh Royal Infirmary and diagnosed with heart attack through a definitive blood test. Of these patients, 93 per cent presented with chest pain as their primary symptom – 93 per cent of men and 93 per cent of women.[10] Absolutely no sex difference was observed. The 'Hollywood heart attack', as it is sometimes known in medical circles, really is the most common way in which the condition presents itself, both for men and for women. The BHF issued a special press release along with the study, choosing a title that really leaves little room for misinterpretation: 'No difference in key heart attack symptoms between men and women'.[11]

Where did the idea that people experience heart attack symptoms differently on account of their sex come from? It tracks back to the 1980s, to around the same time that women began experiencing more heart attacks than ever before.[12] This uptick was likely due to women living longer (the life expectancy advantage of women in the US and the global West peaked in the 1970s[13]) and the fact that women tend to experience heart attacks at a later age than men on account of lifestyle factors.[14] Where women previously were dying of other conditions earlier, they were now living longer – and more likely to experience coronary heart disease as a result. Researchers were quick to notice that women who had heart attacks were more likely to die from them too. This related to the lack of adequate diagnosis – something that persists to this day – and an explanation was sought. Indeed, women report 'less' chest pain than men during heart attack – describing their pain less as intense crushing, and more of a pressure or tightness.[15] This is not to say that the pain is any more or less in either gender. The reasons why men and women may report pain differently – pain that may be, objectively, the same – are manifold. Not only do women tend to experience regular period pain and also more conditions in their lifetime than men[16] (thus leaving them 'pain fatigued'), but there is a good chance they have already experienced the downplaying or even outright gaslighting of previous medical conditions at the hands of a practitioner. We all know the stereotype of the hysterical or hypochondriac female patient. When presenting themselves to a healthcare practitioner, women tend to group symptoms together[17] – a tactic that can best be described as throwing mud at the wall, hoping for something to stick, and to finally be taken seriously – and this can inadvertently distract practitioners from the severity of the key symptom: chest pain.

It's imperative to understand that the theory that women die more from heart attacks because they experience different symptoms from men is incorrect. Research simply does not support it, and yet the idea was and continues to be peddled. At which point, we must ask another question – if this myth is so easily refutable, why has it so stubbornly remained in the public consciousness? Is it because it is easier to ascribe these deaths to ignorance of women's 'different' and 'non-conforming' bodies – to unknown, unexpected symptoms that even the women themselves miss – than to the murkier and less easily remedied problem of women simply not being taken seriously by their doctors? If I wanted an easy life, I would subscribe to the belief that my mum's death was unavoidable. That even the best doctor would have missed the signs of her coronary heart disease. Unfortunately, I know this isn't true.

In this book, we have shown how the poor treatment of people who do not fit into the box get blamed for the very system that fails them. Cis women, trans women and men, non-binary people, queer people, non-white people and intersex people all suffer, in medical terms, for insufficient care – and if that wasn't bad enough, we are supposed to feel like it's all our own fault too. The blame we're subjected to takes many forms. It can be the stigmatising emphasis on certain lifestyle choices, or the chokehold of being called a bad mother. It can be the abnegation of responsibility to fix something because the body is 'faulty' and doesn't *want* to be fixed. It is when the very fact of being a woman is treated as a pathological condition. Or when the genitals we are born with are deemed not good enough for society, even if they're good enough for us.

It may feel as though we have reached a frustrating impasse. Where can we *possibly* go from here? Like me, you may long for more than toothless slogans such as 'Believe her', or 'We're listening!' or, after the worst thing imaginable has already happened, 'Lessons will be learned' – every time there is another high-profile death of a Black woman in childbirth, or another spate of newborn baby injuries and deaths.

There *are*, however, a number of concrete things we can actively campaign for that will improve the material reality of our healthcare. We can insist on being treated like individual people rather than stereotypes, through the implementation of personalised healthcare. We can demand that unacceptable gaps in knowledge about our bodies are filled by better biomedical research. We can campaign for truly equitable access to healthcare, in every country in the world. All of this costs money. The field has been systematically and grossly underfunded – it is time for governments, pharmaceutical companies and international organisations to make good on their promises, and put their money where their mouths are.

We must listen to each other, and we must expect to be heard. At the beginning of this book, I mentioned how so many people generously shared with me their own experiences of medical misogyny, misogynoir, and racial and gender violence. I carry their stories with me now and think of them often. There was the doctor telling his patient that she should expect acute pain in recovery, seeing as her delivery was 'unnatural' compared with vaginal delivery; the man who was told he was being 'a big girl's blouse' for not wanting a pelvic exam without a chaperone; the woman who should stop complaining about the pain of her vaginal dilation therapy because 'vaginas hurt'; the lesbian with vaginismus told that her condition was 'irrelevant' given the presumed nature of her sex life; the brown woman who was told she probably had gestational diabetes because 'Asians overeat'; the cis woman who was denied a smear test because she was 'too old' to be having sex; the intersex patient who was asked, as a child: 'Which one do you want to be?'

Not only do these words convey myriad presuppositions held about the patients – presuppositions that get in the way of the best care or otherwise actively cause harm – but they also prove the power that language has in medical settings. Language creates an identity that determines everything from bedside care to broader care plans, to funding decisions and fundamental research. Healthcare practitioners often have to make quick decisions based on sparse data – What do I think is best for this patient? What do I think this patient needs? – and perceived identities (age, gender, race, for instance) will go towards informing those decisions. This can be harmful for the patient, not just when those identities are incorrectly assigned, but when they are correctly assigned also – because they will always override the individuality of the patient. These words carry and maintain stereotypes. Stereotypes have no place in the hospital.

We must be mindful of how we use language in medical settings. It should never be used to put someone in the wrong box, or into a box they can never get out of. Using gender-inclusive language where we can is a powerful tool in freeing people up from the expectations of gender, and puts attention on their individual bodies and minds, rather than the stereotypical wants and needs socially attached to their gender. To use gender-neutral language is to try and step away from the biases that gendered language is inherently imbued with.

Asking this of a healthcare practitioner is no mean feat. Overworked and underpaid in most global healthcare settings, these people are simultaneously embedded in the broader world outside of the hospital or the doctor's surgery that continually reasserts and reinforces these very same biases – so you may ask: Aren't you asking too much? Is this really the most important thing?

This book seeks to argue that, yes, this *is* of vital importance. Firstly, these biases kill people. Secondly, the biases held in healthcare don't just mirror the biases outside of it, but in many ways they feed and contribute to it. Ideas about 'inferior races', for example, stem from pseudo-scientific arguments, and are perpetually legitimised when one race is treated better than others.

As for my own gynaecological health: I've come to think of it like the sea. For now, the waters are calm and clear. My prolapse seems to have retreated. I have learned to have sex in such a way that won't wake the beast, at least not for now. I know that one day the clouds will gather – the odds are stacked against me – so it's just a matter of time. And I will face that storm when it comes. I am hopeful that things will be better then – the surgical options more specialised, personalised and multiform, and with better success rates too. It's hard not to think of myself as part of a long line of women who have been failed – but the future has to be better; I can't let it not be. There are good days and bad days. You have to laugh – to carry on living, to carry on hoping – or else you'd cry and never stop.

Acknowledgements

The entire team at the Rosie Hospital, Cambridge, especially the midwives who brought our children into the world and managed to keep all three of us alive, and in some of the most adverse working conditions. My doctors Fiona Cornish and Kate Townsend. My midwife and now friend Claire Thompson.

The many people who generously shared their time and expertise. In particular: Mr Mark Slack, Dr John Latimer, Mr Edward Morris, Susanna Stanford, Dr Anne Hanley, Dr Sarah B. Rodriguez, Elizabeth Schmidt.

To friends and colleagues at St Catharine's College, and the Department of Pharmacology, Cambridge.

Our eternally fragrant agent John Ash, his assistant Erika Price and everyone who worked on the book at PEW Literary and CAA. Our editors Poppy Hampson, Becky Hardie, Rose Tomaszewska and the incredible Molly Slight. The team at Chatto and Vintage, especially assistant editor Asia Choudhury, marketing executive Mairéad Zielinksi and publicity manager Jessica Spivey. Emma's brilliant audiobook producer (and emotional support assistant) Lily Ridett, our copy editor Kate Johnson and our specialist sensitivity readers.

All of those who shared their personal experiences with us, especially Pauline Le Tixerant, Ellen Pilsworth and Nasheed Qamar Faruqi. Also, those who reached out to us over Twitter and Instagram; your stories brought us to tears. The campaigners all over the world who work tirelessly and often thanklessly to bring stories of medical misogyny to light.

Supportive and beloved friends, chief among them Sarah Cox, Lindsay Carter, Roxanne Middleton, Natasha Calder, Eamonn Bell, Hannah Nurse, Shira Lapidot, Tsila Zalt, Vita Peacock, Kate Sawyer, Simon Patterson and Kristen MacAskill. Our long-suffering neighbours Marion Cobby, Graham Day and Sam Stokes.

Jolanta and Zbigniew Szewczak for their unflinching generosity, and to Jola, in particular, for sharing with us her story. Our grandmothers Marynia, Danusia, Mary, Angela and Pamela. Our children Hieronim and Orlando, who deserve a better world.

And most of all we wish to thank Ann-Marie Harris. Your absence is like the sky, spread over everything. Please come home.

Notes

Introduction. I Fell Out of My Vagina (And So Could You!)

1 Louise Carroll et al., 'Pelvic Organ Prolapse: The Lived Experience', *PLOS ONE* 17, no. 11 (2 Nov. 2022), e0276788: https://doi.org/10.1371/journal.pone.0276788, accessed 12 December 2024.
2 Mohamed Abdel-fattah et al., 'Primary and Repeat Surgical Treatment for Female Pelvic Organ Prolapse and Incontinence in Parous Women in the UK: A Register Linkage Study', *BMJ Open* 1, no. 2 (1 Jan. 2011), e000206: https://doi.org/10.1136/bmjopen-2011-000206, accessed 12 December 2024.
3 'NHS England: NHS Pelvic Health Clinics to Help Tens of Thousands of Women across the Country', https://www.england.nhs.uk/2021/06/nhs-pelvic-health-clinics-to-help-tens-of-thousands-women-across-the-country/, accessed 15 July 2024.
4 Matthew D. Barber and Christopher Maher, 'Epidemiology and Outcome Assessment of Pelvic Organ Prolapse', *International Urogynecology Journal* 24, no. 11 (1 Nov. 2013), 1783–90: https://doi.org/10.1007/s00192-013-2169-9, accessed 12 December 2024.
5 Lale Say et al., 'Global Causes of Maternal Death: A WHO Systematic Analysis', *The Lancet Global Health* 2, no. 6 (1 June 2014), e323–33: https://doi.org/10.1016/S2214-109X(14)70227-X, accessed 12 December 2024.
6 Jianhua Wu et al., 'Impact of Initial Hospital Diagnosis on Mortality for Acute Myocardial Infarction: A National Cohort Study', *European Heart Journal. Acute Cardiovascular Care* 7, no. 2 (1 Mar. 2018), 139–48: https://doi.org/10.1177/2048872616661693, accessed 12 December 2024.
7 S. Holle et al., 'Sex Differences in Treatment and Outcome of Patients with Cardiogenic Shock Complicating Acute Myocardial Infarction', *European Heart Journal. Acute Cardiovascular Care* 11, no. Supplement 1 (1 May 2022), zuac041.022: https://doi.org/10.1093/ehjacc/zuac041.022, accessed 12 December 2024.

1. You Didn't Do Your Kegels

1 Arnold H. Kegel, 'Progressive Resistance Exercise in the Functional Restoration of the Perineal Muscles', *American Journal of Obstetrics & Gynecology* 56, no. 2 (1 Aug. 1948), 238–48: https://doi.org/10.1016/0002-9378(48)90266-X, accessed 12 December 2024.
2 'Pelvic Organ Prolapse – Treatment', nhs.uk, 20 Oct. 2017: https://www.nhs.uk/conditions/pelvic-organ-prolapse/treatment/, accessed 12 December 2024.
3 'Urinary Incontinence – Non-Surgical Treatment', nhs.uk, 23 Oct. 2017: https://www.nhs.uk/conditions/urinary-incontinence/treatment/, accessed 12 December 2024.
4 'Vulvodynia (Vulval Pain)', nhs.uk, 18 Oct. 2017: https://www.nhs.uk/conditions/vulvodynia/, accessed 12 December 2024.
5 'Vaginismus', nhs.uk, 11 Jan. 2018: https://www.nhs.uk/conditions/vaginismus/, accessed 12 December 2024.
6 'Pelvic Pain', nhs.uk, 19 Oct. 2017: https://www.nhs.uk/conditions/pelvic-pain/, accessed 12 December 2024.
7 'Pain Relief for Endometriosis: Endometriosis UK': https://www.endometriosis-uk.org/pain-relief-endometriosis, accessed 15 July 2024.
8 'Pelvic Pain'.
9 'Elvie Trainer: Smart Pelvic Floor Trainer and App', Elvie, https://www.elvie.com/en-gb/shop/elvie-trainer, accessed 15 July 2021.
10 'Urinary Incontinence'.
11 Patrick McKenzie, Jan Rohozinski, and Gopal Badlani, 'Genetic Influences on Stress Urinary Incontinence', *Current Opinion in Urology* 20, no. 4 (July 2010), 291–95: https://doi.org/10.1097/MOU.0b013e32833a4436, accessed 12 December 2024.
12 Elad Leron et al., 'Overactive Bladder Syndrome: Evaluation and Management', *Current Urology* 11, no. 3 (Mar. 2018), 117–25: https://doi.org/10.1159/000447205, accessed 12 December 2024.
13 Alison Bardsley, 'An Overview of Urinary Incontinence', *British Journal of Nursing* 25, no. 18 (13 Oct. 2016), S14–21: https://doi.org/10.12968/bjon.2016.25.18.S14, accessed 12 December 2024.
14 'Urinary Incontinence'.

15 Chantale Dumoulin, Licia P. Cacciari, and E. Jean C. Hay-Smith, 'Pelvic Floor Muscle Training versus No Treatment, or Inactive Control Treatments, for Urinary Incontinence in Women', *Cochrane Database of Systematic Reviews*, no. 10 (2018): https://doi.org/10.1002/14651858.CD 005654.pub4, accessed 12 December 2024.

16 Stephanie J. Woodley et al., 'Pelvic Floor Muscle Training for Preventing and Treating Urinary and Faecal Incontinence in Antenatal and Postnatal Women', *Cochrane Database of Systematic Reviews*, no. 5 (2020): https://doi.org/10.1002/14651858.CD007471.pub4, accessed 12 December 2024.

17 Suzanne Hagen and Diane Stark, 'Conservative Prevention and Management of Pelvic Organ Prolapse in Women', *Cochrane Database of Systematic Reviews*, no. 12 (2011): https://doi.org/10.1002/14651858.CD003882.pub4, accessed 12 December 2024.

18 Suzanne Hagen et al., 'Individualised Pelvic Floor Muscle Training in Women with Pelvic Organ Prolapse (POPPY): A Multicentre Randomised Controlled Trial', *The Lancet* 383, no. 9919 (1 Mar. 2014), 796–806: https://doi.org/10.1016/S0140-6736(13)61977-7, accessed 12 December 2024.

19 Ting Wang, Zhengfang Wen, and Meng Li, 'The Effect of Pelvic Floor Muscle Training for Women with Pelvic Organ Prolapse: A Meta-Analysis', *International Urogynecology Journal* 33, no. 7 (21 Mar. 2022): https://doi.org/10.1007/s00192-022-05139-z, accessed 12 December 2024.

20 Judith A. Katzmann, *Gill v Ethicon Sàrl*, No. NSD 1590 of 2012 (Federal Court of Australia, 21 Nov. 2019).

21 Katzmann, *Gill v Ethicon Sàrl*, at 1021.

22 Katzmann, *Gill v Ethicon Sàrl*, at 1033.

23 Katzmann, *Gill v Ethicon Sàrl*, at 1094.

24 Katzmann, *Gill v Ethicon Sàrl*, at 1130.

25 Naşide Mangir et al., 'Landmarks in Vaginal Mesh Development: Polypropylene Mesh for Treatment of SUI and POP', *Nature Reviews Urology* 16, no. 11 (Nov. 2019), 675–89: https://doi.org/10.1038/s41585-019-0230-2, accessed 12 December 2024.

26 'Inguinal Hernia Repair', nhs.uk, 23 Oct. 2017: https://www.nhs.uk/conditions/inguinal-hernia-repair/what-happens/, accessed 12 December 2024.

27 Markus Gahleitner and Christian Paulik, 'Polypropylene', in *Ullmann's Encyclopedia of Industrial Chemistry* (Weinheim, 2014), 1–44: https://doi.org/10.1002/14356007.021_004.pub2, accessed 12 December 2024.
28 Katzmann, *Gill v Ethicon Sàrl*, at 93.
29 David F. Williams, 'On the Mechanisms of Biocompatibility', *Biomaterials* 29, no. 20 (July 2008), 2941–53: https://doi.org/10.1016/j.biomaterials.2008.04.023, accessed 12 December 2024.
30 James M. Anderson, Analiz Rodriguez, and David T. Chang, 'Foreign Body Reaction to Biomaterials', *Seminars in Immunology* 20, no. 2 (Apr. 2008), 86–100: https://doi.org/10.1016/j.smim.2007.11.004, accessed 12 December 2024.
31 'First Do No Harm: The Report of the Independent Medicines and Medical Devices Safety Review', Independent Medicines and Medical Devices Safety Review (8 July 2020).
32 H. P. Dietz et al., 'Mechanical Properties of Urogynecologic Implant Materials', *International Urogynecology Journal and Pelvic Floor Dysfunction* 14, no. 4 (Oct. 2003), 239–43; discussion 243: https://doi.org/10.1007/s00192-003-1041-8, accessed 12 December 2024.
33 Katzmann, *Gill v Ethicon Sàrl*, at 173–89.
34 'First Do No Harm'.
35 'First Do No Harm'.
36 Jack Moore, J. T. Armstrong, and Seward H. Wills, 'The Use of Tantalum Mesh in Cystocele with Critical Report of Ten Cases', *American Journal of Obstetrics & Gynecology*, Transactions of the Central Association of Obstetricians and Gynecologists, 69, no. 5 (1 May 1955), 1127–35: https://doi.org/10.1016/0002-9378(55)90109-5, accessed 12 December 2024.
37 Marc Soler, Pierre J. Verhaeghe, and Réne Stoppa, 'Polyester (Dacron®) Mesh', in *Abdominal Wall Hernias: Principles and Management*, edited by Robert Bendavid et al. (New York, NY, 2001), 266–71: https://doi.org/10.1007/978-1-4419-8574-3_35, accessed 12 December 2024.
38 'First Do No Harm'.
39 'Urinary Incontinence: An Inevitable Part of Aging?', National Poll on Healthy Aging, 1 Nov. 2018: https://www.healthyagingpoll.org/reports-more/report/urinary-incontinence-inevitable-part-aging, accessed 12 December 2024.

40 Center for Devices and Radiological Health, 'Premarket Notification 510(k)', FDA (FDA, 12 May 2023): https://www.fda.gov/medical-devices/premarket-submissions-selecting-and-preparing-correct-submission/premarket-notification-510k, accessed 12 December 2024.

41 Carl J. Heneghan et al., 'Trials of Transvaginal Mesh Devices for Pelvic Organ Prolapse: A Systematic Database Review of the US FDA Approval Process', *BMJ Open* 7, no. 12 (1 Dec. 2017), e017125: https://doi.org/10.1136/bmjopen-2017-017125, accessed 12 December 2024.

42 L. Lewis Wall and Douglas Brown, 'The Perils of Commercially Driven Surgical Innovation', *American Journal of Obstetrics & Gynecology* 202, no. 1 (1 Jan. 2010), 30.e1–30.e4: https://doi.org/10.1016/j.ajog.2009.05.031, accessed 12 December 2024.

43 K. C. Kobashi et al., 'Erosion of Woven Polyester Pubovaginal Sling', *Journal of Urology* 162, no. 6 (Dec. 1999), 2070–72: https://doi.org/10.1016/S0022-5347(05)68103-7, accessed 12 December 2024.

44 Wall and Brown, 'The Perils of Commercially Driven Surgical Innovation'.

45 Jonathan Gornall, 'How Mesh Became a Four Letter Word', *BMJ: British Medical Journal* 363 (2018): https://www.jstor.org/stable/26963613, accessed 12 December 2024.

46 Heneghan et al., 'Trials of Transvaginal Mesh Devices for Pelvic Organ Prolapse'.

47 Jonathan Gornall, 'The Trial that Launched Millions of Mesh Implant Procedures: Did Money Compromise the Outcome?', *BMJ* 363 (10 Oct. 2018), k4155: https://doi.org/10.1136/bmj.k4155, accessed 12 December 2024.

48 Ulf Ulmsten and Peter Petros, 'Intravaginal Slingplasty (IVS): An Ambulatory Surgical Procedure for Treatment of Female Urinary Incontinence', *Scandinavian Journal of Urology and Nephrology* 29, no. 1 (1 Mar. 1995), 75–82: https://doi.org/10.3109/00365599509180543, accessed 12 December 2024.

49 U. Ulmsten et al., 'An Ambulatory Surgical Procedure under Local Anesthesia for Treatment of Female Urinary Incontinence', *International Urogynecology Journal and Pelvic Floor Dysfunction* 7, no. 2 (1996): 81–85; discussion 85–86: https://doi.org/10.1007/BF01902378, accessed 12 December 2024.

50 Gornall, 'The Trial that Launched Millions of Mesh Implant Procedures': https://www.bmj.com/content/363/bmj.k4155
51 U. Ulmsten et al., 'A Multicenter Study of Tension-Free Vaginal Tape (TVT) for Surgical Treatment of Stress Urinary Incontinence', *International Urogynecology Journal and Pelvic Floor Dysfunction* 9, no. 4 (1998), 210–13: https://doi.org/10.1007/BF01901606, accessed 12 December 2024.
52 Gornall, 'The Trial that Launched Millions of Mesh Implant Procedures'.
53 Ibid.
54 S. Salvatore et al., 'Prosthetic Surgery for Genital Prolapse: Functional Outcome', *Neurourology and Urodynamics* 21, no. 4 (2002): 10; Christopher Maher et al., 'Surgical Management of Pelvic Organ Prolapse in Women', *Cochrane Database of Systematic Reviews*, no. 4 (2004): https://doi.org/10.1002/14651858.CD004014.pub2, accessed 12 December 2024.
55 Heneghan et al., 'Trials of Transvaginal Mesh Devices for Pelvic Organ Prolapse'.
56 *Batiste* v *McNabb, Johnson & Johnson and Ethicon, Inc.* (District Court of Dallas County, 25 Mar. 2014).
57 *Batiste* v *McNabb, Johnson & Johnson and Ethicon, Inc.* at 48.
58 Bill Madden, 'Pelvic Mesh Litigation – Outcome of the Federal Court of Australia Trial in "*Gill* v *Ethicon Sarl* (No 5)"', *Australian Health Law Bulletin* 28, no. 3 (July 2020), 53–8: https://doi.org/10.3316/agispt.20200813034887, accessed 12 December 2024.
59 Angela Wood and Elizabeth Reed, 'Full Court Dismisses Johnson & Johnson's Appeal against Findings in Pelvic Mesh Class Action', Maddocks: https://www.maddocks.com.au/insights/full-court-dismisses-johnson-johnsons-appeal-against-findings-in-pelvic-mesh-class-action, accessed 28 July 2024.
60 Hannah Devlin, 'Pharma firm sold mesh implant despite pain warnings', *Guardian*, 27 Nov. 2018: https://www.theguardian.com/society/2018/nov/27/vaginal-mesh-implant-sold-despite-warnings-could-cause-pain-johnson-johnson, accessed 12 December 2024.
61 Devlin, 'Pharma firm sold mesh implant despite pain warnings'.
62 Devlin, 'Pharma firm sold mesh implant despite pain warnings'.
63 Hannah Devlin, 'Revealed: Johnson & Johnson's "irresponsible" actions over vaginal mesh implant', *Guardian*, 29 Sept. 2017: https://

www.theguardian.com/society/2017/sep/29/revealed-johnson-johnsons-irresponsible-actions-over-vaginal-mesh-implant, accessed 12 December 2024.

64 Christopher Knaus, 'Johnson & Johnson vaginal mesh presentation featured lingerie-clad women, court told', *Guardian*, 9 Oct. 2017: https://www.theguardian.com/australia-news/2017/oct/09/johnson-johnson-vaginal-mesh-presentation-featured-lingerie-clad-women-court-told, accessed 12 December 2024.

65 Gabrielle Jackson, 'Why don't doctors trust women? Because they don't know much about us', *Guardian*, 1 Sept. 2019: https://www.theguardian.com/books/2019/sep/02/why-dont-doctors-trust-women-because-they-dont-know-much-about-us, accessed 12 December 2024.

66 Kerri Smith, 'Women's Health Research Lacks Funding – in a Series of Charts', *Nature* 617, no. 7959 (May 2023), 28–9: https://doi.org/10.1038/d41586-023-01475-2, accessed 12 December 2024.

67 Hamilton Moses III et al., 'The Anatomy of Medical Research: US and International Comparisons', *JAMA* 313, no. 2 (13 Jan. 2015), 174–89: https://doi.org/10.1001/jama.2014.15939, accessed 12 December 2024.

68 Jonathan Stempel, 'Boston Scientific in $189 million settlement with US states over surgical mesh devices', *Reuters*, 23 Mar. 2021: https://www.reuters.com/article/business/healthcare-pharmaceuticals/boston-scientific-in-189-million-settlement-with-us-states-over-surgical-mesh-idUSKBN2BF29C/, accessed 12 December 2024.

69 Angela Wood and Jemima Stratton, 'Settlement Approval for Pelvic Mesh Class Action Against Johnson & Johnson and Ethicon', Maddocks: https://www.maddocks.com.au/insights/settlement-approval-for-pelvic-mesh-class-action-against-johnson-johnson-and-ethicon, accessed 28 July 2024.

70 Melissa Davey, 'Australia bans transvaginal mesh products as "too risky"', *Guardian*, 29 Nov. 2017: https://www.theguardian.com/society/2017/nov/30/australia-bans-transvaginal-mesh-products-as-too-risky, accessed 12 December 2024.

71 'Pelvic Organ Prolapse – Treatment', accessed 12 December 2024.

72 Thomas F. Baskett (ed.), 'Le Fort, Léon Clément (1829–1893): Le Fort Operation', in *Eponyms and Names in Obstetrics and Gynaecology*, 3rd edition

(Cambridge, 2019), 236: https://doi.org/10.1017/9781108421706.190, accessed 12 December 2024.

73 Ali Azadi et al., 'Chapter 49: Obliterative Procedures', in *Ostergard's Textbook of Urogynecology: Female Pelvic Medicine & Reconstructive Surgery* (Philadelphia, PA, 2022).

74 Michelle E. Koski et al., 'Colpocleisis for Advanced Pelvic Organ Prolapse', *Urology* 80, no. 3 (1 Sept. 2012), 542–46: https://doi.org/10.1016/j.urology.2012.06.009, accessed 12 December 2024.

2. No Pain, No Gain

1 'Agenda: Board of Examiners for Nursing' (Department of Public Health, 15 June 2022): https://portal.ct.gov/dph/public-health-hearing-office/board-of-examiners-for-nursing/meeting-agendas-and-minutes, accessed 12 December 2024.

2 'Yale Agrees to Pay $308K to Resolve Allegations of Violations of Controlled Substances Act', 4 Oct. 2022: https://www.justice.gov/usao-ct/pr/yale-agrees-pay-308k-resolve-allegations-violations-controlled-substances-act, accessed 12 December 2024.

3 'Nurse Pleads Guilty to Tampering with Fentanyl Vials Intended for Patients at Fertility Clinic', United States Attorney's Office, District of Connecticut, 2 Mar. 2021: https://www.justice.gov/usao-ct/pr/nurse-pleads-guilty-tampering-fentanyl-vials-intended-patients-fertility-clinic, accessed 12 December 2024.

4 Susan Burton et al., *The Retrievals* (podcast), Ep. 4, 'The Clinic', *The New York Times*, 27 July 2023: https://www.nytimes.com/2023/07/27/podcasts/serial-the-retrievals-yale-fertility-clinic.html, accessed 12 December 2024.

5 Burton et al., *The Retrievals* (podcast), Ep. 3, 'The Sentence', 13 July 2023: https://www.nytimes.com/2023/07/13/podcasts/serial-the-retrievals-yale-fertility-clinic.html, accessed 12 December 2024.

6 Burton et al., *The Retrievals* (podcast), Ep. 1: 'The Patients', *The New York Times*, 29 June 2023: https://www.nytimes.com/2023/06/29/podcasts/serial-the-retrievals-yale-fertility-clinic.html, accessed 12 December 2024.

7 Gulam Bahadur et al., 'Correlation of IVF Outcomes and Number of Oocytes Retrieved: A UK Retrospective Longitudinal Observational Study of 172 341 Non-Donor Cycles', *BMJ Open* 13, no. 1 (2 Jan. 2023), e064711: https://doi.org/10.1136/bmjopen-2022-064711, accessed 12 December 2024.

8 Andrew Steptoe, 'Biology: Changing the World – a Tribute to Patrick Steptoe, Robert Edwards and Jean Purdy', *Human Fertility* 18, no. 4 (2 Oct. 2015), 232–3: https://doi.org/10.3109/14647273.2015.1077657, accessed 12 December 2024.

9 Josh Halliday, 'Female nurse who played crucial role in IVF ignored on plaque', *Guardian*, 9 June 2019: https://www.theguardian.com/society/2019/jun/10/jean-purdy-female-nurse-who-played-crucial-role-in-ivf-ignored-on-plaque, accessed 12 December 2024.

10 Martin H. Johnson et al., 'Why the Medical Research Council Refused Robert Edwards and Patrick Steptoe Support for Research on Human Conception in 1971', *Human Reproduction* 25, no. 9 (Sept. 2010), 2157–74: https://doi.org/10.1093/humrep/deq155, accessed 12 December 2024.

11 'The First IVF Baby Was Born 40 Years Ago Today', *ABC News*, 24 July 2018: https://www.abc.net.au/news/science/2018-07-25/first-ivf-baby-louise-joy-brown-turns-40/10017032, accessed 12 December 2024.

12 Bart C. J. M. Fauser, 'Towards the Global Coverage of a Unified Registry of IVF Outcomes', *Reproductive BioMedicine Online* 38, no. 2 (1 Feb. 2019), 133–37: https://doi.org/10.1016/j.rbmo.2018.12.001, accessed 12 December 2024.

13 'Universal Declaration of Human Rights', United Nations: https://www.un.org/en/about-us/universal-declaration-of-human-rights, accessed 19 July 2024.

14 Ethics Committee of the American Society for Reproductive Medicine, 'Disparities in Access to Effective Treatment for Infertility in the United States: An Ethics Committee Opinion', *Fertility and Sterility* 104, no. 5 (Nov. 2015), 1104–10: https://doi.org/10.1016/j.fertnstert.2015.07.1139, accessed 12 December 2024.

15 Nicole Knight, 'A Global View on IVF Treatment and Access', Empowered Women's Health, https://www.volusonclub.net/empow

ered-womens-health/a-global-view-of-ivf-treatment-and-access/, accessed 8 Aug. 2022.

16 Benjamin J. Peipert et al., 'Impact of in Vitro Fertilization State Mandates for Third Party Insurance Coverage in the United States: A Review and Critical Assessment', *Reproductive Biology and Endocrinology* 20 (4 Aug. 2022), 111: https://doi.org/10.1186/s12958-022-00984-5, accessed 12 December 2024.

17 Courtney Rubin, 'Are Pricey Fertility Treatments Helping Women Have Babies . . . Or Preying on Them?', Women's Health, 19 Oct. 2019: https://www.womenshealthmag.com/health/a29136055/fertility-treatment-add-on-accessories/, accessed 12 December 2024.

18 Rubin, 'Are Pricey Fertility Treatments . . .'.

19 E. A. Spencer et al., 'Claims for Fertility Interventions: A Systematic Assessment of Statements on UK Fertility Centre Websites', *BMJ Open* 6, no. 11 (1 Nov. 2016), e013940: https://doi.org/10.1136/bmjopen-2016-013940, accessed 12 December 2024.

20 'From Assisted Hatching to Embryo Glue, Most IVF "Add-Ons" Rest on Shaky Science, Studies Find', *STAT* (blog), 5 Nov. 2019: https://www.statnews.com/2019/11/05/ivf-add-ons-shaky-science-studies/, accessed 12 December 2024.

21 'UK Fertility Regulator Launches Improved Ratings for Fertility Treatment "Add-Ons"', HFEA: https://www.hfea.gov.uk/about-us/news-and-press-releases/2023/uk-fertility-regulator-launches-improved-ratings-for-fertility-treatment-add-ons/, accessed 20 July 2024.

22 Rubin, 'Are Pricey Fertility Treatments . . .'.

23 Rubin, 'Are Pricey Fertility Treatments . . .'.

24 'From Assisted Hatching to Embryo Glue . . .'.

25 Sarah Lensen et al., 'A Randomized Trial of Endometrial Scratching before In Vitro Fertilization', *New England Journal of Medicine* 380, no. 4 (24 Jan. 2019), 325–34: https://doi.org/10.1056/NEJMoa1808737, accessed 12 December 2024.

26 S. Lensen, L. Sadler, and C. Farquhar, 'Endometrial Scratching for Subfertility: Everyone's Doing It', *Human Reproduction* 31, no. 6 (1 June 2016), 1241–44: https://doi.org/10.1093/humrep/dew053, accessed 12 December 2024.

27 Steven D. Schrock and Carolyn Harraway-Smith, 'Labor Analgesia', *American Family Physician* 85, no. 5 (1 Mar. 2012), 447–54.
28 Katherine Arendt and Scott Segal, 'Why Epidurals Do Not Always Work', *Reviews in Obstetrics and Gynecology* 1, no. 2 (2008), 49–55: https://www.ncbi.nlm.nih.gov/pmc/articles/PMC2505163/, accessed 12 December 2024.
29 'Incidence of Epidural Hematoma, Infection, and Neurologic Injury in Obstetric Patients with Epidural Analgesia/Anesthesia', *Obstetric Anesthesia Digest* 27, no. 1 (Mar. 2007), 4: https://journals.lww.com/obstetricanesthesia/citation/2007/03000/incidence_of_epidural_hematoma,_infection,_and.3.aspx, accessed 12 December 2024.
30 'Pain Relief in Labour', nhs.uk, 2 Dec. 2020: https://www.nhs.uk/pregnancy/labour-and-birth/what-happens/pain-relief-in-labour/, accessed 12 December 2024.
31 Millicent Anim-Somuah et al., 'Epidural versus Non-epidural or No Analgesia for Pain Management in Labour', *Cochrane Database of Systematic Reviews*, no. 5 (2018), https://doi.org/10.1002/14651858.CD000331.pub4/, accessed 12 December 2024.
32 Rachel J. Kearns et al., 'Epidural Analgesia during Labour and Severe Maternal Morbidity: Population Based Study', *BMJ* 385 (22 May 2024), e077190: https://doi.org/10.1136/bmj-2023-077190/, accessed 12 December 2024.
33 G. A. Skowronski, 'Pain Relief in Childbirth: Changing Historical and Feminist Perspectives', *Anaesthesia and Intensive Care* 43, no. 1 Supplement (July 2015), 25–28: https://doi.org/10.1177/0310057X150430S106, accessed 12 December 2024.
34 Alexander J. Butwick, Cynthia A. Wong, and Nan Guo, 'Maternal Body Mass Index and Use of Labor Neuraxial Analgesia: A Population-Based Retrospective Cohort Study', *Anesthesiology* 129, no. 3 (1 Sept. 2018), 448–58: https://doi.org/10.1097/ALN.0000000000002322, accessed 12 December 2024.
35 Jacek Furmanik, 'Labour Epidural Analgesia in Poland in 2009 – a Survey', *Anaesthesiology Intensive Therapy* 45, no. 3 (Sept. 2013), 149–52: https://doi.org/10.5603/AIT.2013.0031, accessed 12 December 2024.
36 The Epidural and Position Trial Collaborative Group, 'Upright versus Lying Down Position in Second Stage of Labour in Nulliparous

Women with Low Dose Epidural: BUMPES Randomised Controlled Trial', *BMJ* 359 (18 Oct. 2017), j4471: https://doi.org/10.1136/bmj.j4471, accessed 12 December 2024.

37 Camille Le Ray and Nathalie Lelong, 'Les Enquêtes Nationales Périnatales: Les naissances, le suivi à deux mois et les établissement. Situation et évolution depuis 2016' (Paris: Centre de Recherche en Epidémiologie et Statistiques, Oct. 2022): https://cress-umr1153.fr/fr/project/les-enquetes-nationales-perinatales/, accessed 12 December 2024.

38 Sezin Topçu, 'Adopting an "Unlearner" Technology? Knowledge Battles over Pharmaceutical Pain Relief in Childbirth in Post-1968 France', *Reproductive Biomedicine & Society Online* 13 (1 Aug. 2021), 1–13: https://doi.org/10.1016/j.rbms.2021.03.002, accessed 12 December 2024.

39 Amelia Hill, '"I asked three times for an epidural": Why are women being denied pain relief during childbirth?', *Guardian*, 4 Mar. 2020: https://www.theguardian.com/lifeandstyle/2020/mar/04/i-asked-three-times-for-an-epidural-why-are-women-being-denied-pain-relief, accessed 12 December 2024.

40 Joanna Moorhead, 'Epidurals are for wimps', *Independent*, 22 May 2006: https://www.independent.co.uk/life-style/health-and-families/health-news/epidurals-are-for-wimps-479369.html, accessed 12 December 2024.

41 I. Loudon, 'Deaths in Childbed from the Eighteenth Century to 1935', *Medical History* 30, no. 1 (Jan. 1986), 1–41: https://doi.org/10.1017/s0025727300045014, accessed 12 December 2024.

42 'Hysteroscopy Action', Hysteroscopy Action: https://www.hysteroscopyaction.org.uk/, accessed 21 July 2024.

43 Shirish S. Sheth et al., 'Sonographic Evaluation of Uterine Volume and Its Clinical Importance', *Journal of Obstetrics and Gynaecology Research* 43, no. 1 (2017), 185–89: https://doi.org/10.1111/jog.13189, accessed 12 December 2024.

44 'AAGL Practice Report: Practice Guidelines for the Management of Hysteroscopic Distending Media: (Replaces Hysteroscopic Fluid Monitoring Guidelines. J Am Assoc Gynecol Laparosc. 2000;7:167–168.)', *Journal of Minimally Invasive Gynecology* 20, no. 2 (1 Mar. 2013), 137–48: https://doi.org/10.1016/j.jmig.2012.12.002, accessed 12 December 2024.

45 Baskett (ed.), 'Pantaleoni, D Commander (*c.*1869): Hysteroscopy', in *Eponyms and Names*, 310: https://doi.org/10.1017/9781108421706.251, accessed 12 December 2024.

46 Baskett (ed.), 'Pantaleoni, D Commander . . .'.

47 'Hysteroscopy', nhs.uk, 23 Oct. 2017: https://www.nhs.uk/conditions/hysteroscopy/, accessed 12 December 2024.

48 P. De Iaco et al., 'Acceptability and Pain of Outpatient Hysteroscopy', *Journal of the American Association of Gynecologic Laparoscopists* 7, no. 1 (Feb. 2000), 71–75: https://doi.org/10.1016/s1074-3804(00)80012-2, accessed 12 December 2024.

49 Juliana A. de Carvalho Schettini et al., 'Pain Evaluation in Outpatients Undergoing Diagnostic Anesthesia-Free Hysteroscopy in a Teaching Hospital: A Cohort Study', *Journal of Minimally Invasive Gynecology* 14, no. 6 (1 Nov. 2007), 729–35: https://doi.org/10.1016/j.jmig.2007.05.009, accessed 12 December 2024.

50 Jessica Furseth, 'When women are denied pain relief during invasive procedures', *Vice* (blog), 16 Jan. 2019: https://www.vice.com/en/article/zmdday/is-hysteroscopy-painful-womens-health, accessed 12 December 2024.

51 'NHS Hysteroscopy Treatment', Hansard, UK Parliament, 31 Jan. 2023: https://hansard.parliament.uk/commons/2023-01-31/debates/6964ABD5-815F-4C26-8759-50EE1CB04E5B/NHSHysteroscopy-Treatment, accessed 12 December 2024.

52 'Causes of Cervical Cancer', nhs.uk, 20 Oct. 2017: https://www.nhs.uk/conditions/cervical-cancer/causes/, accessed 12 December 2024.

53 Stephen W. Leslie, Hussain Sajjad, and Sandeep Kumar, 'Genital Warts', in *StatPearls* (Treasure Island, FL, 2024): http://www.ncbi.nlm.nih.gov/books/NBK441884/, accessed 12 December 2024.

54 'HPV and Cancer – National Cancer Institute', 3 Jan. 2019: https://www.cancer.gov/about-cancer/causes-prevention/risk/infectious-agents/hpv-and-cancer, accessed 12 December 2024.

55 Tatyana S. Gurina and Lary Simms, 'Histology, Staining', in *StatPearls* (Treasure Island, FL, 2024): http://www.ncbi.nlm.nih.gov/books/NBK557663/, accessed 12 December 2024.

56 'When You'll Be Invited for Cervical Screening', nhs.uk, 14 July 2023: https://www.nhs.uk/conditions/cervical-screening/when-youll-be-invited/, accessed 12 December 2024.

57 P. Sasieni, J. Adams, and J. Cuzick, 'Benefit of Cervical Screening at Different Ages: Evidence from the UK Audit of Screening Histories', *British Journal of Cancer* 89, no. 1 (7 July 2003), 88–93: https://doi.org/10.1038/sj.bjc.6600974, accessed 12 December 2024.

58 'Women's Health: Sex, Intimacy, and Menopause: National Poll on Healthy Aging', 11 May 2022: https://www.healthyagingpoll.org/reports-more/report/womens-health-sex-intimacy-and-menopause, accessed 12 December 2024.

59 Clare Gilham, Emma J. Crosbie, and Julian Peto, 'Cervical Cancer Screening in Older Women', *BMJ* 372 (5 Feb. 2021), n280: https://doi.org/10.1136/bmj.n280, accessed 12 December 2024.

60 Anonymous, 'Let's Talk About . . . Smear Tests after Menopause', Jo's Cervical Cancer Trust, 15 Oct. 2019: https://www.jostrust.org.uk/about-us/news-and-blog/smear-tests-after-menopause, accessed 12 December 2024.

61 'Cervical Screening Saves Lives – Evaluating the National Campaign – PHE Screening', 28 Sept. 2021: https://phescreening.blog.gov.uk/2021/09/28/cervical-screening-saves-lives/, accessed 12 December 2024.

62 Kirsty F. Bennett et al., 'Barriers to Cervical Screening and Interest in Self-Sampling Among Women Who Actively Decline Screening', *Journal of Medical Screening* 25, no. 4 (Dec. 2018), 211–17: https://doi.org/10.1177/0969141318767471, accessed 12 December 2024.

63 'Barriers to Cervical Screening among 25–29 Year Olds', Jo's Cervical Cancer Trust, 15 June 2017: https://www.jostrust.org.uk/about-us/our-research-and-policy-work/our-research/barriers-cervical-screening-among-25-29-year-olds, accessed 12 December 2024.

64 'Barriers to Cervical Screening among 25–29 Year Olds'.

65 'Embarrassment Makes Women Avoid Smear Tests, Charity Says', *BBC News*, 22 Jan. 2018: https://www.bbc.com/news/health-42747892, accessed 12 December 2024.

66 'Women reveal the reasons they don't go for smear tests', *Independent*, 21 Jan. 2019: https://www.independent.co.uk/life-style/

smear-test-cervical-screening-attend-reason-embarrassment-jos-cervical-cancer-trust-a8738416.html, accessed 12 December 2024.

67 'Endometriosis': https://www.who.int/news-room/fact-sheets/detail/endometriosis, accessed 21 July 2024.

68 Ping Teresa Yeh et al., 'Self-Sampling for Human Papillomavirus (HPV) Testing: A Systematic Review and Meta-Analysis', *BMJ Global Health* 4, no. 3 (14 May 2019), e001351: https://doi.org/10.1136/bmjgh-2018-001351, accessed 12 December 2024.

69 Alison M. Berner et al., 'Attitudes of Transgender Men and Non-Binary People to Cervical Screening: A Cross-Sectional Mixed-Methods Study in the UK', *British Journal of General Practice* 71, no. 709 (1 Aug. 2021), e614–25: https://doi.org/10.3399/BJGP.2020.0905, accessed 12 December 2024.

70 'Trans Lives Survey 2021: Enduring the UK's Hostile Environment': https://transactual.org.uk/wp-content/uploads/TransLivesSurvey 2021.pdf, accessed 12 December 2024.

71 Sarah M. Peitzmeier et al., 'Female-to-Male Patients Have High Prevalence of Unsatisfactory Paps Compared to Non-Transgender Females: Implications for Cervical Cancer Screening', *Journal of General Internal Medicine* 29, no. 5 (May 2014), 778–84: https://doi.org/10.1007/s11606-013-2753-1, accessed 12 December 2024.

72 'NHS England: NHS Gives Women Human Papillomavirus Virus (HPV) Home Testing Kits to Cut Cancer Deaths': https://www.england.nhs.uk/2021/02/nhs-gives-women-hpv-home-testing-kits-to-cut-cancer-deaths/, accessed 16 January 2022.

73 Rebecca Landy et al., 'Non-Speculum Sampling Approaches for Cervical Screening in Older Women: Randomised Controlled Trial', *British Journal of General Practice* 72, no. 714 (1 Jan. 2022), e26–33: https://doi.org/10.3399/BJGP.2021.0350, accessed 12 December 2024.

74 Jerome L. Belinson et al., 'The Mexican Cervical Cancer Screening Trial: Self-Sampling for Human Papillomavirus with Unaided Visual Inspection as a Secondary Screen', *International Journal of Gynecologic Cancer* 19, no. 1 (1 Jan. 2009): https://doi.org/10.1111/IGC.0b013e318197f479, accessed 12 December 2024.

75 'How to Use a Vaginal Dilator', Memorial Sloan Kettering Cancer Center: https://www.mskcc.org/cancer-care/patient-education/how-use-vaginal-dilator, accessed 3 June 2022.

76 Kat Macey et al., 'Women's Experiences of Using Vaginal Trainers (Dilators) to Treat Vaginal Penetration Difficulties Diagnosed as Vaginismus: A Qualitative Interview Study', *BMC Women's Health* 15, no. 1 (20 June 2015), 49: https://doi.org/10.1186/s12905-015-0201-6, accessed 12 December 2024.

77 Peggy J. Kleinplatz, 'Sex Therapy for Vaginismus: A Review, Critique, and Humanistic Alternative', *Journal of Humanistic Psychology* 38, no. 2 (1 Apr. 1998), 51–81: https://doi.org/10.1177/00221678980382004, accessed 12 December 2024.

78 William H. Masters and Virginia E. Johnson, *Human Sexual Inadequacy* (Boston, MA, 1970), p. 281.

79 Marie-Andrée Lahaie et al., 'Vaginismus: A Review of the Literature on the Classification/Diagnosis, Etiology and Treatment', *Women's Health* 6, no. 5 (1 Sept. 2010), 705–19: https://doi.org/10.2217/WHE.10.46, accessed 12 December 2024.

80 C. P. Roberts, M. J. Haber, and J. A. Rock, 'Vaginal Creation for Müllerian Agenesis', *American Journal of Obstetrics & Gynecology* 185, no. 6 (Dec. 2001), 1349–52; discussion 1352–3: https://doi.org/10.1067/mob.2001.119075, accessed 12 December 2024.

81 A. Ketheeswaran et al., 'Vaginal Dilation in Mayer-Rokitansky-Kuster-Hauser (MRKH) Syndrome', *Journal of Minimally Invasive Gynecology* 22, no. 6 (1 Nov. 2015), S103–4: https://doi.org/10.1016/j.jmig.2015.08.279, accessed 12 December 2024.

82 Oluyemisi A. Adeyemi-Fowode and Jennifer E. Dietrich, 'Assessing the Experience of Vaginal Dilator Use and Potential Barriers to Ongoing Use among a Focus Group of Women with Mayer-Rokitansky-Küster-Hauser Syndrome', *Journal of Pediatric and Adolescent Gynecology* 30, no. 4 (1 Aug. 2017), 491–94: https://doi.org/10.1016/j.jpag.2017.02.002, accessed 12 December 2024.

83 Adeyemi-Fowode and Dietrich, 'Assessing the Experience of Vaginal Dilator Use . . .'.

84 'Vaginal Dilators and MRKH: Information for Patients, Relatives and Carers', Imperial College Healthcare NHS Trust, Feb. 2019: https://www.imperial.nhs.uk/-/media/website/patient-information-leaflets/childrens-services/disorders-of-sexual-development-and-adolescent-gynaecology/

vaginal-dilator-therapy-for-mrkh.pdf?rev=a8ca71f3f08b4d54a2a dec2480783970, accessed 12 December 2024.
85 John A. Rock et al., 'Success Following Vaginal Creation for Müllerian Agenesis', *Fertility and Sterility* 39, no. 6 (1 June 1983), 809–13: https://doi.org/10.1016/S0015-0282(16)47121-9, accessed 12 December 2024.
86 A. D'Alberton and F. Santi, 'Formation of a Neovagina by Coitus', *Obstetrics and Gynecology* 40, no. 5 (Nov. 1972), 763–64.

3. We're Listening

1 Kristen R. Ghodsee, *Why Women Have Better Sex Under Socialism: And Other Arguments for Economic Independence* (London, 2018).
2 '6 lat programu Rodzina 500+. Inwestycja, która opłaca się wszystkim', Ministerstwo Rodziny, Pracy i Polityki Społecznej, 1 Apr. 2022: https://www.gov.pl/web/rodzina/6-lat-programu-rodzina-500-inwestycja-ktora-oplaca-sie-wszystkim, accessed 12 December 2024.
3 Barbara Baranowska et al., 'Is There Respectful Maternity Care in Poland? Women's Views About Care during Labor and Birth', *BMC Pregnancy and Childbirth* 19, no. 1 (23 Dec. 2019), 520: https://doi.org/10.1186/s12884-019-2675-y, accessed 12 December 2024.
4 'An International Collaboration Investigating Childbirth-Related Trauma across the World', City, University of London (City, University of London, 16 July 2023): https://www.city.ac.uk/news-and-events/news/2023/07/international-collaboration-investigating-childbirth-related-trauma-across-world, accessed 12 December 2024.
5 Julia Leinweber et al., 'Developing a Woman-Centered, Inclusive Definition of Traumatic Childbirth Experiences: A Discussion Paper', *Birth* 49, no. 4 (2022), 687–96: https://doi.org/10.1111/birt.12634.
6 https://pubmed.ncbi.nlm.nih.gov/34242670/, accessed 12 December 2024.
7 Diana Bužinskienė, Živilė Sabonytė-Balšaitienė, and Tomas Poškus, 'Perianal Diseases in Pregnancy and After Childbirth: Frequency, Risk Factors, Impact on Women's Quality of Life and Treatment Methods', *Frontiers in Surgery* 9 (18 Feb. 2022): 788823: https://doi.org/10.3389/fsurg.2022.788823m, accessed 12 December 2024.

8 Chris Kettle and Susan Tohill, 'Perineal Care', *BMJ Clinical Evidence* 2008 (24 Sept. 2008): 1401.

9 Bužinskienė, Sabonytė-Balšaitienė, and Poškus, 'Perianal Diseases . . .', accessed 12 December 2024.

10 John O. L. DeLancey et al., 'Pelvic Floor Injury during Vaginal Birth Is Life-Altering and Preventable: What Can We Do About It?', *American Journal of Obstetrics & Gynecology* 230, no. 3 (1 Mar. 2024): 279-294.e2: https://doi.org/10.1016/j.ajog.2023.11.1253, accessed 12 December 2024.

11 Cassandra N. Ramar, and W. R. Grimes, 'Perineal Lacerations', in *StatPearls* (Treasure Island, FL, 2024): http://www.ncbi.nlm.nih.gov/books/NBK559068/, accessed 12 December 2024.

12 İsmet Gün, Bülent Doğan, and Özkan Özdamar, 'Long- and Short-Term Complications of Episiotomy', *Turkish Journal of Obstetrics and Gynecology* 13, no. 3 (Sept. 2016): 144–48: https://doi.org/10.4274/tjod.00087, accessed 12 December 2024.

13 'Urinary Retention Following Childbirth', Cambridge University Hospitals: https://www.cuh.nhs.uk/patient-information/urinary-retention-following-childbirth/, accessed 21 July 2024.

14 Monika Thakur and Angesh Thakur, 'Uterine Inversion', in *StatPearls* (Treasure Island, FL, 2024): http://www.ncbi.nlm.nih.gov/books/NBK525971/, accessed 12 December 2024.

15 Aaron J. Seidman and Marco A. Siccardi, 'Postpartum Pubic Symphysis Diastasis', in *StatPearls* (Treasure Island, FL, 2024): http://www.ncbi.nlm.nih.gov/books/NBK537043/, accessed 12 December 2024.

16 J.-Y. Maigne, F. Rusakiewicz, and M. Diouf, 'Postpartum Coccydynia: A Case Series Study of 57 Women', *European Journal of Physical and Rehabilitation Medicine* 48, no. 3 (Sept. 2012): 387–92.

17 'Postpartum Haemorrhage': https://www.who.int/teams/sexual-and-reproductive-health-and-research-(srh)/areas-of-work/maternal-and-perinatal-health/postpartum-haemorrhage, accessed 21 July 2024.

18 'WHO Announces the First Meeting of the Postpartum Haemorrhage (PPH) Bundle Guideline Development Subgroup': https://www.who.int/news/item/14-08-2023-who-announces-the-first-meeting-of-the-postpartum-haemorrhage-(pph)-bundle-guideline-development-subgroup, accessed 21 July 2024.

19 'Maternal Mortality': https://www.who.int/news-room/fact-sheets/detail/maternal-mortality, accessed 21 July 2024.
20 Cheryl Tatano Beck, Sue Watson, and Robert K. Gable, 'Traumatic Childbirth and Its Aftermath: Is There Anything Positive?', *Journal of Perinatal Education* 27, no. 3 (June 2018): 175–84: https://doi.org/10.1891/1058-1243.27.3.175, accessed 12 December 2024.
21 Anna Suarez and Vera Yakupova, 'Past Traumatic Life Events, Postpartum PTSD, and the Role of Labor Support', *International Journal of Environmental Research and Public Health* 20, no. 11 (4 June 2023): 6048: https://doi.org/10.3390/ijerph20116048, accessed 12 December 2024.
22 Beck, Watson, and Gable, 'Traumatic Childbirth and Its Aftermath'.
23 Mari Greenfield and Zoe Darwin, 'Trans and Non-Binary Pregnancy, Traumatic Birth, and Perinatal Mental Health: A Scoping Review', *International Journal of Transgender Health* 22, no. 1–2: 203–16: https://doi.org/10.1080/26895269.2020.1841057, accessed 21 July 2024.
24 For further reading see: https://www.transpregnancyproject.com/wp-content/uploads/2024/03/Trans-Pregnancy-policy-review-UK.pdf.
25 https://www.transpregnancyproject.com/wp-content/uploads/2024/03/Trans-Pregnancy-policy-review-UK.pdf, accessed 12 December 2024.
26 'Information on Testosterone Hormone Therapy: Gender Affirming Health Program': https://transcare.ucsf.edu/article/information-testosterone-hormone-therapy, accessed 21 July 2024.
27 Angela Leung et al., 'Assisted Reproductive Technology Outcomes in Female-to-Male Transgender Patients Compared with Cisgender Patients: A New Frontier in Reproductive Medicine', *Fertility and Sterility* 112, no. 5 (1 Nov. 2019), 858–65: https://doi.org/10.1016/j.fertnstert.2019.07.014, accessed 12 December 2024.
28 Alexis Light et al., 'Family Planning and Contraception Use in Transgender Men', *Contraception* 98, no. 4 (Oct. 2018), 266–69: https://doi.org/10.1016/j.contraception.2018.06.006, accessed 12 December 2024.
29 'I'm Trans. Does Birth Control Affect HRT Treatment?': https://www.plannedparenthood.org/blog/im-trans-does-birth-control-affect-hrt-treatment, accessed 21 July 2024.
30 Juno Obedin-Maliver and Harvey J. Makadon, 'Transgender Men and Pregnancy', *Obstetric Medicine* 9, no. 1 (Mar. 2016), 4–8: https://doi.org/10.1177/1753495X15612658, accessed 12 December 2024.

31 Ayesha Hassan et al., 'Pregnancy in a Transgender Male: A Case Report and Review of the Literature', *Case Reports in Endocrinology* 2022 (29 June 2022), 6246867: https://doi.org/10.1155/2022/6246867, accessed 12 December 2024.

32 Atsuko Yoshida et al., 'Transgender Man Receiving Testosterone Treatment Became Pregnant and Delivered a Girl: A Case Report', *Journal of Obstetrics and Gynaecology Research* 48, no. 3 (Mar. 2022): 866–68: https://doi.org/10.1111/jog.15145, accessed 12 December 2024.

33 'Improving Trans and Non-Binary Experiences of Maternity Services', Mid and South Essex Integrated Care System, 26 May 2023: https://www.midandsouthessex.ics.nhs.uk/get-involved/insights/improving-trans-and-non-binary-experiences-of-maternity-services/, accessed 12 December 2024.

34 Elizabeth Kukura, 'Reconceiving Reproductive Health Systems: Caring for Trans, Nonbinary, and Gender-Expansive People During Pregnancy and Childbirth', *Journal of Law, Medicine & Ethics* 50, no. 3: 471–88: https://doi.org/10.1017/jme.2022.88, accessed 21 July 2024.

35 Alexis Hoffkling, Juno Obedin-Maliver, and Jae Sevelius, 'From Erasure to Opportunity: A Qualitative Study of the Experiences of Transgender Men around Pregnancy and Recommendations for Providers', *BMC Pregnancy and Childbirth* 17, no. 2 (8 Nov. 2017), 332: https://doi.org/10.1186/s12884-017-1491-5, accessed 12 December 2024.

36 'Birth Trauma Inquiry an Important First Step in Reducing Traumatic Births, Says City Expert', City, University of London (City, University of London, 13 May 2024), https://www.city.ac.uk/news-and-events/news/2024/may/birth-trauma-inquiry-response-susan-ayers, accessed 12 December 2024.

37 Donna Ockenden, 'Final Report of the Ockenden Review': https://www.gov.uk/government/publications/final-report-of-the-ockenden-review, accessed 21 July 2024.

38 'Shropshire caesarean rate is the lowest in England', *Shropshire Star*, 7 Dec. 2011: https://www.shropshirestar.com/news/2011/12/07/shropshire-caesarean-rate-is-the-lowest-in-england/, accessed 12 December 2024.

39 Denis Campbell, 'Jeremy Hunt orders investigation into baby deaths at NHS Trust', *Guardian*, 12 Apr. 2017: https://www.theguardian.com/

society/2017/apr/12/jeremy-hunt-orders-investigation-into-baby-deaths-at-nhs-trust, accessed 12 December 2024.
40 Richard Vize, 'Ockenden Report Exposes Failures in Leadership, Teamwork, and Listening to Patients', *BMJ* 376 (31 Mar. 2022), o860: https://doi.org/10.1136/bmj.o860, accessed 12 December 2024.
41 Ockenden, 'Final Report of the Ockenden Review', 118.
42 J. Moorhead, 'Are you too posh to push?', *Daily Mail*, 26 Jan. 1999, 36–37.
43 'Shropshire Caesarean rate is the lowest in England'.
44 Donna Ockenden, 'Emerging Findings and Recommendations from the Independent Review of Maternity Services at the Shrewbury and Telford Hospital NHS Trust', 10 Dec. 2020: https://assets.publishing.service.gov.uk/government/uploads/system/uploads/attachment_data/file/943011/Independent_review_of_maternity_services_at_Shrewsbury_and_Telford_Hospital_NHS_Trust.pdf, accessed 12 December 2024.
45 Ockenden, 'Emerging Findings . . .', 14.
46 Ockenden, 'Emerging Findings . . .', 15.
47 'Ockenden Review: Summary of Findings, Conclusions and Essential Actions', gov.uk: https://www.gov.uk/government/publications/final-report-of-the-ockenden-review/ockenden-review-summary-of-findings-conclusions-and-essential-actions, accessed 21 July 2024.
48 'Birth Reflections', Medway NHS: https://www.medway.nhs.uk/services/birth-reflections/, accessed 21 July 2024.
49 S. Rose et al., 'Psychological Debriefing for Preventing Post Traumatic Stress Disorder (PTSD)', *Cochrane Database of Systematic Reviews*, no. 2 (2002): https://doi.org/10.1002/14651858.CD000560, accessed 12 December 2024.
50 Rhonda Small, Judith Lumley, and Liesje Toomey, 'Midwife-Led Debriefing after Operative Birth: Four to Six Year Follow-up of a Randomised Trial [ISRCTN24648614]', *BMC Medicine* 4 (1 Mar. 2006), 3: https://doi.org/10.1186/1741-7015-4-3, accessed 12 December 2024.
51 Jessica Cornwell, '"I blamed myself for almost dying after birth"', *Mail Online*, 11 May 2022: https://www.dailymail.co.uk/femail/article-10806405/As-report-lays-bare-catastrophic-maternity-care-mother-describes-shattering-experience.html, accessed 12 December 2024.

52 Jessica Cornwell, *Birth Notes: A Memoir of Trauma, Motherhood and Recovery* (London, 2022).
53 Ockenden, 'Final Report of the Ockenden Review'.
54 Denis Campbell, 'Austerity has led to NHS quality of care declining in key areas, study finds', *Guardian*, 5 July 2023: https://www.theguardian.com/society/2023/jul/05/austerity-has-led-to-nhs-quality-of-care-deteriorating-across-the-board-study-finds, accessed 12 December 2024.
55 Andrew Gregory, 'Deadly cancer treatment delays now "routine" in NHS, say damning reports', *Guardian*, 12 June 2024: https://www.theguardian.com/society/article/2024/jun/13/deadly-cancer-treatment-delays-routine-nhs, accessed 12 December 2024.
56 'How Does the US Healthcare System Compare to Other Countries?', *Peter G. Peterson Foundation* (blog), https://www.pgpf.org/blog/2023/07/how-does-the-us-healthcare-system-compare-to-other-countries, accessed 29 July 2024.
57 'One in 5 Women Reported Mistreatment While Receiving Maternity Care', Centers for Disease Control and Prevention, 1 Jan. 2016: https://www.cdc.gov/media/releases/2023/s0822-vs-maternity-mistreatment.html, accessed 12 December 2024.
58 'Hear Her Campaign', Centers for Disease Control and Prevention, 3 May 2024: https://www.cdc.gov/hearher/index.html, accessed 12 December 2024.
59 'One in 5 Women Reported Mistreatment While Receiving Maternity Care'.

4. Go Natural

1 Carl O'Brien, '"I'll Never Forget the Pain. It Was Excruciating"', *Irish Times*, 27 Nov. 2013: https://www.irishtimes.com/news/health/i-ll-never-forget-the-pain-it-was-excruciating-1.1608531, accessed 12 December 2024.
2 'Symphysiotomies', *Woman's Hour* (BBC Radio 4, 9 Dec. 2002): https://www.bbc.co.uk/radio4/womanshour/2002_50_mon_01.shtml, accessed 12 December 2024.

3 C. B. Wykes et al., 'Symphysiotomy: A Lifesaving Procedure', *BJOG: An International Journal of Obstetrics & Gynaecology* 110, no. 2 (2003), 219–21: https://doi.org/10.1046/j.1471-0528.2003.02001.x, accessed 12 December 2024.

4 A. P. Barry, 'Symphysiotomy or Pubiotomy; Why, When, and How?', *Irish Journal of Medical Science* Vol. 27 (Feb. 1951), 49–73: https://doi.org/10.1007/BF02966281, accessed 12 December 2024.

5 Baskett (ed.), 'Sigault, Jean René (b. 1740), Symphysiotomy', in *Eponyms and Names*, 386: https://doi.org/10.1017/9781108421706.309, accessed 12 December 2024.

6 Baskett (ed.), 'Baudelocque, Jean-Louis (1746–1810), Baudelocque's Diameter', in *Eponyms and Names*, 34: https://doi.org/10.1017/9781108421706.027, accessed 12 December 2024.

7 Leah Hazard, *Womb: The Inside Story of Where We All Began* (London, 2023) p. 15.

8 'Cesarean Section – A Brief History: Part 1', Exhibitions, National Institutes of Health (US National Library of Medicine), 1: https://www.nlm.nih.gov/exhibition/cesarean/part1.html, accessed 23 July 2024.

9 Sulochana Dhakal-Rai et al., 'A Brief History and Indications for Cesarean Section', *Journal of Patan Academy of Health Sciences* 8, no. 3 (31 Dec. 2021), 101–11: https://doi.org/10.3126/jpahs.v8i3.27657, accessed 12 December 2024.

10 'Cesarean Section – A Brief History: Part 3', Exhibitions, National Institutes of Health (US National Library of Medicine), 3: https://www.nlm.nih.gov/exhibition/cesarean/part3.html, accessed 23 July 2024.

11 'Cesarean Section – A Brief History: Part 3'.

12 Oonagh Walsh, 'Report on Symphysiotomy in Ireland 1944–1984' (Department of Health, Government of Ireland, 1 July 2014): https://www.gov.ie/en/publication/8535fb-report-on-symphysiotomy-in-ireland-1944-1984-professor-oonagh-walsh/, accessed 12 December 2024.

13 Homa Khaleeli, 'Symphysiotomy – Ireland's brutal alternative to caesareans', *Guardian*, 12 Dec. 2014: https://www.theguardian.com/lifeandstyle/2014/dec/12/symphysiotomy-irelands-brutal-alternative-to-caesareans, accessed 12 December 2024.

14 Walsh, 'Report on Symphysiotomy in Ireland . . .'.

15 Miriam Lord, 'Yes, Yes, Yes. A Resounding, Emphatic Yes', *Irish Times*, 25 May 2018: https://www.irishtimes.com/news/politics/miriam-lord-yes-yes-yes-a-resounding-emphatic-yes-1.3508854, accessed 23 July 2024.

16 'Is There a Limit to How Many C-Sections a Person Can Have?', Mayo Clinic, https://www.mayoclinic.org/tests-procedures/c-section/expert-answers/c-sections/faq-20058380, accessed 23 July 2024.

17 'Will a VBAC Work for You?', Mayo Clinic: https://www.mayoclinic.org/healthy-lifestyle/labor-and-delivery/in-depth/vbac/art-20044869, accessed 23 July 2024.

18 Khaleeli, 'Symphysiotomy – Ireland's Brutal Alternative to Caesareans'.

19 Maureen H. Clark, 'The Surgical Symphysiotomy *Ex Gratia* Payment Scheme' (Minister for Health, Republic of Ireland, 19 Oct. 2016), 181: https://assets.gov.ie/43053/b58b223e633b4123abec37475ebdbe1e.pdf, accessed 12 December 2024.

20 Clark, 'Surgical Symphysiotomy . . .', 182.

21 Pope Pius XII, 'Text of Address by Pope Pius XII on the Science and Morality of Painless Childbirth', *Linacre Quarterly* 23, no. 2 (1 May 1956): https://epublications.marquette.edu/lnq/vol23/iss2/2, accessed 12 December 2024.

22 Ioanna A. Ramoutsaki, Helen Askitopoulou, and Eleni Konsolaki, 'Pain Relief and Sedation in Roman Byzantine Texts: *Mandragoras Officinarum*, *Hyoscyamos Niger* and *Atropa Belladonna*', International Congress Series, The History of Anesthesia, 1242 (1 Dec. 2002), 43–50: https://doi.org/10.1016/S0531-5131(02)00699-4, accessed 12 December 2024.

23 Klaus Meyer, 'Dem Morphin auf der Spur', *Pharmazeutische Zeitung*, 12 Apr. 2004: https://www.pharmazeutische-zeitung.de/titel-16-2004/, accessed 12 December 2024.

24 Ryan LeVasseur and Sukumar P. Desai, 'Ebenezer Hopkins Frost (1824–1866): William T. G. Morton's First Identified Patient and Why He Was Invited to the Ether Demonstration of October 16, 1846', *Anesthesiology* 117, no. 2 (1 Aug. 2012), 238–42: https://doi.org/10.1097/ALN.0b013e31825f01b7, accessed 12 December 2024.

25 A. G. McKenzie, 'The Bicentenary of James Young Simpson (1811–1870)', *Anaesthesia* 66, no. 6 (2011), 438–40: https://doi.org/10.1111/j.1365-2044.2011.06768.x, accessed 12 December 2024.

26 Michael A. E. Ramsay, 'John Snow, MD: Anaesthetist to the Queen of England and Pioneer Epidemiologist', *Proceedings (Baylor University Medical Center)* 19, no. 1 (Jan. 2006), 24–28: https://www.ncbi.nlm.nih.gov/pmc/articles/PMC1325279/, accessed 12 December 2024.

27 Donald Caton, *What a Blessing She Had Chloroform: The Medical and Social Response to the Pain of Childbirth from 1800 to the Present* (New Haven, CT, 1999).

28 William Camann, 'A History of Pain Relief During Childbirth', in *The Wondrous Story of Anesthesia*, edited by Edmond I Eger II, Lawrence J. Saidman, and Rod N. Westhorpe (New York, NY, 2014), 847–58: https://doi.org/10.1007/978-1-4614-8441-7_62, accessed 12 December 2024.

29 'Doctors Disagree on Twilight Sleep: Death of First American Patient Renews Discussion of Painless Childbirth. Overestimated, Says One. Great Boon and Will Become Universal When Intelligently Used, Another Declares', *The New York Times*, 24 Aug. 1915: https://www.nytimes.com/1915/08/24/archives/doctors-disagree-on-twilight-sleep-death-of-first-american-patient.html, accessed 12 December 2024.

30 Camann, 'History of Pain Relief During Childbirth'.

31 Margarete J. Sandelowski, *Pain, Pleasure, and American Childbirth: From the Twilight Sleep to the Read Method, 1914–1960* (Westport, CT, 1984).

32 Sandelowski, *Pain, Pleasure, and American Childbirth*.

33 'The Fog', *Mad Men*, AMC, 13 Sept. 2009.

34 Faith Gibson, 'Traveling Through Time to Normal Birth', *Birth* 38, no. 3 (2011), 266–68: https://doi.org/10.1111/j.1523-536X.2011.00493.x, accessed 12 December 2024.

35 Donald Caton, 'Who Said Childbirth Is Natural?: The Medical Mission of Grantly Dick Read', *Anesthesiology* 84, no. 4 (1 Apr. 1996), 955–64: https://doi.org/10.1097/00000542-199604000-00024, accessed 12 December 2024.

36 Grantly Dick-Read, *Childbirth Without Fear: The Principles and Practice of Natural Childbirth*, 2nd edition (London, 2013).

37 M. A. Monto, 'Lamaze and Bradley Childbirth Classes: Contrasting Perspectives toward the Medical Model of Birth', *Birth* (Berkeley, CA) 23, no. 4 (Dec. 1996), 193–201: https://doi.org/10.1111/j.1523-536x.1996.tb00492.x, accessed 12 December 2024.

38 'Tokophobia (Fear of Childbirth): Causes, Symptoms & Treatment', Cleveland Clinic: https://my.clevelandclinic.org/health/diseases/22711-tokophobia-fear-of-childbirth, accessed 12 December 2024.

39 Karin Demšar et al., 'Tokophobia (Fear of Childbirth): Prevalence and Risk Factors', *Journal of Perinatal Medicine* 46, no. 2 (23 Feb. 2018), 151–54: https://doi.org/10.1515/jpm-2016-0282, accessed 12 December 2024.

40 'Overview: Caesarean Birth, Guidance', NICE (NICE, 31 Mar. 2021): https://www.nice.org.uk/guidance/ng192, accessed 12 December 2024.

41 'Your Right to a Caesarean Birth', Birthrights, https://birthrights.org.uk/factsheets/right-to-a-c-section/, accessed 23 July 2024.

42 'Your Right to a Caesarean Birth'.

43 'Maternal Request Caesarean' (Birthrights, Aug. 2018): https://birthrights.org.uk/wp-content/uploads/2018/08/Final-Birthrights-MRCS-Report-2108-1.pdf, accessed 12 December 2024.

44 Sharon Sung et al., 'Cesarean Delivery', in *StatPearls* (Treasure Island, FL, 2024): http://www.ncbi.nlm.nih.gov/books/NBK546707/, accessed 12 December 2024.

45 'Maternal Mortality Ratio', *CIA : The World Factbook*, https://www.cia.gov/the-world-factbook/field/maternal-mortality-ratio/country-comparison/, accessed 23 July 2024.

46 K. S. Joseph et al., 'Maternal Mortality in the United States: Recent Trends, Current Status, and Future Considerations', *Obstetrics & Gynecology* 137, no. 5 (May 2021), 763: https://doi.org/10.1097/AOG.0000000000004361, accessed 12 December 2024.

47 Rie Sakai-Bizmark et al., 'Evaluation of Hospital Cesarean Delivery-Related Profits and Rates in the United States', *JAMA Network Open* 4, no. 3 (19 Mar. 2021), e212235: https://doi.org/10.1001/jamanetworkopen.2021.2235, accessed 12 December 2024.

48 Zahra Shahshahan et al., 'Caesarean Section in Iran', *The Lancet* 388, no. 10039 (2 July 2016), 29–30: https://doi.org/10.1016/S0140-6736(16)30899-6, accessed 12 December 2024.

49 'Financial Incentives to Doctors and the High Rates of Caesarean Births', *LSE Business Review* (blog), 24 Sept. 2021: https://blogs.lse.ac.uk/businessreview/2021/09/24/financial-incentives-to-doctors-and-the-high-rates-of-caesarean-births/, accessed 12 December 2024.

50 Mahboubeh Shirzad et al., 'Prevalence of and Reasons for Women's, Family Members', and Health Professionals' Preferences for Cesarean Section in Iran: A Mixed-Methods Systematic Review', *Reproductive Health* 18, no. 1 (2 Jan. 2021), 3: https://doi.org/10.1186/s12978-020-01047-x, accessed 12 December 2024.

51 'How the Marketing of Formula Milk Influences Our Decisions on Infant Feeding' (World Health Organisation and United Nations Children's Fund, 22 Feb. 2022): https://www.who.int/publications/i/item/9789240044609, accessed 12 December 2024.

52 'Breastfeeding', WHO, https://www.who.int/health-topics/breastfeeding, accessed 28 July 2024.

53 'UK "World's Worst" at Breastfeeding', *BBC News*, 29 Jan. 2016: https://www.bbc.com/news/health-35438049, accessed 12 December 2024.

54 'Baby Formula Prices: Soaring Costs Devastating Family Finances – Survey', *BBC News*, 13 Dec. 2023: https://www.bbc.com/news/uk-67701180, accessed 12 December 2024.

55 'Midwife Numbers Drop by 600 in the Year since Minister Admitted England Was 2000 Midwives Short', Royal College of Midwives, https://www.rcm.org.uk/media-releases/2022/july/rcm-calls-for-improvements-in-staffing-to-enable-better-breastfeeding-support/, accessed 23 July 2024.

56 Stanley Ip et al., 'Breastfeeding and Maternal and Infant Health Outcomes in Developed Countries', *Evidence Report/Technology Assessment*, no. 153 (Apr. 2007), 1–186.

57 Sophie Borland, 'Breastfeeding boom: middle-class mothers lead the charge with 90% rejecting formula milk', *Daily Mail*, 21 June 2011: https://www.dailymail.co.uk/health/article-2006246/Breast-feeding-boom-Middle-class-mothers-lead-charge-rates-rocket.html, accessed 12 December 2024.

58 Anna Momigliano, 'Breast-feeding Isn't Free. This Is How Much It Really Costs', *Washington Post*, 21 May 2019: https://www.washingtonpost.com/lifestyle/2019/05/28/breast-feeding-isnt-free-this-is-how-much-it-really-costs/, accessed 12 December 2024.

59 Eliane Glaser, 'It's class, not whether a baby is breastfed, that determines life chances', *Guardian*, 24 Nov. 2014: https://www.theguardian.

com/commentisfree/2014/nov/24/class-baby-breastfed-life-chances-inequality, accessed 12 December 2024.

60 Christie del Castillo-Hegyi, 'Letter to Doctors and Parents About the Dangers of Insufficient Exclusive Breastfeeding', *Fed is Best Foundation* (blog), 18 Apr. 2015: https://fedisbest.org/2015/04/letter-to-doctors-and-parents-about-the-dangers-of-insufficient-exclusive-breastfeeding/, accessed 12 December 2024.

61 'Mothers & Others: Guide to Pregnancy, Feeding and Parenting' (RL Advertising, Publishing Division, n.d.): http://www.mothersguide.co.uk/, accessed 12 December 2024.

62 Rose Stokes, '"The darkest period of my life": I struggled to breastfeed – then a drug sent me spiralling', *Guardian*, 30 May 2024: https://www.theguardian.com/lifeandstyle/article/2024/may/30/the-darkest-period-of-my-life-i-struggled-to-breastfeed-then-a-drug-sent-me-spiralling, accessed 12 December 2024.

63 Stokes, '"The darkest period of my life" . . .'.

64 Jack Newman and Teresa Pitman, *Dr Jack Newman's Guide to Breastfeeding*, 1st edition (Canada, 2009).

65 Jojanneke E. van Amesfoort, Norah M. Van Mello, and Renate van Genugten, 'Lactation Induction in a Transgender Woman: Case Report and Recommendations for Clinical Practice', *International Breastfeeding Journal* 19, no. 1 (11 Mar. 2024), 18: https://doi.org/10.1186/s13006-024-00624-1, accessed 12 December 2024.

66 Michael Searles, 'Trans-women's milk as good as breast milk, says NHS trust', *Telegraph*, 18 Feb. 2024: https://www.telegraph.co.uk/news/2024/02/18/trans-womens-milk-as-good-as-breast-milk-says-nhs-trust/, accessed 12 December 2024.

5. Sacrifice Yourself

1 Abortion Act 1967, Pub. L. No. 1967 c. 87 (1967): https://www.legislation.gov.uk/ukpga/1967/87/contents, accessed 12 December 2024.

2 'Abortion Statistics, England and Wales: 2020', Accredited Official Statistics (Department of Health and Social Care, UK, 4 May 2022):

https://www.gov.uk/government/statistics/abortion-statistics-for-england-and-wales-2020/abortion-statistics-england-and-wales-2020, accessed 12 December 2024.

3. Tobi Thomas, 'Outrage at jail sentence for woman who took abortion pills later than UK limit', *Guardian*, 12 June 2023: https://www.theguardian.com/world/2023/jun/12/woman-in-uk-jailed-for-28-months-over-taking-abortion-pills-after-legal-time-limit, accessed 12 December 2024.
4. Thomas, 'Outrage at Jail Sentence . . .'.
5. Alexandra Topping, 'Woman jailed for taking abortion pills after time limit to be freed from prison', *Guardian*, 18 July 2023: https://www.theguardian.com/uk-news/2023/jul/18/carla-foster-woman-jailed-obtaining-tablets-pregnancy-freed-appeal, accessed 12 December 2024.
6. 'Mama Izabeli z Pszczyny: Przecież to powinien być mój grób, a nie jej', *Fakt*, 5 Nov. 2021: https://www.fakt.pl/wydarzenia/polska/slask/pszczyna-smierc-ciezarnej-izabeli-mama-30-latki-nie-kryje-emocji/ytc338v, accessed 12 December 2024.
7. 'Mama Izabeli z Pszczyny'.
8. 'Wstrząsające ustalenia o śmierci Izy z Pszczyny. Powtarzała: Chcę żyć, nie chce umierać', *Fakt*, 5 Nov. 2021: https://www.fakt.pl/wydarzenia/polska/pszczyna-smierc-30-letniej-izabeli-wstrzasajaca-relacja-bliskich/qczgzzs, accessed 12 December 2024.
9. 'Woman Dies after Abortion Request "Refused" at Galway Hospital', *BBC News*, 14 Nov. 2012: https://www.bbc.com/news/uk-northern-ireland-20321741, accessed 12 December 2024.
10. Joe Parkin Daniels et al., 'Killed by abortion laws: five women whose stories we must never forget', *Guardian*, 7 May 2022: https://www.theguardian.com/global-development/2022/may/07/killed-by-abortion-laws-five-women-whose-stories-we-must-never-forget, accessed 12 December 2024.
11. Daniels et al., 'Killed by abortion laws . . .'.
12. Katarzyna Borkowska, 'Prawo aborcyjne w Polsce – rys historyczny', *Studia Prawnoustrojowe*, no. 62 (20 Dec. 2023): https://doi.org/10.31648/sp.9145, accessed 12 December 2024.
13. Mark Savage, 'The Law of Abortion in the Union of Soviet Socialist Republics and the People's Republic of China: Women's Rights in

Two Socialist Countries', *Stanford Law Review* 40, no. 4 (1988), 1027–117: https://doi.org/10.2307/1228777, accessed 12 December 2024.

14 'Rozporządzenie Prezydenta Rzeczypospolitej z Dnia 11 Lipca 1932 r. – Kodeks Karny', Dz.U. 1932 nr 60 poz. 571 § (1932): https://isap.sejm.gov.pl/isap.nsf/DocDetails.xsp?id=WDU19320600571, accessed 12 December 2024.

15 Waldemar Kowalski, 'Hoser: "W PRL 800 tys. aborcji rocznie", Aborcja była wtedy legalna i masowa, ale nie aż tak – wyjaśniamy', *naTemat*, 21 Jan. 2015: http://natemat.pl/130773,aborcja-w-prl-byla-legalna-i-masowa-abp-hoser-widzi-w-tym-przyczyne-samobojczej-polityki, accessed 12 December 2024.

16 'Janda wezwała kobiety do strajku i się zaczęło. Dziesiątki tysięcy osób skrzykują się na Facebooku', gazeta.pl, 26 Sept. 2016: https://wiadomosci.gazeta.pl/wiadomosci/7,114883,20746998,kobiety-chca-strajkowac-ws-aborcji-wykladowca-uw-napisala.html, accessed 12 December 2024.

17 'Trybunał Konstytucyjny: Planowanie Rodziny, Ochrona Płodu Ludzkiego i Warunki Dopuszczalności Przerywania Ciąży', https://trybunal.gov.pl/postepowanie-i-orzeczenia/wyroki/art/11300-planowanie-rodziny-ochrona-plodu-ludzkiego-i-warunki-dopuszczalnosci-przerywania-ciazy, accessed 24 July 2024.

18 'Strajk Kobiet', 9 Mar. 2022: https://strajkkobiet.eu/, accessed 12 December 2024.

19 'The Daughter of a Saint Speaks of Her Mother's Holiness', *National Catholic Register*, 12 Sept. 2011: https://www.ncregister.com/news/the-daughter-of-a-saint-speaks-of-her-mothers-holiness/, accessed 12 December 2024.

20 'Gianna Beretta Molla (1922–1962), Biography', https://www.vatican.va/news_services/liturgy/saints/ns_lit_doc_20040516_beretta-molla_en.html, accessed 24 July 2024.

21 Alison McIntyre, 'Doctrine of Double Effect', in *The Stanford Encyclopedia of Philosophy*, edited by Edward N. Zalta, Spring 2019 (Stanford University, 2019): https://plato.stanford.edu/archives/spr2019/entries/double-effect/, accessed 12 December 2024.

22 'Święta Gianna Beretta Molla na nowym znaczku – Poczta Polska', 28 Apr. 2022: https://www.poczta-polska.pl/news/swieta-gianna-beretta-molla-na-nowym-znaczku/, accessed 12 December 2024.

23 René Girard, *I See Satan Fall Like Lightning*, trans. James G. Williams (New York, NY, 2001), p. 70.
24 'Six Months Post-Roe, 24 US States Have Banned Abortion or Are Likely to Do So: A Roundup', Guttmacher Institute, 9 Jan. 2023: https://www.guttmacher.org/2023/01/six-months-post-roe-24-us-states-have-banned-abortion-or-are-likely-do-so-roundup, accessed 12 December 2024.
25 'The World's Abortion Laws', Center for Reproductive Rights, https://reproductiverights.org/maps/worlds-abortion-laws/, accessed 24 July 2024.
26 'The World's Abortion Laws'.
27 Richard Armitage, 'Abortion in Northern Ireland: Decriminalisation, COVID-19 and Recent Data', *The Lancet Regional Health – Europe* 15 (1 Apr. 2022): https://doi.org/10.1016/j.lanepe.2022.100349, accessed 12 December 2024.
28 Eleni Courea, 'MPs propose decriminalising abortion up to 24 weeks', *Guardian*, 8 Apr. 2024: https://www.theguardian.com/world/2024/apr/08/mps-propose-decriminalising-abortion-up-to-24-weeks-england-wales-stella-creasy, accessed 12 December 2024.
29 'Suski: wciąż czasem kobiety umierają przy porodach, ale nie ma to związku z żadną decyzją TK', Polska Agencja Prasowa SA, https://www.pap.pl/aktualnosci/news%2C987944%2Csuski-wciaz-czasem-kobiety-umieraja-przy-porodach-ale-nie-ma-zwiazku-z, accessed 24 July 2024.

6. Choose Joy

1 Mikhail Mikhaĭlovich Bakhtin, *Rabelais and His World*, trans. Helene Iswolsky (Bloomington, IN, 1984), p. 26.
2 Mi Kyung Kong and Sang Wook Bai, 'Surgical Treatments for Vaginal Apical Prolapse', *Obstetrics & Gynecology Science* 59, no. 4 (13 July 2016), 253–60: https://doi.org/10.5468/ogs.2016.59.4.253, accessed 12 December 2024.
3 Julija Makajeva, Carolina Watters, and Panos Safioleas, 'Cystocele', in *StatPearls* (Treasure Island, FL, 2024): http://www.ncbi.nlm.nih.gov/books/NBK564303/, accessed 12 December 2024.
4 Mark D. Walters, '19 – Surgical Correction of Anterior Vaginal Wall Prolapse', in *Urogynecology and Reconstructive Pelvic Surgery*, 3rd edition,

edited by Mark D. Walters and Mickey M. Karram (Philadelphia, 2007), 234–45: https://doi.org/10.1016/B978-0-323-02902-5.50025-3, accessed 12 December 2024.

5 Christopher Maher et al., 'Surgery for Women with Apical Vaginal Prolapse', *Cochrane Database of Systematic Reviews*, no. 10 (2016): https://doi.org/10.1002/14651858.CD012376, accessed 12 December 2024; Christopher Maher et al., 'Surgery for Women with Anterior Compartment Prolapse', *Cochrane Database of Systematic Reviews*, no. 11 (2016): https://doi.org/10.1002/14651858.CD004014.pub6, accessed 12 December 2024; Alex Mowat et al., 'Surgery for Women with Posterior Compartment Prolapse', *Cochrane Database of Systematic Reviews*, no. 3 (2018): https://doi.org/10.1002/14651858.CD012975, accessed 12 December 2024.

6 National Childbirth Trust, 'Nearly Half of New Mothers with Mental Health Problems Don't Get Diagnosed or Treated', National Childbirth Trust, 10 Oct. 2018: https://www.nct.org.uk/about-us/media/news/nearly-half-new-mothers-mental-health-problems-dont-get-diagnosed-or-treated, accessed 12 December 2024.

7 Sehar K. Raza, and Syed Raza, 'Postpartum Psychosis', in *StatPearls* (Treasure Island, FL, 2024): http://www.ncbi.nlm.nih.gov/books/NBK544304/, accessed 12 December 2024.

8 'NHS England: Perinatal Mental Health', https://www.england.nhs.uk/mental-health/perinatal/, accessed 25 July 2024.

9 'Frances Wellburn Suicide: Inquest Told of Gaps in Care', *BBC News*, 23 Mar. 2022: https://www.bbc.com/news/uk-england-york-north-yorkshire-60847972, accessed 12 December 2024.

10 'Mental health services failing to consider impact of menopause, putting women at risk of suicide', Sky News, https://news.sky.com/story/mental-health-services-failing-to-consider-impact-of-menopause-putting-women-at-risk-of-suicide-12840229, accessed 25 July 2024.

11 'Mental health services failing to consider impact of menopause, putting women at risk of suicide'.

12 Debra L. Karch et al., 'Surveillance for Violent Deaths – National Violent Death Reporting System, 16 States, 2009', *Morbidity and Mortality Weekly Report. Surveillance Summaries* (Washington DC, 2002) 61, no. 6 (14 Sept. 2012), 1–43; 'Statistical Report: Near to Real-Time Suspected Suicide Surveillance (nRTSSS) for England for the 15 Months to Apr. 2024',

Official Statistics (Office for Health Improvement and Disparities, UK Government, 25 July 2024): https://www.gov.uk/government/statistics/near-to-real-time-suspected-suicide-surveillance-nrtsss-for-england/statistical-report-near-to-real-time-suspected-suicide-surveillance-nrtsss-for-england-for-the-15-months-to-august-2023, accessed 12 December 2024; 'Deaths by Suicide over Time', Official Statistics (Australian Institute of Health and Welfare, Australian Government, 3 Nov. 2023): https://www.aihw.gov.au/suicide-self-harm-monitoring/data/deaths-by-suicide-in-australia/suicide-deaths-over-time, accessed 12 December 2024.

13 'Menopause: Diagnosis and Management', National Institute for Health and Care Excellence (NICE, 12 Nov. 2015): https://www.nice.org.uk/guidance/ng23, accessed 12 December 2024.

14 Megan Herson and Jayashri Kulkarni, 'Hormonal Agents for the Treatment of Depression Associated with the Menopause', *Drugs & Aging* 39, no. 8 (2022), 607–18: https://doi.org/10.1007/s40266-022-00962-x, accessed 12 December 2024.

15 Elizabeth Siegel Watkins, *The Estrogen Elixir: A History of Hormone Replacement Therapy in America* (Baltimore, MD, 2010), p. 34.

16 Robert A. Wilson and Thelma A. Wilson, 'The Fate of the Nontreated Postmenopausal Woman: A Plea for the Maintenance of Adequate Estrogen from Puberty to the Grave', *Journal of the American Geriatrics Society* 11, no. 4 (1963), 347–62: https://doi.org/10.1111/j.1532-5415.1963.tb00068.x, accessed 12 December 2024.

17 Robert A. Wilson, *Feminine Forever* (London, 1966).

18 Watkins, *Estrogen Elixir*, p. 49.

19 Elizabeth Siegel Watkins, '"Doctor, Are You Trying to Kill Me?": Ambivalence About the Patient Package Insert for Estrogen', *Bulletin of the History of Medicine* 76, no. 1 (2002), 84–104: https://www.jstor.org/stable/44446152, accessed 12 December 2024.

20 Watkins, *Estrogen Elixir*.

21 Robert A. Wilson, 'Which Hormone to Take and When', *Vogue*, June 1966.

22 'Bazaar's Over-40 Guide on Health, Looks, Sex', *Harper's Bazaar*, Aug. 1973.

23 Watkins, *Estrogen Elixir*, p. 247.

24 Randi Hutter Epstein, *Aroused: The History of Hormones and How They Control Just About Everything*, 1st edition (New York, NY, 2018), p. 186.

25 Roger A. Lobo et al., 'Back to the Future: Hormone Replacement Therapy as Part of a Prevention Strategy for Women at the Onset of Menopause', *Atherosclerosis* 254 (1 Nov. 2016), 282–90: https://doi.org/10.1016/j.atherosclerosis.2016.10.005, accessed 12 December 2024.

26 Jennifer Gunter, *The Menopause Manifesto: Own Your Health with Facts and Feminism* (London, 2021), p. 213.

27 'Women's Health Initiative', https://www.whi.org/, accessed 25 July 2024.

28 Jacques E. Rossouw et al., 'Risks and Benefits of Estrogen plus Progestin in Healthy Postmenopausal Women: Principal Results From the Women's Health Initiative Randomized Controlled Trial', *JAMA* 288, no. 3 (17 July 2002), 321–33: https://doi.org/10.1001/jama.288.3.321, accessed 12 December 2024.

29 Adam L. Hersh, Marcia L. Stefanick, and Randall S. Stafford, 'National Use of Postmenopausal Hormone Therapy: Annual Trends and Response to Recent Evidence', *JAMA* 291, no. 1 (7 Jan. 2004), 47–53: https://doi.org/10.1001/jama.291.1.47, accessed 12 December 2024.

30 Laurie Pahus et al., 'Patient Distrust in Pharmaceutical Companies: An Explanation for Women Under-Representation in Respiratory Clinical Trials?', *BMC Medical Ethics* 21, no. 1 (13 Aug. 2020), 72: https://doi.org/10.1186/s12910-020-00509-y, accessed 12 December 2024.

31 Neil Vargesson, 'Thalidomide-induced Teratogenesis: History and Mechanisms', *Birth Defects Research* 105, no. 2 (June 2015), 140–56: https://doi.org/10.1002/bdrc.21096, accessed 12 December 2024.

32 Robert L. Brent, 'Drug Testing in Animals for Teratogenic Effects: Thalidomide in the Pregnant Rat', *Journal of Pediatrics* 64, no. 5 (1 May 1964), 762–70: https://doi.org/10.1016/S0022-3476(64)80626-0, accessed 12 December 2024.

33 Lancelot Hogben, 'The Hogben Test', *BMJ* 2, no. 4485 (21 Dec. 1946), 962–63: https://www.ncbi.nlm.nih.gov/pmc/articles/PMC2054960/, accessed 12 December 2024.

34 Sarah Rainey, '"Is this the forgotten thalidomide?"', *Telegraph*, 12 May 2014: https://www.telegraph.co.uk/news/health/10819186/Is-this-the-forgotten-thalidomide.html, accessed 12 December 2024.

35 Carl Heneghan et al., 'Oral Hormone Pregnancy Tests and the Risks of Congenital Malformations: A Systematic Review and Meta-Analysis',

F1000Research 7 (29 Jan. 2019), 1725: https://doi.org/10.12688/f1000research.16758.2, accessed 12 December 2024.

36 Marieke Veurink, Marlies Koster, and Lolkje T. W. de Jong-van den Berg, 'The History of DES, Lessons to Be Learned', *Pharmacy World and Science* 27, no. 3 (1 June 2005), 139–43: https://doi.org/10.1007/s11096-005-3663-z, accessed 12 December 2024.

37 Elisabeth Mahase, 'Sodium Valproate Continues to Be Prescribed in Hundreds of Pregnancies, Data Show', *BMJ* 377 (21 Apr. 2022), o1013: https://doi.org/10.1136/bmj.o1013, accessed 12 December 2024.

38 Hersh, Stefanick, and Stafford, 'National Use of Postmenopausal Hormone Therapy'.

39 Angelo Cagnacci and Martina Venier, 'The Controversial History of Hormone Replacement Therapy', *Medicina* 55, no. 9 (18 Sept. 2019), 602: https://doi.org/10.3390/medicina55090602, accessed 12 December 2024.

40 Jacques E. Rossouw et al., 'Postmenopausal Hormone Therapy and Risk of Cardiovascular Disease by Age and Years Since Menopause', *JAMA* 297, no. 13 (4 Apr. 2007), 1465–77: https://doi.org/10.1001/jama.297.13.1465, accessed 12 December 2024.

41 'The Global Wellness Industry Is Now Worth $5.6 Trillion', *Bloomberg*, 9 Nov. 2023: https://www.bloomberg.com/news/articles/2023-11-09/the-global-wellness-industry-is-now-worth-5-6-trillion, accessed 12 December 2024.

42 Clare Patton, Marisa McVey, and Ciara Hackett, 'Enough of the "Snake Oil": Applying a Business and Human Rights Lens to the Sexual and Reproductive Wellness Industry', *Business and Human Rights Journal* 7, no. 1 (Feb. 2022), 12–28: https://doi.org/10.1017/bhj.2021.51, accessed 12 December 2024.

43 Nicholas B. Tiller, John P. Sullivan, and Panteleimon Ekkekakis, 'Baseless Claims and Pseudoscience in Health and Wellness: A Call to Action for the Sports, Exercise, and Nutrition-Science Community', *Sports Medicine* (Auckland, NZ) 53, no. 1 (Jan. 2023), 1–5: https://doi.org/10.1007/s40279-022-01702-2, accessed 12 December 2024.

44 Terry Nguyen, 'The Wellness World's Conspiracy Problem Is Linked to Orientalism', Vox, 16 July 2021: https://www.vox.com/the-goods/22577558/wellness-world-qanon-conspiracy-orientalism, accessed 12 December 2024.

45 'What's Goop?: The Story Behind the Brand': https://goop.com/whats-goop/, accessed 25 July 2024.
46 'What's Goop . . .'.
47 Taffy Brodesser-Akner, 'How Goop's Haters Made Gwyneth Paltrow's Company Worth $250 Million', *The New York Times*, 25 July 2018: https://www.nytimes.com/2018/07/25/magazine/big-business-gwyneth-paltrow-wellness.html, accessed 12 December 2024.
48 Sarah Bailey, 'Gwyneth Unveiled', *Harper's Bazaar*, 11 Apr. 2013: https://www.harpersbazaar.com/celebrity/latest/news/g2647/gwyneth-paltrow-interview-0513/, accessed 12 December 2024.
49 Esther Zuckerman, 'Gwyneth Paltrow Has Written the Bible of Laughable Hollywood Neuroticism', *The Atlantic* (blog), 12 Mar. 2013: https://www.theatlantic.com/culture/archive/2013/03/gwyneth-paltrow-its-all-good-book/317493/, accessed 12 December 2024.
50 'Gwyneth Paltrow's Guide to Living Your Best Life: 12 Bonkers Ideas', *Harper's Bazaar*, 8 Jan. 2021: https://www.harpersbazaar.com/uk/culture/culture-news/news/a39740/gwyneth-paltrow-guide-to-life/, accessed 12 December 2024.
51 Magali Robert, 'Second-Degree Burn Sustained after Vaginal Steaming', *Journal of Obstetrics and Gynaecology Canada* 41, no. 6 (1 June 2019), 838–39: https://doi.org/10.1016/j.jogc.2018.07.013, accessed 12 December 2024.
52 Jennifer Gunter, 'Gwyneth Paltrow Says Steam Your Vagina, an OB/GYN Says Don't', *Dr Jen Gunter* (blog), 27 Jan. 2015: https://drjengunter.com/2015/01/27/gwyneth-paltrow-says-steam-your-vagina-an-obgyn-says-dont/, accessed 12 December 2024.
53 Jacques Ravel, Inmaculada Moreno, and Carlos Simón, 'Bacterial Vaginosis and its Association with Infertility, Endometritis, and Pelvic Inflammatory Disease', *American Journal of Obstetrics & Gynecology* 224, no. 3 (1 Mar. 2021), 251–57: https://doi.org/10.1016/j.ajog.2020.10.019, accessed 12 December 2024; Lindsey K. Jennings and Diann M. Krywko, 'Pelvic Inflammatory Disease', in *StatPearls* (Treasure Island, FL, 2024): http://www.ncbi.nlm.nih.gov/books/NBK499959/, accessed 12 December 2024.
54 Gwyneth Paltrow and Ingrid Fetell Lee, 'Finding Joy Again', *The Goop* (podcast): https://www.globalplayer.com/podcasts/episodes/7DraiVv/, accessed 25 July 2024.

55 Gerda Endemann, 'Menopause and Perimenopause', *Goop* (blog), 8 Aug. 2021: https://goop.com/wellness/health/menopause-and-perimenopause/, accessed 12 December 2024.

56 Endemann, 'Menopause and Perimenopause'.

57 Beck, Watson, and Gable, 'Traumatic Childbirth and Its Aftermath'.

58 Pauline Slade, Andrea Murphy, and Emma Hayden, 'Identifying Post-Traumatic Stress Disorder after Childbirth', *BMJ* 377 (10 May 2022), e067659: https://doi.org/10.1136/bmj-2021-067659, accessed 12 December 2024.

59 Thomas A. Fergus, David P. Valentiner, and Jacob B. Holzman, 'The Combination of Health Anxiety and Somatic Symptoms: Examining Associations With Health-Related Beliefs and Gender Differences', *Journal of Cognitive Psychotherapy* 28, no. 4 (2014), 274–86: https://doi.org/10.1891/0889-8391.28.4.274, accessed 12 December 2024.

60 David Westergaard et al., 'Population-Wide Analysis of Differences in Disease Progression Patterns in Men and Women', *Nature Communications* 10, no. 1 (8 Feb. 2019), 666: https://doi.org/10.1038/s41467-019-08475-9, accessed 12 December 2024.

61 Eleni S. Tsamantioti and Heba Mahdy, 'Endometriosis', in *StatPearls* (Treasure Island, FL, 2024): http://www.ncbi.nlm.nih.gov/books/NBK567777/, accessed 12 December 2024.

62 Allyson C. Bontempo and Lisa Mikesell, 'Patient Perceptions of Misdiagnosis of Endometriosis: Results from an Online National Survey', *Diagnosis* (Berlin, Germany) 7, no. 2 (26 May 2020), 97–106: https://doi.org/10.1515/dx-2019-0020, accessed 12 December 2024.

63 Rodrigo de P. Sepulcri and Vivian F. do Amaral, 'Depressive Symptoms, Anxiety, and Quality of Life in Women with Pelvic Endometriosis', *European Journal of Obstetrics & Gynecology and Reproductive Biology* 142, no. 1 (1 Jan. 2009), 53–6: https://doi.org/10.1016/j.ejogrb.2008.09.003, accessed 12 December 2024.

64 Nicky Hudson, 'The Missed Disease? Endometriosis as an Example of "Undone Science"', *Reproductive Biomedicine & Society Online* 14 (13 Aug. 2021), 20–27: https://doi.org/10.1016/j.rbms.2021.07.003, accessed 12 December 2024.

65 Brigitte Leeners et al., 'The Effect of Pregnancy on Endometriosis – Facts or Fiction?', *Human Reproduction Update* 24, no. 3 (1 May 2018),

290–99: https://doi.org/10.1093/humupd/dmy004, accessed 12 December 2024.
66 Leeners et al., 'The Effect of Pregnancy on Endometriosis . . .', accessed 12 December 2024.
67 Carlo Bulletti et al., 'Endometriosis and Infertility', *Journal of Assisted Reproduction and Genetics* 27, no. 8 (Aug. 2010), 441–47: https://doi.org/10.1007/s10815-010-9436-1, accessed 12 December 2024.
68 'Stress Relief from Infertility', Mayo Clinic Health System, https://www.mayoclinichealthsystem.org/hometown-health/speaking-of-health/infertility-and-stress, accessed 25 July 2024.
69 Michael Obladen, 'Birthmark and Blemish: The Doctrine of Maternal Imagination', in *Oxford Textbook of the Newborn: A Cultural and Medical History*, Oxford Textbooks in Paediatrics (Oxford, 2021): https://doi.org/10.1093/med/9780198854807.003.0026, accessed 12 December 2024.
70 Joanne Limburg, 'Once upon a life: Joanne Limburg', *Guardian*, 3 Apr. 2010: https://www.theguardian.com/lifeandstyle/2010/apr/04/joanne-limburg-poet-depression-miscarriage, accessed 12 December 2024.

7. Stop Complaining

1 'Saving Lives, Improving Mothers' Care: Lessons Learned to Inform Maternity Care from the UK and Ireland Confidential Enquiries into Maternal Deaths and Morbidity 2019-21' (MBRRACE-UK, Oct. 2023): https://www.npeu.ox.ac.uk/assets/downloads/mbrrace-uk/reports/maternal-report-2023/MBRRACE-UK_Maternal_Compiled_Report_2023.pdf, accessed 12 December 2024.
2 Joseph et al., 'Maternal Mortality in the United States', accessed 12 December 2024.
3 Diane Taylor, 'The tragedy of Rianna and baby Aisha: Why a teenager gave birth all alone in a prison cell', *Guardian*, 2 Aug. 2023: https://www.theguardian.com/society/2023/aug/02/the-tragedy-of-rianna-and-baby-aisha-cleary-teenager-gave-birth-all-alone-in-a-prison-cell.
4 Taylor, 'The tragedy of Rianna and baby Aisha . . .'.
5 Taylor, 'The tragedy of Rianna and baby Aisha . . .'.
6 Taylor, 'The tragedy of Rianna and baby Aisha . . .'.

7 Taylor, 'The tragedy of Rianna and baby Aisha . . .'.
8 Saraswathi Vedam et al., 'The Giving Voice to Mothers Study: Inequity and Mistreatment during Pregnancy and Childbirth in the United States', *Reproductive Health* 16, no. 1 (11 June 2019), 77: https://doi.org/10.1186/s12978-019-0729-2, accessed 12 December 2024.
9 Liz Hamel et al., 'KFF/The Undefeated Survey on Race and Health' (KFF, 13 Oct. 2020): https://www.kff.org/report-section/kff-the-undefeated-survey-on-race-and-health-main-findings/, accessed 12 December 2024.
10 Toni Morrison, *The Bluest Eye* (London, 2022), pp. 121–22.
11 Kelly M. Hoffman et al., 'Racial Bias in Pain Assessment and Treatment Recommendations, and False Beliefs About Biological Differences Between Blacks and Whites', *Proceedings of the National Academy of Sciences of the United States of America* 113, no. 16 (19 Apr. 2016), 4296–4301: https://doi.org/10.1073/pnas.1516047113, accessed 12 December 2024.
12 Linda Villarosa, 'How False Beliefs in Physical Racial Difference Still Live in Medicine Today', *The New York Times*, 14 Aug. 2019, https://www.nytimes.com/interactive/2019/08/14/magazine/racial-differences-doctors.html: https://www.nytimes.com/interactive/2019/08/14/magazine/racial-differences-doctors.html, accessed 12 December 2024.
13 John Brown, *Slave Life in Georgia: A Narrative of the Life, Sufferings, and Escape of John Brown, a Fugitive Slave, Now in England*, edited by Louis A. Chamerovzow (London, 1855), p. 48: https://hdl.handle.net/2027/coo.31924032774527?urlappend=%3Bseq=128, accessed 12 December 2024.
14 Villarosa, 'How False Beliefs in Physical Racial Difference Still Live in Medicine Today'.
15 L. L. Wall, 'The Medical Ethics of Dr J Marion Sims: A Fresh Look at the Historical Record', *Journal of Medical Ethics* 32, no. 6 (June 2006), 346–50: https://doi.org/10.1136/jme.2005.012559, accessed 12 December 2024.
16 Hoffman et al., 'Racial Bias in Pain Assessment and Treatment Recommendations, and False Beliefs About Biological Differences Between Blacks and Whites'.
17 John E. Snyder et al., 'Black Representation in the Primary Care Physician Workforce and Its Association With Population Life Expectancy and Mortality Rates in the US', *JAMA Network Open* 6, no. 4 (14 Apr.

2023), e236687: https://doi.org/10.1001/jamanetworkopen.2023.6687, accessed 12 December 2024.

18 Marcella Alsan, Owen Garrick, and Grant Graziani, 'Does Diversity Matter for Health? Experimental Evidence from Oakland', *American Economic Review* 109, no. 12 (Dec. 2019), 4071–111: https://doi.org/10.1257/aer.20181446, accessed 12 December 2024.

19 Brad N. Greenwood et al., 'Physician–Patient Racial Concordance and Disparities in Birthing Mortality for Newborns', *Proceedings of the National Academy of Sciences* 117, no. 35 (1 Sept. 2020), 21194–200: https://doi.org/10.1073/pnas.1913405117, accessed 12 December 2024.

20 Tom Abate, 'Nobel Winner's Theories Raise Uproar in Berkeley: Geneticist's Views Strike Many as Racist, Sexist', SFGATE, 13 Nov. 2000: https://www.sfgate.com/science/article/Nobel-Winner-s-Theories-Raise-Uproar-in-Berkeley-3236584.php, accessed 12 December 2024.

21 H. B. Chin et al., 'Racial Disparities in Seeking Care for Help Getting Pregnant', *Paediatric and Perinatal Epidemiology* 29, no. 5 (Sept. 2015), 416–25: https://doi.org/10.1111/ppe.12210, accessed 12 December 2024.

22 John A. Sampson, 'Peritoneal Endometriosis due to Menstrual Dissemination of Endometrial Tissue into Peritoneal Cavity', *American Journal of Obstetrics & Gynecology* 14 (1927), 422–69: https://cir.nii.ac.jp/crid/1574231876116149888, accessed 12 December 2024.

23 David Byron Redwine, 'Was Sampson Wrong?', *Fertility and Sterility* 78, no. 4 (Oct. 2002), 686–93: https://doi.org/10.1016/s0015-0282(02)03329-0, accessed 12 December 2024.

24 O. Bougie et al., 'Influence of Race/Ethnicity on Prevalence and Presentation of Endometriosis: A Systematic Review and Meta-Analysis', *BJOG: An International Journal of Obstetrics & Gynaecology* 126, no. 9 (2019), 1104–15: https://doi.org/10.1111/1471-0528.15692, accessed 12 December 2024.

25 George H. Shade, Mieke Lane, and Michael P. Diamond, 'Endometriosis in the African American Woman – Racially, a Different Entity?', *Gynecological Surgery* 9, no. 1 (Feb. 2012), 59–62: https://doi.org/10.1007/s10397-011-0685-5, accessed 12 December 2024.

26 Donald L. Chatman, 'Endometriosis in the Black Woman', *American Journal of Obstetrics & Gynecology* 125, no. 7 (1 Aug. 1976), 987–89: https://doi.org/10.1016/0002-9378(76)90502-0, accessed 12 December 2024.

27 Carrie B. Oser et al., 'African American Women and Sexually Transmitted Infections: The Contextual Influence of Unbalanced Sex Ratios and Individual Risk Behaviors', *Journal of Drug Issues* 47, no. 4 (Oct. 2017), 543–61: https://doi.org/10.1177/0022042616678610, accessed 12 December 2024.

28 Runzhi Wang et al., 'Association of Neighborhood Economic Status and Race With Developing Pelvic Inflammatory Disease After Sexually Transmitted Infections', *Obstetrics and Gynecology* 142, no. 4 (Oct. 2023), 948–55: https://doi.org/10.1097/AOG.0000000000005341, accessed 12 December 2024.

29 US Preventive Services Task Force, 'Screening for Hypertensive Disorders of Pregnancy: US Preventive Services Task Force Final Recommendation Statement', *JAMA* 330, no. 11 (19 Sept. 2023), 1074–82: https://doi.org/10.1001/jama.2023.16991, accessed 12 December 2024.

30 'Why Black Women Face a High Risk of Pregnancy Complications', Harvard School of Public Health, 25 Feb. 2019: https://www.hsph.harvard.edu/news/hsph-in-the-news/black-women-pregnancy-complications/, accessed 12 December 2024.

31 Juanita J. Chinn, Iman K. Martin, and Nicole Redmond, 'Health Equity Among Black Women in the United States', *Journal of Women's Health* 30, no. 2 (1 Feb. 2021), 212–19: https://doi.org/10.1089/jwh.2020.8868, accessed 12 December 2024.

32 Tyler Mitchell, 'Beyoncé in Her Own Words: Her Life, Her Body, Her Heritage', *Vogue*, 6 Aug. 2018: https://www.vogue.com/article/beyonce-september-issue-2018, accessed 12 December 2024.

33 'Dr Chaniece Wallace (1990–2020)', *Contemporary OB/GYN*, 30 Oct. 2020: https://www.contemporaryobgyn.net/view/dr-chaniece-wallace-1990-2020-, accessed 12 December 2024.

34 Shahd A. Karrar, Daniel J. Martingano, and Peter L. Hong, 'Preeclampsia', in *StatPearls* (Treasure Island, FL, 2024): http://www.ncbi.nlm.nih.gov/books/NBK570611/, accessed 12 December 2024.

35 'Dr Chaniece Wallace (1990–2020)'.

36 Marian F. MacDorman et al., 'Racial and Ethnic Disparities in Maternal Mortality in the United States Using Enhanced Vital Records, 2016–2017', *American Journal of Public Health* 111, no. 9 (Sept. 2021), 1673–81:

https://doi.org/10.2105/AJPH.2021.306375/, accessed 12 December 2024.

37 'Tori Bowie: American Three-Time Olympic Medallist Died from Complications in Childbirth', *BBC Sport*, 13 June 2023: https://www.bbc.com/sport/athletics/65887510/, accessed 12 December 2024.

38 'Saving Lives, Improving Mothers' Care . . .'.

39 Mary Beth Flanders-Stepans, 'Alarming Racial Differences in Maternal Mortality', *Journal of Perinatal Education* 9, no. 2 (2000), 50–51: https://doi.org/10.1624/105812400X87653, accessed 12 December 2024.

40 Lauren Chaloner, '"They didn't believe I was in labour" says black mother "ignored" by midwives', *Independent*, 18 Apr. 2023: https://www.independent.co.uk/news/health/maternity-labour-black-mothers-midwives-b2321307.html, accessed 12 December 2024.

41 Susan Devaney, 'Meet the Duo Fiercely Campaigning to Change the Black Maternity Experience', *British Vogue*, 4 May 2021: https://www.vogue.co.uk/beauty/article/five-x-more-black-maternity-experience, accessed 12 December 2024.

42 '2024 Black Maternal Health Week', Black Mamas Matter Alliance, https://blackmamasmatter.org/bmhw-2024/, accessed 26 July 2024.

43 'About Five X More', Five X More, https://fivexmore.org/about, accessed 26 July 2024.

44 'The New Government Must Commit to Transformative Change to Save More Babies' Lives', Sands, 8 July 2024: http://www.sands.org.uk/about-sands/media-centre/news/2024/07/new-government-must-commit-transformative-change-save-more, accessed 12 December 2024.

45 Tinuke Awe et al., 'The Black Maternity Experience Survey: A Nationwide Study of Black Women's Experiences of Maternity Services in the United Kingdom', Five X More, May 2022: https://static1.squarespace.com/static/5ee11f70fe99d54ddeb9ed4a/t/628a8756365828292ccb7712/1653245787911/The+Black+Maternity+Experience+Report.pdf, accessed 12 December 2024.

8. You Had a Baby

1. Jean Garnett, 'Scenes from an Open Marriage', *The Paris Review* (blog), 29 June 2022: https://www.theparisreview.org/blog/2022/06/29/scenes-from-an-open-marriage/, accessed 12 December 2024.
2. Rob Modic, 'Burt's Accuser Indicted', *Dayton Daily News*, 22 Aug. 1990.
3. James C. Burt and Joan Burt, *Surgery of Love* (New York, NY, 1975).
4. Sarah B. Rodriguez, *The Love Surgeon: A Story of Trust, Harm, and the Limits of Medical Regulation*, Critical Issues in Health and Medicine (New Brunswick, NJ, 2020), pp. 1–2.
5. Rodriguez, *Love Surgeon*, p. 128.
6. Rodriguez, *Love Surgeon*, p. 12.
7. Rodriguez, *Love Surgeon*, pp. 12–13.
8. Rodriguez, *Love Surgeon*, p. 13.
9. Rodriguez, *Love Surgeon*, p. 11.
10. Rodriguez, *Love Surgeon*, p. 128.
11. Rodriguez, *Love Surgeon*, p. 108.
12. Rodriguez, *Love Surgeon*, p. 108.
13. Rodriguez, *Love Surgeon*, p. 156.
14. Rodriguez, *Love Surgeon*, p. 176.
15. Montgomery Brower, 'James Burt's "Love Surgery" Was Supposed to Boost Pleasure, But Some Patients Say It Brought Pain', *People*, 27 Mar. 1989.
16. 'Ohio Woman Still Scarred By "Love" Doctor's Sex Surgery', *ABC News*, 6 Dec. 2012: https://abcnews.go.com/Health/ohio-woman-writes-book-love-doctor-mutilated-sex/story?id=17897317, accessed 12 December 2024.
17. Brower, 'James Burt's "Love Surgery" . . .'
18. Alice E. Adams, 'Molding Women's Bodies: The Surgeon as Sculptor', in *Bodily Discursions: Genders, Representations, Technologies*, edited by Deborah S. Wilson, and Christine Moneera Laennec, SUNY Series in Postmodern Culture (Albany, NY, 1997).
19. Sara Spettel and Mark Donald White, 'The Portrayal of J. Marion Sims' Controversial Surgical Legacy', *Journal of Urology* 185, no. 6 (June 2011): https://doi.org/10.1016/j.juro.2011.01.077, accessed 12 December 2024.

20 Meagan Flynn, 'Statue of "Father of Gynecology", Who Experimented on Enslaved Women, Removed from Central Park', *Washington Post*, 18 Apr. 2018: https://www.washingtonpost.com/news/morning-mix/wp/2018/04/18/statue-of-father-of-gynecology-who-experimented-on-enslaved-women-removed-from-central-park/, accessed 12 December 2024.

21 Lalita Kaplish, 'A Nasty History of the Vaginal Speculum', *Wellcome Collection*, 26 Sept. 2023: https://wellcomecollection.org/articles/ZRGkCBcAACYAq7rT, accessed 12 December 2024.

22 William H. Masters and Virginia E. Johnson, *Human Sexual Response* (Boston, MA, 1966).

23 James G. Pfaus et al., 'The Whole versus the Sum of Some of the Parts: Toward Resolving the Apparent Controversy of Clitoral versus Vaginal Orgasms', *Socioaffective Neuroscience & Psychology* 6 (25 Oct. 2016), 10.3402/snp.v6.32578: https://doi.org/10.3402/snp.v6.32578, accessed 12 December 2024.

24 Rachel E. Gross, *Vagina Obscura: An Anatomical Voyage* (New York, NY, 2022), p. 34.

25 Elizabeth Sheehan, 'Victorian Clitoridectomy: Isaac Baker Brown and His Harmless Operative Procedure', *Medical Anthropology Newsletter* 12, no. 4 (1981), 9–15: https://www.jstor.org/stable/647794, accessed 12 December 2024.

26 Adams, 'Molding Women's Bodies: The Surgeon as Sculptor'.

27 Rhett N. Willis et al., 'Labiaplasty Minora Reduction', in *StatPearls* (Treasure Island, FL, 2024): http://www.ncbi.nlm.nih.gov/books/NBK448086/, accessed 12 December 2024.

28 'Meet Dr. Alinsod', *South Coast Urogynecology* (blog): https://urogyn.org/about-us/meet-dr-alinsod/, accessed 26 July 2024.

29 'Labia Minora Plasty', *South Coast Urogynecology* (blog): https://urogyn.org/avs_minora/, accessed 26 July 2024.

30 'Vampire Wing Lift – Labia Majora Augmentation', *South Coast Urogynecology* (blog): https://urogyn.org/vampire-wing-lift-labia-majora-augmentation/, accessed 26 July 2024.

31 Maya Dusenbery, *Doing Harm: The Truth About How Bad Medicine and Lazy Science Leave Women Dismissed, Misdiagnosed, and Sick*, 1st edition (New York, NY, 2017), p. 14.

32 'ICD-11', WHO, https://icd.who.int/en, accessed 26 July 2024.
33 'GA13.2 Hypertrophy of Vulva', ICD-11: https://icd.who.int/browse/2024-01/mms/en#1318576293, accessed 26 July 2024.
34 'Labiaplasty (Vulval Surgery)', nhs.uk, 26 Jan. 2023: https://www.nhs.uk/conditions/cosmetic-procedures/cosmetic-surgery/labiaplasty/, accessed 12 December 2024.
35 Sarah B. Rodriguez, 'The History of Female Genital Cosmetic Surgery in the United States: From Marginal to Mainstream', in *Female Genital Cosmetic Surgery: Solution to What Problem?*, edited by Lih-Mei Liao and Sarah M. Creighton (Cambridge, 2019), pp. 33–41: https://doi.org/10.1017/9781108394673.004, accessed 12 December 2024.
36 Jillian Lloyd et al., 'Female Genital Appearance: "Normality" Unfolds', *BJOG: An International Journal of Obstetrics & Gynaecology* 112, no. 5 (2005), 643–46: https://doi.org/10.1111/j.1471-0528.2004.00517.x, accessed 12 December 2024.
37 Heinrich Loeb, 'Harnröhrencapacität und Tripperspritzen', *Münchener Medizinische Wochenschrift* 46, no. 2 (1899), 1016–18.
38 H. Wessells, T. F. Lue, and J. W. McAninch, 'Penile Length in the Flaccid and Erect States: Guidelines for Penile Augmentation', *Journal of Urology* 156, no. 3 (Sept. 1996), 995–97.
39 Rodriguez, 'History of Female Genital Cosmetic Surgery . . .'.
40 Rodriguez, 'History of Female Genital Cosmetic Surgery . . .'.
41 Deborah A. Sullivan, *Cosmetic Surgery: The Cutting Edge of Commercial Medicine in America* (New Brunswick, NJ, 2001), p. 74.
42 'ISAPS International Survey on Aesthetic/Cosmetic Procedures Performed in 2019', International Society of Aesthetic Plastic Surgery, 2020: https://www.isaps.org/it/discover/about-isaps/global-statistics/reports-and-press-releases/global-survey-2019-full-report-and-press-releases-english/, accessed 12 December 2024.
43 'Global Survey 2019: Full Report and Press Releases (English)', https://www.isaps.org/discover/about-isaps/global-statistics/reports-and-press-releases/global-survey-2019-full-report-and-press-releases-english/, accessed 26 July 2024.
44 Rodriguez, 'History of Female Genital Cosmetic Surgery . . .'.
45 Dorothy Shaw and Nicole Todd, 'Chapter 5: Drivers and Dilemmas of Female Genital Cosmetic Surgery', in *Ethical Issues in Women's Healthcare:*

Practice and Policy, edited by Lori d'Agincourt-Canning et al. (Oxford, 2019): https://doi.org/10.1093/med/9780190851361.003.0005, accessed 12 December 2024.

46 Jennifer A. Hayes and Meredith J. Temple-Smith, 'New Context, New Content – Rethinking Genital Anatomy in Textbooks', *Anatomical Sciences Education* 15, no. 5 (2022), 943–56: https://doi.org/10.1002/ase.2173, accessed 12 December 2024.

47 Shaw and Todd, 'Drivers and Dilemmas of Female Genital Cosmetic Surgery'.

48 Jennifer Gunter, *The Vagina Bible: The Vulva and the Vagina – Separating the Myth from the Medicine* (London, 2019), p. 167.

49 'Labiaplasty (Vulval Surgery)'.

50 'Aesthetic Vaginal Surgery', The Scarlett Phoenix / Dr Alexandra Runnels, 10 Apr. 2023: https://thescarlettphoenix.com/aesthetic-vaginal-surgery/, accessed 12 December 2024.

51 'Aesthetic Vaginal Surgery'.

52 Daniel C. Sasson, Christine A. Hamori, and Otto J. Placik, 'Labiaplasty: The Stigma Persists', *Aesthetic Surgery Journal* 42, no. 6 (18 May 2022), 638–43: https://doi.org/10.1093/asj/sjab335, accessed 12 December 2024.

53 Arianne Shahvisi, '"FGM" vs. Female "Cosmetic" Surgeries: Why Do They Continue to Be Treated Separately?', *International Journal of Impotence Research* 35, no. 3 (May 2023), 187–91: https://doi.org/10.1038/s41443-021-00514-8, accessed 12 December 2024.

54 Gross, *Vagina Obscura*, p. 42.

55 Sasson, Hamori, and Placik, 'Labiaplasty'.

56 'Female Genital Mutilation: The Crown Prosecution Service', 16 August 2023; updated 30 July 2024: https://www.cps.gov.uk/legal-guidance/female-genital-mutilation, accessed 26 July 2024.

57 Lindy McDougall, *The Perfect Vagina: Cosmetic Surgery in the Twenty-First Century* (Bloomington, IN, 2021), p. 12.

58 Hong Jiang et al., 'Selective versus Routine Use of Episiotomy for Vaginal Birth', *Cochrane Database of Systematic Reviews*, no. 2 (2017): https://doi.org/10.1002/14651858.CD000081.pub3, accessed 12 December 2024.

59 Kyle Barjon and Heba Mahdy, 'Episiotomy', in *StatPearls* (Treasure Island, FL, 2024): http://www.ncbi.nlm.nih.gov/books/NBK546675/, accessed 12 December 2024.

60 'Episiotomy: When It's Needed, When It's Not', Mayo Clinic, https://www.mayoclinic.org/healthy-lifestyle/labor-and-delivery/in-depth/episiotomy/art-20047282, accessed 7 September 2022.
61 'Female Genital Tract Surgery', BAPRAS, https://www.bapras.org.uk/public/patient-information/surgery-guides/female-genital-tract-surgery, accessed 7 September 2022.
62 Vanessa Barbara, 'Latin America Claims to Love Its Mothers. Why Does It Abuse Them?', *The New York Times*, 11 Mar. 2019: https://www.nytimes.com/2019/03/11/opinion/latin-america-obstetric-violence.html, accessed 12 December 2024.
63 Christine J. Parisien, and Marvin L. Corman, 'The Secca® Procedure for the Treatment of Fecal Incontinence: Definitive Therapy or Short-Term Solution', *Clinics in Colon and Rectal Surgery* 18, no. 1 (Feb. 2005), 42–5: https://doi.org/10.1055/s-2005-864080, accessed 12 December 2024.
64 'Endoscopic Radiofrequency Therapy of the Anal Sphincter for Faecal Incontinence: Guidance', National Institute for Health and Care Excellence (NICE, 25 May 2011): https://www.nice.org.uk/guidance/ipg393, accessed 12 December 2024.
65 McDougall, *The Perfect Vagina*, p. 78.
66 'Labiaplasty (Vulval Surgery)', accessed 12 December 2024.
67 Sara Rodrigues, 'From Vaginal Exception to Exceptional Vagina: The Biopolitics of Female Genital Cosmetic Surgery', *Sexualities* 15, no. 7 (1 Oct. 2012), 778–94: https://doi.org/10.1177/1363460712454073, accessed 12 December 2024.
68 Joseph J. Pariser and Nicholas Kim, 'Transgender Vaginoplasty: Techniques and Outcomes', *Translational Andrology and Urology* 8, no. 3 (June 2019), 241–47: https://doi.org/10.21037/tau.2019.06.03, accessed 12 December 2024.
69 'Standards of Care for the Health of Transgender and Gender Diverse People, Version 8', *International Journal of Transgender Health*: https://www.tandfonline.com/doi/pdf/10.1080/26895269.2022.2100644, accessed 12 December 2024.
70 https://pubmed.ncbi.nlm.nih.gov/39385869/, accessed 12 December 2024.
71 https://pubmed.ncbi.nlm.nih.gov/37105933/, accessed 12 December 2024.
72 Gross, *Vagina Obscura*.
73 Gabriel Veber Moisés da Silva et al., 'Male-to-Female Gender-Affirming Surgery: 20-Year Review of Technique and Surgical Results', *Frontiers*

in Surgery 8 (5 May 2021): https://doi.org/10.3389/fsurg.2021.639430, accessed 12 December 2024.

74 Shon Faye, *The Transgender Issue: Trans Justice Is Justice for All* (London, 2022), p. 77.

75 https://www.transhealthcare.org/vaginoplasty/, accessed 12 December 2024.

9. Which Box Do I Tick?

1 Christiane Völling, *Ich war Mann und Frau. Mein Leben als Intersexuelle* (Köln, 2010), p. 13.
2 Ifeanyi I. Momodu, Brian Lee, and Gurdeep Singh, 'Congenital Adrenal Hyperplasia', in *StatPearls* (Treasure Island, FL, 2024): http://www.ncbi.nlm.nih.gov/books/NBK448098/, accessed 12 December 2024.
3 Andrea Brandt and Barbara Supp, 'Sexualität: Und Gott schuf das dritte Geschlecht', *Der Spiegel*, 12 Dec. 2007: https://www.spiegel.de/spiegel/a-517983.html, accessed 12 December 2024.
4 Anna Maitland, *In re Völling*, no. 25 O 179/07 (Landgericht Köln, 6 Feb. 2008).
5 Völling, *Ich war Mann und Frau*, p. 44.
6 Maitland, *In re Völling*.
7 Brandt and Supp, 'Sexualität'.
8 Maitland, *In re Völling*.
9 Catherine Harper, *Intersex*, 1st edition (Oxford; New York, NY, 2007), p. 2.
10 Sigmund Freud, 'Lecture XXXIII: Femininity', in *The Standard Edition of the Complete Psychological Works of Sigmund Freud*, 24 vols, vol. 22, *New Introductory Lectures On Psycho-Analysis and Other Works (1932–1936)*, edited by James Strachey (London, 1964), pp. 112–35.
11 Harper, *Intersex*, p. 2.
12 Maitland, *In re Völling*.
13 Maitland, *In re Völling*.
14 Maitland, *In re Völling*.
15 Maitland, *In re Völling*.
16 Völling, *Ich war Mann und Frau*, p. 96.
17 Brandt and Supp, 'Sexualität'.

18 'How Common Is Intersex?', Intersex Society of North America, 22 Aug. 2009: https://web.archive.org/web/20090822212522/http://www.isna.org/faq/frequency/, accessed 12 December 2024.
19 https://interactadvocates.org/faq/, accessed 12 December 2024.
20 'Cleft Lip & Palate', National Institute of Dental and Craniofacial Research: https://www.nidcr.nih.gov/health-info/cleft-lip-palate, accessed 27 July 2024.
21 https://www.degruyter.com/document/doi/10.18574/nyu/9780814731895.003.0009/pdf, accessed 12 December 2024.
22 Anne Fausto-Sterling, 'The Five Sexes', *The Sciences* 33, no. 2 (1993), 20–24: https://doi.org/10.1002/j.2326-1951.1993.tb03081.x, accessed 12 December 2024.
23 'UN Free & Equal: Intersex', United Nations Office of the High Commissioner for Human Rights, https://www.unfe.org/en/know-the-facts/challenges-solutions/intersex, accessed 27 July 2024.
24 Melanie Blackless et al., 'How Sexually Dimorphic Are We? Review and Synthesis', *American Journal of Human Biology: The Official Journal of the Human Biology Council* 12, no. 2 (Mar. 2000), 151–66: https://doi.org/10.1002/(SICI)1520-6300(200003/04)12:2<151::AID-AJHB1>3.0.CO;2-F, accessed 12 December 2024.
25 https://journals.sagepub.com/doi/10.1177/0306312718757081, accessed 12 December 2024.
26 Momodu, Lee, and Singh, 'Congenital Adrenal Hyperplasia'.
27 Shikha Singh and Stella Ilyayeva, 'Androgen Insensitivity Syndrome', in *StatPearls* (Treasure Island, FL, 2024): http://www.ncbi.nlm.nih.gov/books/NBK542206/, accessed 12 December 2024.
28 Carole Samango-Sprouse et al., 'Klinefelter Syndrome and Turner Syndrome', *Pediatrics in Review* 42, no. 5 (1 May 2021), 272–74: https://doi.org/10.1542/pir.2020-004028, accessed 12 December 2024.
29 'Intersex Conditions', Intersex Society of North America: https://isna.org/faq/conditions/, accessed 27 July 2024.
30 Elizabeth Reis, *Bodies in Doubt: An American History of Intersex* (Baltimore, MD, 2009), p. 121.
31 Reis, *Bodies*, p. 3.
32 Reis, *Bodies*, pp. 8–15.
33 Reis, *Bodies*, pp. 45–54.

34 Reis, *Bodies*, p. xii.
35 Reis, *Bodies*, pp. 59–68.
36 Reis, *Bodies*, pp. 45–46.
37 Reis, *Bodies*, p. xiii.
38 Alice Domurat Dreger, *Hermaphrodites and the Medical Invention of Sex*, 1st edition (Cambridge, MA, 1998), p. 158.
39 David Andrew Griffiths, 'Diagnosing sex: Intersex and "sex change" in Britain 1930–1955', *Sexualities* 21, no. 3 (17 Jan. 2018), 476–95: https://journals.sagepub.com/doi/10.1177/1363460717740339, accessed 12 December 2024.
40 Jemima Repo, 'The Birth of Gender: Social Control, Hermaphroditism, and the New Postwar Sexual Apparatus', in *The Biopolitics of Gender*, edited by Jemima Repo (Oxford, 2015): https://doi.org/10.1093/acprof:oso/9780190256913.003.0002, accessed 12 December 2024.
41 Harper, *Intersex*, p. 47.
42 *Secret Intersex*, documentary, WAGtv, 2004.
43 Harper, *Intersex*, p. 29.
44 Dreger, *Hermaphrodites and the Medical Invention of Sex*, p. 190.
45 *Secret Intersex*.
46 Harper, *Intersex*, p. 30.
47 Harper, *Intersex*, p. 30.
48 Harper, *Intersex*, pp. 34–35.
49 Harper, *Intersex*, p. 35.
50 Harper, *Intersex*, p. 34.
51 Morgan Holmes, 'In(to)Visibility: Intersexuality in the Field of Queer', in *Looking Queer: Body Image and Identity in Lesbian, Bisexual, Gay, and Transgender Communities*, edited by Dawn Atkins, Haworth Gay and Lesbian Studies (Birmingham, NY, 1998), p. 224.
52 Holmes, 'In(to)Visibility . . .', p. 225.
53 Harper, *Intersex*, p. 43.
54 John Colapinto, *As Nature Made Him: The Boy Who Was Raised as a Girl* (New York, NY, 2000), p. 49.
55 Colapinto, *As Nature Made Him*, pp. 50–52.
56 'David Reimer, 38, Subject of the John/Joan Case', *The New York Times*, 12 May 2004: https://www.nytimes.com/2004/05/12/us/david-reimer-38-subject-of-the-john-joan-case.html, accessed 12 December 2024.

57 Alice D. Dreger and April M. Herndon, 'Progress and Politics in the Intersex Rights Movement: Feminist Theory in Action', *GLQ: A Journal of Lesbian and Gay Studies* 15, no. 2 (1 Apr. 2009), 199–224: https://doi.org/10.1215/10642684-2008-134, accessed 12 December 2024.
58 Harper, *Intersex*, p. 44.
59 Colapinto, *As Nature Made Him*, pp. 86–88.
60 Colapinto, *As Nature Made Him*, pp. 86–88.
61 Harper, *Intersex*, p. 44.
62 John Money and Anke A. Ehrhardt, *Man & Woman: Boy & Girl* (Baltimore, MD, 1972).
63 'Dr Money and the Boy with No Penis', *Horizon*, BBC Two, 4 Nov. 2004.
64 'David Reimer, 38, Subject of the John/Joan Case'.
65 Harper, *Intersex*, p. 45.
66 Benedict Carey, 'John William Money, 84, Sexual Identity Researcher, Dies', *The New York Times*, 11 July 2006: https://www.nytimes.com/2006/07/11/us/11money.html, accessed 12 December 2024.
67 Maitland, *In re Völling*.
68 StopIGM.org, 'Nuremberg Hermaphrodite Lawsuit: Michaela "Micha" Raab Wins Damages and Compensation for Intersex Genital Mutilations!', StopIGM.org, 17 Dec. 2015: https://stopigm.org/nuremberg-hermaphrodite-lawsuit-damages-and-compensation-for-intersex-genital-mutilations/, accessed 12 December 2024.
69 Völling, *Ich war Mann und Frau*.
70 Brandt and Supp, 'Sexualität'.
71 Maitland, *In re Völling*.
72 Maitland, *In re Völling*.
73 *Secret Intersex*.
74 Harper, *Intersex*, p. 36.
75 Völling, *Ich war Mann und Frau*, p. 116.
76 Judith Butler, *Undoing Gender*, 1st edition (New York; London, 2004), p. 64.
77 Butler, *Undoing Gender*, p. 65.
78 'Malta Declaration' in *The Legal Status of Intersex Persons*, edited by Jens M. Scherpe et al. (Cambridge, 2018), pp. 7–10: https://www.cambridge.org/core/books/abs/legal-status-of-intersex-persons/malta-declaration/EC07BEA9EFC219346352D531DD6CBC03, accessed 12 December 2024.

79 Kieran Guilbert, 'Surgery and sterilization scrapped in Malta's benchmark LGBTI law', *Reuters*, 1 April 2015: https://www.reuters.com/article/lifestyle/surgery-and-sterilization-scrapped-in-maltas-benchmark-lgbti-law-idUSKBN0MS4ZD/, accessed 12 December 2024.

Conclusion. Cause of Death: Woman

1 'Heart Disease Facts', CDC, 24 July 2024: https://www.cdc.gov/heart-disease/data-research/facts-stats/index.html, accessed 12 December 2024.
2 Jing Liu et al., 'Age-Stratified Sex Disparities in Care and Outcomes in Patients With ST-Elevation Myocardial Infarction', *American Journal of Medicine* 133, no. 11 (Nov. 2020), 1293–1301.e1: https://doi.org/10.1016/j.amjmed.2020.03.059, accessed 12 December 2024.
3 Wu et al., 'Impact of Initial Hospital Diagnosis on Mortality for Acute Myocardial Infarction', accessed 12 December 2024.
4 Gudny Stella Gudnadottir et al., 'Gender Differences in Coronary Angiography, Subsequent Interventions, and Outcomes among Patients with Acute Coronary Syndromes', *American Heart Journal* 191 (Sept. 2017), 65–74: https://doi.org/10.1016/j.ahj.2017.06.014, accessed 12 December 2024.
5 Min Zhao et al., 'Sex Differences in Cardiovascular Medication Prescription in Primary Care: A Systematic Review and Meta-Analysis', *Journal of the American Heart Association: Cardiovascular and Cerebrovascular Disease* 9, no. 11 (20 June 2020), e014742: https://doi.org/10.1161/JAHA.119.014742, accessed 12 December 2024.
6 Kyle J. Schulte and Harvey N. Mayrovitz, 'Myocardial Infarction Signs and Symptoms: Females vs. Males', *Cureus* 15, no. 4 (13 Apr. 2023), e37522: https://doi.org/10.7759/cureus.37522, accessed 12 December 2024.
7 Hoa L. Nguyen et al., 'Age and Sex Differences in Duration of Prehospital Delay in Patients with Acute Myocardial Infarction: A Systematic Review', *Circulation: Cardiovascular Quality and Outcomes* 3, no. 1 (Jan. 2010), 82–92: https://doi.org/10.1161/CIRCOUTCOMES.109.884361, accessed 12 December 2024.

8 'Summary Report: Outpatient Appointments by Gender', NHS England, 8 Oct. 2020: https://digital.nhs.uk/data-and-information/publications/statistical/hospital-outpatient-activity/2019-20/summary-report---gender, accessed 12 December 2024.
9 'No Difference in Key Heart Attack Symptoms Between Men and Women', British Heart Foundation: https://www.bhf.org.uk/what-we-do/news-from-the-bhf/news-archive/2019/august/no-difference-in-key-heart-attack-symptoms-between-men-and-women, accessed 12 December 2024.
10 Amy V. Ferry et al., 'Presenting Symptoms in Men and Women Diagnosed With Myocardial Infarction Using Sex-Specific Criteria', *Journal of the American Heart Association* 8, no. 17 (Sept. 2019), e012307: https://doi.org/10.1161/JAHA.119.012307, accessed 12 December 2024.
11 'No Difference in Key Heart Attack Symptoms Between Men and Women'.
12 Barbara Sadick, 'Women Die from Heart Attacks More Often Than Men. Here's Why – and What Doctors Are Doing About It', *Time*, 1 Apr. 2019: https://time.com/5499872/women-heart-disease/, accessed 12 December 2024.
13 Claudia Goldin and Adriana Lleras-Muney, 'XX > XY?: The Changing Female Advantage in Life Expectancy', *Journal of Health Economics* 67 (Sept. 2019), 102224: https://doi.org/10.1016/j.jhealeco.2019.102224, accessed 12 December 2024.
14 A. H. E. M. Maas, and Y. E. A. Appelman, 'Gender Differences in Coronary Heart Disease', *Netherlands Heart Journal* 18, no. 12 (Dec. 2010), 598–602: https://www.ncbi.nlm.nih.gov/pmc/articles/PMC3018605/, accessed 12 December 2024.
15 Schulte and Mayrovitz, 'Myocardial Infarction Signs and Symptoms'.
16 Vedavati Patwardhan et al., 'Differences Across the Lifespan Between Females and Males in the Top 20 Causes of Disease Burden Globally: A Systematic Analysis of the Global Burden of Disease Study 2021', *The Lancet Public Health* 9, no. 5 (1 May 2024), e282–94: https://doi.org/10.1016/S2468-2667(24)00053-7, accessed 12 December 2024.
17 Arthur J. Barsky, Heli M. Peekna, and Jonathan F. Borus, 'Somatic Symptom Reporting in Women and Men', *Journal of General Internal Medicine* 16, no. 4 (Apr. 2001), 266–75: https://doi.org/10.1046/j.1525-1497.2001.00229.x, accessed 12 December 2024.

Index

Abe, Clotilde Rebecca 157
abortion 7, 67, 91, 92, 109–20, 157
access to healthcare, equitable 10, 157, 212
Adams, Alice E. 166, 168
Addenbrooke's, Cambridge 83
African Americans 100, 151, 154–5, 194
Agency for Healthcare Research and Quality, US 102–3
Alinsod, Red 169–71, 175, 177, 179
amenorrhoea (cessation of menstrual periods) 77
American College of Physicians (ACP) 128
American Medical Systems 32, 34
American Society of Reproductive Medicine (ASRM) 45
anaemia 144, 148, 158
anaesthesia 39, 40, 43, 54–5, 89, 92–6, 110, 166, 190, 194–5
Anderson-Bialis, Deborah 47
androgen insensitivity syndrome (AIS) 193
angiogram 209
anovulation (cessation of ovulation) 77
anterior colporrhaphy 121
anti-psychosis medication 125
anxiety 72, 76, 97, 106, 110, 123, 136, 137, 139, 140–41, 143, 180, 207
Apogee mesh 32
appendectomy 188
aromatase excess syndrome 193
Avaulta Solo mesh 32
Awe, Tinuke 156–7
Ayers, Susan 79

'baby blues' 137
bacterial infection 4, 76, 188
Baker Brown, Isaac 167–8
Bard Medical 32
Barry, Arthur 91–2
Batiste, Linda 34
Baudelocque, Jean-Louis/Baudelocque's diameter 88

Beckham, Victoria 81
Behan, Matilda 86–7, 90
Biden, Joe 120
bilateral orchidectomy 199
biomaterial 26–7
Birthrights 97
birth trauma 68–85, 137, 178
Black Mamas Matter Alliance (BMMA) 157
Black Maternal Health Week 157
Black people 7, 143–58, 166, 194, 212
  Black women 144–58, 166
  Black men 7, 156
blame 3, 6–7, 10, 15, 21, 35–6, 40, 43, 140–41, 155, 193, 211–12
bleeding 4, 48, 53–4, 75, 76, 84, 110, 112, 116, 138, 160, 165
Bonaparte, Marie 167
Boston Scientific 30–31, 38
Bourn Hall Clinic 44
Bowie, Tori 154–5
Bradley, Robert 96
breast cancer 7, 129
breastfeeding 72, 101–8, 137
British Association of Plastic Reconstructive and Aesthetic Surgeons 178
British Journal of Obstetrics and Gynaecology 151
British Medical Journal 80
British Pregnancy Advisory Service (BPAS) 114
Brown, John 149
Brown, Louise 45
Brown, Lyn 55
Browning, Jimmie Dean 165
Burt, James C. 162–8
Butler, Judith 203–4

C-section 76, 79–83, 86–101, 108, 116, 153
Cambridge University 44
Campaign Against Painful Hysteroscopy 54–5
cancer 7–8, 37–8, 53, 55–8, 60–62, 85, 129, 130, 131, 163, 171

Cardozo, Linda 36
Carmody, Mrs Francis X. 94
Carr, Lindsey 154
Catholic Church 87, 88, 90, 91, 117, 118
CDC (Centers for Disease Control and Prevention), US 47
   'Hear Her' campaign 85
Center for Reproductive Rights 119–20
Centre for Evidence-Based Medicine at the University of Oxford 46, 130
cervical cancer 38
   screening (smear test) 11, 55–62, 212
cervix 9, 17, 53–4, 55, 56, 60, 75, 110, 138, 191
Chatman, Donald 152
childbirth 6
   birth debriefing services 83–4
   birth protocols 100
   birth trauma 68–85, 136–7, 178
   Black women and *see* Black women
   C-section and *see* C-section
   epidural and 1, 3, 5, 8, 48–52, 108
   female genital cosmetic surgery (FGCS) and 168–85
   hypnobirthing 51
   labour 48–50, 52, 68, 69, 73–6, 80–84, 86, 88, 89, 90, 92–5, 98, 107, 115, 116, 130, 144–6, 156, 164, 177
   maternal imagination 140–41
   maternal mortality rates 76, 88, 89, 100, 147, 153, 154, 155, 157
   miscarriage 7, 47, 116, 130, 141–2
   natural birth movement 51, 96
   pain relief during, origins of 92–6
   postpartum depression 76, 78
   prolapse and *see* prolapse
   six-week check 8, 9, 14, 98
   tokophobia/fear of pain during 96–7
   vaginal birth 18, 81–2, 89, 90, 91, 96–101, 103, 108, 110, 212
chloroform 93, 94
chronic fatigue syndrome (CFS) 37, 170
Clayton, Janine Austin 37
Cleary, Aisha 146–7
Cleary, Rianna 144–7
Cleveland Clinic 97
clinical research
   clinical trials 18–20, 24, 26, 27, 30, 31, 32–5, 38, 42, 47, 50, 62, 83, 93, 115, 129, 131
   gaps in 37, 212

   inclusion of female subjects in 37
   racism and 155
   US influence on 38
clitoris 15, 163–5, 167–70, 173, 181, 182, 192, 194
   clitoridectomy (surgical removal of the clitoris) 167–8
coccyx (tailbone) 75
Cochrane 50, 122
congenital anomalies 109, 116, 130, 140
Colapinto, John: *As Nature Made Him: The Boy Who Was Raised as a Girl* 200
colpocleisis 39–40
communism 72–4, 117–18
Competition and Markets Authority, UK government 102
congenital adrenal hyperplasia (CAH) 187–8, 190, 192–3
Contemporary OB/GYN 154
'contested' conditions 37, 170
contraception 78, 91, 92, 109
Cornwell, Jessica: *Birth Notes* 84, 98
coronary heart disease 7, 207, 208–11
Covid-19 55, 62, 114, 116
craniotomy 88
Creasy, Stella 120
cube pessary 183–4
'Czarny Poniedziałek' (Black Monday) 118

Dawson, Diane 24–5, 35
Del Castillo-Hegyi, Christie 103–5
dementia 7
Department of Health and Social Care, UK 52
Department of Justice, UK 147
Depo-Testosterone 78
depression 7, 25, 78, 106, 124–7, 135–7, 139–40, 142, 148, 201
   antidepressant medication 106, 126, 201
   postpartum 76
diabetes 47, 100, 212
Dick-Read, Grantly 95–6; *Childbirth Without Fear* 96
diethylstilbestrol (DES) 130
dilatation and evacuation 110
dilator therapy 62–5
disabilities 8, 104, 110, 114, 118, 141, 148
Doctrine of Double Effect 119
domperidone 105–7
dopamine 105
double cryptorchidism (undescended testicles) 188

Downtown Presbyterian Hospital, Albuquerque, New Mexico 103
Dreger, Alice 196
Duffield, Rosie 107
Dusenbery, Maya: *Doing Harm* 170

eclampsia 76, 154–5
Edinburgh Royal Infirmary 210
Edwards, Robert 44–5
egg-retrieval 44
Elvie Trainer 15–17
endometrial scratching 45, 47–8
endometriosis 4, 7, 14, 37, 57, 59–60, 138–40, 151–2, 155
endoscopy 53
epidural 1, 3, 5, 8, 48–52, 108
episiotomy 74, 75, 97, 108, 163, 164, 177–9
Ethicon 22–4, 25, 26, 27, 28, 31–4, 36
ethnic minority people 7, 194. *See also* Black men *and* Black women
European Convention on Human Rights (ECHR): Article 8 97
European Union (EU) 97

Fausto-Sterling, Anne 192
Faye, Shon: *The Transgender Issue* 182–3
FDA (Food and Drug Administration), US 27, 30–31, 32, 33–4, 38, 128
    Premarket Approval 30–31
    Section 510(k) rule 30
Fed is Best Foundation 104
Federal Court of Australia 23, 35
Felix, Allyson 155
female genital cosmetic surgery (FGCS) 168–85
female genital mutilation (FGM) 57, 175, 176–7
female pseudo-hermaphroditism 189
feminism 94
fentanyl 41–2, 43
fertility 7
    abortion and 109
    add-ons 45–6
    Black women and 150–51
    endometriosis and *see* endometriosis
    infertility 7, 8, 41, 43–8, 63, 77, 89, 92, 109, 134, 135, 139–40, 141, 150–51, 157, 193
    IVF 42–8, 52, 65–6
    MRKH and 63

testosterone and 77
vaginal steaming and 134, 135
FertilityIQ 47
'Finding Joy Again' (podcast interview) 135
fistula 7, 18, 31, 87, 88, 149, 166, 177
Five X More 157, 158
Fleming, Alexander 90
formula milk 101–5, 108
Foster, Carla 114–15
Freud, Sigmund 167, 190

Garnett, Jean 159
gender-affirming care 66, 77–8, 79, 183
    gender-affirming hormone therapies (GAHT) 77
gender violence 6, 8, 90, 212
genital surgery 58, 59, 183, 194–6
Ghodsee, Kristen R.: *Why Women Have Better Sex Under Socialism* 73
Gill, Kathryn 21–4, 35, 36
'Giving Voice to the Mothers' study 147
Goldfarb-Newman Protocol 107
Goop 132–6
Grace (friend of author) 143–4, 147–8, 149, 155–6
Gross, Rachel E.: *Vagina Obscura* 176, 182
Gunter, Jen: *The Menopause Manifesto* 128–9, 135, 174
gynaecologist 13, 14, 15, 16, 29, 32, 36, 44, 66, 90, 127, 128–9, 135, 151, 152, 162, 163, 165, 173–4, 179, 183–5
Gynemesh PS 24, 32

haemorrhoids 75
Halappanavar, Savita 116
Halban, Josef 167
Hamilton, Thomas 149
Harper, Catherine: *Intersex* 189–90, 196–8
Harris, Andrzej 1, 3, 5, 10, 14, 68, 72, 108, 122, 123, 159, 160, 184, 186, 205, 206–7
Hazard, Leah 88–9
Health Issues Centre 38
Health Services Safety Investigations Body (HSSIB) 126
heart attack 7, 116, 129, 209–11
heartburn 143, 147–8
heart disease 7, 100, 207–11
hermaphrodite 189–90, 192, 194
hernia 17, 25–8, 29, 31, 32

HFEA (the Human Fertilisation and Embryology Authority) 46, 47
Holmes, Morgan 198
hormone replacement therapy (HRT) 126–36, 202, 207
HPV (human papillomavirus) 56–7, 60, 62
Human Sexual Response report 167
Hunt, Jeremy 80
'husband stitch' ix, 179
hypochondria 136, 138, 211
hypertensive disorders 76
hypovolaemic shock 76
hysterectomy 6, 118, 163–6, 184
hysteria, female 167, 211
hysteroscopy 52–5, 66, 67

Idaho, US, Biden's government sues (2022) 120
idiopathic foot neuropathy 41
immune system 27, 28, 43, 47, 56, 138
incontinence 7, 13–14, 16, 18, 21, 25, 75, 86–7, 122, 177, 178, 179, 183, 184, 197
  bladder incontinence 7, 165
  overflow incontinence 18
  stress urinary incontinence (SUI) 13, 17–20, 23–4, 25, 28, 29–30, 31, 33, 38
  total incontinence 18
  urge incontinence 18
incubator 70–71, 115
infant feeding 101–2, 106
infertility 7, 8, 41, 43–8, 63, 77, 89, 92, 109, 134, 135, 139–40, 141, 150–51, 157, 193
inflammation 4, 27, 138, 152, 207
inguinal hernia 25
insomnia 77, 78, 207
intersex people 7, 8, 186–205, 211, 212
Iran 100–101
Ireland 86–7, 91, 116, 120
IVF (*in vitro* fertilization) 42–8, 52, 65–6

jaundice 103, 104
Jo's Cervical Cancer Trust 58–60
John/Joan case 199–201
John Paul II, Pope 118
Johnson & Johnson 23–4, 30–36, 38
Johnson, Virginia E. 63
Journal of the American Medical Association 38
Journal of Perinatal Education 137
Journal of Urology 31

Kaiser Family Foundation 147
Kegel aid 13–15
Kegel, Alfred 13
Kegel muscle 164
Kegels *see* pelvic-floor exercises
King's College Hospital, London 36
Kleinplatz, Peggy J. 63
Klinefelter syndrome 193
Knuddelbär (Hungarian Vizsla) 160–61

labia
  labia minora 163, 164, 168, 169, 182
  labial laxity 169, 179
  labiaplasty 59, 168–82
labour, birth 48–50, 52, 68, 69, 73–6, 80–84, 86, 88, 89, 90, 92–5, 98, 107, 115, 116, 130, 144–6, 156, 164, 177
Labour Party 107, 120, 157
labour within the home 74
lactation 103–7
Lamaze, Fernand 96
laminaria tent 54
Laurent, Bo 192
Le Fort, Léon Clément 39–40
Lee, Ingrid Fetell: *Joyful: The Surprising Power of Ordinary Things to Create Extraordinary Happiness* 135
Leopold, Prince 93
lichen sclerosus 174
lidocaine gel 66
Lim, Anita 61–2
Limburg, Joanne 141
listening to patients 79, 82–5, 156–7, 212
liver failure 47, 154
'love surgery' 162–7

Machado, Carmen Maria: 'The Husband Stitch' ix
Mad Men 95
Madison, Tianna 155
Magdalene laundries 90
Malta Declaration (2013) 204
Margolis, Tom 23
Martin, Bill 31
Masters, William H. 63, 167
maternal imagination 140–41
maternal mortality rates 76, 88, 89, 100, 147, 153, 154, 155, 157

Mayer-Rokitansky-Küster-Hauser (MRKH) syndrome 63–4, 65, 193
Mayo Clinic 139–40, 178
MBRRACE-UK Report 155, 157
McDougall, Lindy 177; *The Perfect Vagina* 179–80
medical misogyny 6, 8, 11, 194, 212
Medical Research Council 44
Medscand 32–3
Meigs, Charles 94
menopause 53–4, 57, 125–36, 207
mental health 14, 76, 83, 97, 106, 114, 121–42, 189
  'baby blues' 137
  anti-psychosis medication 125
  anxiety *see* anxiety
  burden of responsibility 140–41
  depression *see* depression
  endometriosis and 138–40
  hormone replacement therapy (HRT) 126–36
  maternal imagination 140–41
  menopause and 125–36
  miscarriage and 141–2
  paranoia 124–6
  perinatal psychosis 124–6, 142, 143
  positive mindset 141
  psychological birth trauma 136–7
  PTSD *see* post-traumatic stress disorder (PTSD)
  self-blame after pregnancy loss 140
  SSD (somatic symptom syndrome) 137
  therapy 122–4
Mersilene 32
mesh, vaginal 21–39, 131
mifepristone 110, 114
miscarriage 7, 47, 116, 130, 141–2
misoprostol 110, 114
Molla, Gianna Beretta 118–19
Money, John 195–6, 198–201
Monticone, Donna 41–3
Moorhead, Joanna: 'Epidurals are for wimps' 52
morning sickness 124, 130
morphine 92–5
Morrissey, Jacqueline 90, 91
Morrison, Toni: *The Bluest Eye* 148–9
mortality gap 157
Morton, William 93
motherhood, sacrifice and 118–19
'Mothers & Others Guide' 104
myalgic encephalomyelitis (ME) 37

National Birthday Trust Fund 94
National Childbirth Trust (NCT) 123, 143
National Institutes of Health (NIH), US 37
National Maternity Hospital, Dublin 86, 91
National Twilight Sleep Association 94
'natural' term 108
nausea 5, 77, 207
neovagina 63, 64, 65, 182
New England Journal of Medicine 48
New York Times 37, 42, 199–200
NHS (National Health Service) 4, 39, 45–6, 57, 59, 77
  abortion and 114
  Alcohol Brief Intervention programme 112–13
  Black women and 147
  C-section and 80, 83 85, 87, 99
  Kegel aids and 15
  epidural and 49, 51–2
  FGCS and 171, 174, 180, 184
  hysteroscopy 54, 55
  mental health and 122, 125
  MRKH 65
  Ockenden Report into the Shrewsbury and Telford Hospital Trust scandal (2022) 79–83, 85
  understaffing 80–81, 85
  waiting times 77, 85
  'YouScreen' 61–2
NICE (National Institute for Health and Care Excellence) 97, 126, 181
Nobel Prize 44, 150
non-binary people 60–61, 78, 79, 211
Northern Ireland, abortion decriminalised in (2019) 120
Northwestern University 175, 196

O'Connor, Marie 90
Obstetrics and Gynecology 65
Ockenden Report into the Shrewsbury and Telford Hospital Trust scandal (2022) 79–83, 85
oestrogen 127, 128, 131, 136, 192, 193
oocyte (egg) quantity 77
opioid addiction 41
optimum gender rearing model 199
ovaries 78, 138, 188–91, 193, 195, 202
  ovarian cancer 8, 38, 163
  ovarian cysts 14, 191
  ovarian reserve 77

overactive bladder syndrome 18
ovotesticular syndrome 193

pain 4, 7, 22, 23, 24, 29, 36, 41–67
  anaesthesia and 39, 40, 43, 54–5, 89, 92–6, 110, 166, 190, 194–5
  birth trauma and 69–71, 75, 77, 86–7
  Black people and 148–9, 152, 156–7
  childbirth, origins of relief in 92–6
  chronic pain 8, 13, 14, 25, 50, 86–7, 122, 138, 166, 175
  dilator therapy and 62–7, 212
  endometriosis and 138
  epidural and 1, 3, 5, 8, 48–52, 108
  FGCS and 173–5, 178
  gender and 210–11
  heart attack and 208–11
  hysteroscopies and 52–5
  IVF 42–8
  opioid addiction 41–4
  relief 42–3, 49–55, 66–7, 69, 92–6, 108, 156, 207
  sex and 161–6
  smear test 55–62
  tokophobia 96–8
  tolerance 149–50
  twilight sleep and 94–6
Paltrow, Gwyneth 132–5
pan-hysterocolpectomy 39
Pantaleóni, Diomede 53–4
paranoia 124–6
Parkinson's disease 105
pelvic floor/pelvic-floor exercises 13–20, 28, 39, 40, 75, 164
pelvic inflammatory disease (PID) 152
penicillin 90
penis 63, 160, 164, 167, 181, 189, 195, 198–9
  penile inversion vaginoplasty 182–3
  penile skin 181
Pepperall, Sir Edward 115
perinatal psychosis 124–6, 142, 143
perinea 13, 75, 178
period, menstrual 14, 74, 77, 106, 109, 130, 134, 135, 138, 139, 151, 210–11
pessary 7, 15, 39, 183–4
pethidine 66
Phillips, Janet 162–5
phimosis 198–9
Pirogov, Nikolay 93–4

pituitary gland 105
Pius XII, Pope 92
placenta 75, 84
Planned Parenthood 78
Poland 51, 68–9, 73, 74, 115–19, 120, 183
polypropylene 22, 23, 24–5, 26, 27, 32
pornography 173, 176, 200
posterior colporrhaphy 122
postpartum period 19, 75, 76, 78, 99, 105, 159
post-traumatic stress disorder (PTSD) 76–7, 83, 137
Prawo i Sprawiedliwość (Law and Justice) (PiS) 118, 120
pre-eclampsia 152–6, 158
pregnancy 77
  abortion and *see* abortion
  Black women and 143–8, 152–5, 156, 157
  fertility and *see* fertility
  friends, time of making new 143
  mental health and 124–5, 130, 139–42
  mistreatment rates during 147–9
  pre-eclampsia and *see* pre-eclampsia
  preparation classes 100
  SUI and 18–19, 30
  tests 130
  trans men and 77–9, 202
Premarin 129
Prempro 129
Primodos 130
Proceedings of the National Academy of Sciences 148–9
prolactin 105
prolapse 2–25, 32, 38–40, 48, 75, 136, 140, 177, 207, 213–14
  anterior colporrhaphy and 121–2
  C-section 87, 98, 99, 108
  colpocleisis and *see* colpocleisis
  epidural and 48, 52
  hysterectomy and 6
  pelvic-floor exercises and *see* pelvic–floor exercises
  pessary and *see* pessary
  posterior colporrhaphy 122
  rates 4
  repair surgery 6, 39–40, 121–2, 164, 178, 179, 184
  sacral colpopexy 121–2
  sacrospinous ligament fixation 121
  sex and 159
  term 4

uterosacral ligament fixation 121
vaginal mesh and *see* mesh, vaginal
vault prolapse 184
Prolene 27–8
Prolift Total 22
prostate cancer 37
ProteGen 31, 32, 33, 34
pubiotomy 87, 90
Purdy, Jane 44–5

Reimer, Brian 199–201
Reimer, David 198–203
Reis, Elizabeth: *Bodies in Doubt* 194
Reyes, Olga 116
Roberts, Barbra 165
Rodriguez, Sarah B. 171–2, 173
Royal Academy of Surgery of France 88
Royal College of Midwives 102
Royal Oldham Hospital 44
Royal Shrewsbury Hospital 79
Runnels, Alexandra 174–5

sacral colpopexy 121–2
sacrospinous ligament fixation 121
Sajbor, Izabela 115–20
Sampson, John A. 151
Sanders, Ann 24, 25, 35
Sanofi 130
Saumlnger, Max 90
scar tissue 27, 138, 175
Schering AG 130
scopolamine 94
scrotal skin 181, 182
Secret Intersex (documentary) 196
sepsis 76, 116, 117, 186, 205
sex 1, 7, 21, 30, 36, 39, 40, 57, 62, 159–85
　Black people and 150–52, 155
　clitoris and *see* clitoris
　dilator therapy and 63–4
　female genital cosmetic surgery (FGCS) and 168–76
　female genital mutilation (FGM) and 176–7
　Human Sexual Response report 167
　'husband stitch' and 179
　labiaplasty and 168–73
　'love surgery' 162–7
　pain during 36, 62, 134, 138, 152, 161, 165, 174, 178
　pornography 173, 176, 200

　prolapse and 159–62
sexology 63, 192, 195, 199
sexual abuse 90, 201
sexual inversion 194
sexual satisfaction 64
sexual trauma 20
sexual violence 18
sexually transmitted infections 56, 152
Shahvisi, Arianne 175–6
Shrewsbury and Telford Hospital Trust 79–81, 83, 85
Sigault, Jean René 87–8
Simpson, James 93
Sims, John Marion 90, 149, 166–7
six-week check 8, 9, 14, 98
Skolkvik, Van 13
slings 28–9, 31, 32, 34, 121
Smith, Cathy 81
Snow, John 93
socialism 73, 117
sodium valproate 130
Sofradim 34
Souchot, Madame 88
Soviet Union 117
Spain, Alex 91
SSD (somatic symptom syndrome) 137
Stalin, Joseph 117
Steptoe, Patrick 44–5
Stokes, Rose 105–6
Suski, Marek 120
symphysiotomy 87–92, 108
Szewczak, Jola 68–74
Szewczak, Zbigniew 68, 69, 71–3

tension-free vaginal tape (TVT) 33
testosterone 61, 77–8, 193, 200
testovarectomy (surgical removal of testicles and ovaries) 190–91
thalidomide 129–30, 131
Third International Intersex Forum (2013) 204
Thompson, Louise 196–8, 202–3
tokophobia 96–7
trans people 7, 60–61, 66, 77, 78, 79, 107, 181, 182–3, 204–5, 211. *See also* intersex people
Triangle Silicone-Coated Sling and Surgical Mesh 34
trust in healthcare 77, 129, 131–2, 135, 136, 142, 179, 180, 182
Turner syndrome 193

Tusk, Donald 120
twilight sleep 94–6
Tyco Healthcare 34

Ulmsten, Ulf 32–5
United Nations (UN)
　Human Rights Committee 90
　Universal Declaration of Human Rights adopted by (1948) 45
University Hospitals Sussex NHS Foundation Trust 107
University of Glasgow 50
University of Oxford; Centre for Evidence-Based Medicine 46, 130
University of Virginia Medical School 148–9
University of Yale Reproductive Endocrinology and Infertility clinic 40
uterus 7, 9, 39, 47, 52–4, 57, 63, 75, 78, 84, 89, 90, 91, 110, 118, 134, 138, 151, 190–91, 196, 202
　uterine cancer 37
　uterine vaginal prolapse 121, 122, 164
　uterine wall 47–8, 84, 110
　uterosacral ligament fixation 121

vacuum aspiration 110
Vadasz, Danny 38
vagina 24
　colpocleisis/surgical closure of 39–40
　dilator therapy 62–5
　FGCS and see female genital cosmetic surgery (FGCS)
　FGM and see female genital mutilation (FGM)
　HPV and see HPV
　'love surgery' and 163–5
　menopause and 57
　neovagina 63, 64, 65, 182
　pelvic-floor exercises and 13–18, 20
　prolapse and 3–9, 121–2, 164
　tension-free vaginal tape (TVT) 33
　vaginal atresia 193

vaginal births 18, 81–2, 89, 90, 91, 96–101, 103, 108, 110, 212
vaginal cancers 130
vaginal fistula 31, 88, 149, 166
vaginal mesh devices 21–39 see also mesh, vaginal
vaginal orgasm 167
vaginal steaming 134–5
vaginal wellness 132–6, 142
vaginismus 7, 14, 20, 57, 62–3, 212
vaginoplasty 6, 65, 181, 182, 183, 197
vampire wing lift 169, 179
Victoria, Queen 93
Vogue 128, 156–7
Völling, Christiane 187–92, 201–3
　Ich war Mann und Frau ('I Was Man and Woman') 203
vulvodynia 14, 174

Wallace, Anthony 153
Wallace, Chaniece B. 153–4
Wallace, Charlotte 154
Watkins, Elizabeth Siegel: *The Estrogen Elixir: A History of Hormone Replacement Therapy in America* 128
Watson, James: 'Sun and Sex' 150
Weeping Willows 122–3
Wellburn, Frances 125–6, 136
wellness 132–5, 142, 155
Wilson Research Foundation 127, 128
Wilson, Robert 127–8: *Feminine Forever* 127–8
Winnicott, Donald: *Babies and Their Mothers* 143
Women's Health Initiative (WHI) 129, 131
Woodhouse, Christopher 196
World Health Organisation (WHO) 60, 76
　International Classification of Diseases (ICD) 170
World Professional Association for Transgender Health (WPATH) 181
Wyeth 129